In View of Academic Careers and Career-Making Scholars

Innovative Ideas for Institutional Reform

In View of Academic Careers and Career-Making Scholars

Innovative Ideas for Institutional Reform

by

Victor N. Shaw
California State University–Northridge

INFORMATION AGE PUBLISHING, INC.
Charlotte, NC • www.infoagepub.com

Library of Congress Cataloging-in-Publication Data

Shaw, Victor N.
  In view of academic careers and career-making scholars : innovative ideas for institutional reform / by Victor N. Shaw.
    p. cm.
  Includes bibliographical references.
  ISBN 978-1-59311-885-3 (pbk.) – ISBN 978-1-59311-886-0 (hardcover)
  1. Universities and colleges–Faculty. 2. College teachers–Employment. 3. Universities and colleges–Administration. I. Title.
  LB2331.7.S52 2008
  378.1'2023–dc22
                                                    2007050972

Please address correspondence to:
  Victor N. Shaw
  Department of Sociology
  California State University
  18111 Nordhoff Street
  Northridge, CA 91330-8318
  Telephone: (818) 677-7311
  Facsimile: (818) 677-2059
  Email: victor.shaw@csun.edu

Copyright © 2008 Information Age Publishing Inc.

All rights reserved. No part of this publication may be reproduced, stored in a retrieval system, or transmitted in any form or by any electronic or mechanical means, or by photocopying, microfilming, recording or otherwise without written permission from the publisher.

Printed in the United States of America

CONTENTS

Introduction xi

1 The Academic Career Pathway 1
   Background and Analysis 1
   Innovation and Reform 9
      Reform 1: Establish a Career-Sensitive Reward System 9
      Reform 2: Set up a Career-Consistent Evaluation System 10
      *Reform 3: Improve Career-Counseling Services at the Employment
         Organization* 12
      *Reform 4: Improve Career-Counseling Services at the
         Disciplinary Association* 13
      Reform 5: Systemize Career-Related Publications 15

2 Education and Training 17
   Background and Analysis 17
   Innovation and Reform 20
      Reform 1: Strengthen Training in Academic Skills 20
      Reform 2: Cultivate Academic Ways of Life 21
      Reform 3: Provide Guided Exposures to Academia 22
      Reform 4: Depersonalize Graduate Education 23
      Reform 5: Provide Opportunities for Student Exchange and Transfer . . . 25

3 Job Search and Change 27
   Background and Analysis 27
   Innovation and Reform 31
      Reform 1: Blind Review of Applications 31
      Reform 2: Eliminate Letters of Reference 32
      Reform 3: Academic Equalization 33
      *Reform 4: Eliminate Job Interviewing Services by Academic
         Associations* 35
      *Reform 5: Standardize Advertisements for Job Openings
         in a Discipline* 36

vi CONTENTS

4 Organizational Employment 39
　Background and Analysis. 39
　Innovation and Reform 43
　　Reform 1: Make Faculty Exchange a Standard Practice 43
　　Reform 2: Rotate for Academic Management 44
　　Reform 3: Create a Duty-Indicative Ranking System. 46
　　Reform 4: Separate Positions from Ranks 47
　　*Reform 5: Stop Formation of a Part-Time Teaching Profession/
　　a Floating Research Underclass.* 49

5 Professional Network 53
　Background and Analysis. 53
　Innovation and Reform 57
　　Reform 1: Create a Network of Information on Funding 58
　　*Reform 2: Convert Funding upon Promise to Funding
　　upon Outcome* 59
　　Reform 3: Create a Network of Information on Publishing 60
　　Reform 4: Create a Profession of Agents for Academic Publishing 62
　　Reform 5: Establish a Service-Oriented Publishing System 64

6 The Degree 67
　Background and Analysis. 67
　Innovation and Reform 70
　　*Reform 1: Track Job Placement at Disciplinary Associations
　　by Ph.D. Conferring Institutions.* 70
　　*Reform 2: Track Job Performance at Employment
　　by Ph.D. Conferring Institutions.* 71
　　*Reform 3: Track Rank Advancement at Employment
　　by Ph.D. Conferring Institutions.* 73
　　*Reform 4: Track Publications at Leading Outlets
　　by Ph.D. Conferring Institutions.* 74
　　*Reform 5: Track Rank Distribution at Disciplinary
　　Associations by Ph.D. Conferring Institutions* 75

7 Position 77
　Background and Analysis. 77
　Innovation and Reform 79
　　Reform 1: Create a Fast Track for Rank Advancement 79
　　*Reform 2: Create Department, College, and University
　　Professorships.* 81
　　*Reform 3: Use Ad Hoc Committees for Fast Track Rank Advancement,
　　Endowment Positions, and Institutional Professorships* 82
　　Reform 4: Create a Flat Academic Management 83
　　*Reform 5: Distinguish Service from Honor Positions
　　at Academic Associations* 84

Contents vii

8 Publication 87
    Background and Analysis 87
    Innovation and Reform 89
        Reform 1: Establish a General Rating System for All
            Academic Publications 90
        Reform 2: Conduct Regular Surveys of Concerned
            Publication Outlets at Disciplinary Associations 91
        Reform 3: Sponsor Regular Publication Contests
            at Disciplinary Associations 92
        Reform 4: Establish a Future-Oriented Journal for Each Discipline 93
        Reform 5: Establish a Backward-Looking Journal for Each Discipline ... 94

9 Teaching 97
    Background and Analysis 97
    Innovation and Reform 99
        Reform 1: Provide a Week-long Workshop on Teaching
            for New Faculty Members 100
        Reform 2: Promote Peer Coaching 101
        Reform 3: Neutralize Peer Evaluations 102
        Reform 4: Standardize Student Evaluations 103
        Reform 5: Regularize Institutional Teaching Awards 104

10 Presentation 107
    Background and Analysis 107
    Innovation and Reform 110
        Reform 1: Do Not Meet for the Sake of Meeting 111
        Reform 2: Strengthen Academic Standards 112
        Reform 3: Diversify Conference Programs 113
        Reform 4: Publish Conference Proceedings 114
        Reform 5: Make Academic Conventions Not-For-Profit Events ... 115

11 Service 117
    Background and Analysis 117
    Innovation and Reform 120
        Reform 1: Clarify Service 121
        Reform 2: Specify Service Qualifications 122
        Reform 3: Standardize Service Recruitment 123
        Reform 4: Make Service an Open Process for the Academicians Served .. 124
        Reform 5: Make Service an Equal Opportunity for the
            Serving Academicians 125

12 Grants 127
    Background and Analysis 127
    Innovation and Reform 130
        Reform 1: Balance Grants with Awards 130
        Reform 2: Create a Common Grant Market 132

     Reform 3: Establish a User-Friendly Grant System................134
     Reform 4: Simplify Grant Processes...........................135
     Reform 5: Strengthen Grant Reviews..........................136

13 Awards..139
    Background and Analysis....................................139
    Innovation and Reform......................................142
     Reform 1: Establish and Expand Academic Awards for Students and Junior Scholars......................................143
     Reform 2: Create Special Awards for Creative Ideas and Revolutionary Breakthroughs...144
     Reform 3: Publicize and Promote Academic Awards..............145
     Reform 4: Make Government an Authoritative Player in Academic Awards....................................146
     Reform 5: Keep the Spirit of Competition, Meritocracy, and Excellence through Academic Awards.............................148

14 Academic Associations......................................151
    Background and Analysis....................................151
    Innovation and Reform......................................154
     Reform 1: Be Service-Oriented................................155
     Reform 2: Be Knowledge-Driven..............................156
     Reform 3: Represent the Ordinary.............................158
     Reform 4: Celebrate the Exceptional...........................159
     Reform 5: Balance Representation, Service, and Tradition with Excellence, Leadership, and Change...................160

15 Tenure..163
    Background and Analysis....................................163
    Innovation and Reform......................................166
     Reform 1: Separate Tenure from Rank.........................167
     Reform 2: Make It a Standard: Ten Years for Tenure.............168
     Reform 3: Strengthen Post-Tenure Review......................169
     Reform 4: Offer only a Limited Number of Tenure................170
     Reform 5: Establish a Floating Tenure System across Academia......171

16 Scholarly Identity..173
    Background and Analysis....................................174
    Innovation and Reform......................................177
     Reform 1: Clarify Standards..................................177
     Reform 2: Specify Expectations................................178
     Reform 3: Provide Models...................................179

Reform 4: Allow for Deviations 181
Reform 5: Promote Diversity and Vitality 182

Conclusion 185

References 189

About the Author 197

INTRODUCTION

Career making is a universal phenomenon in the modern and postmodern epoch. From the original need of earning a living, to the personal aspiration for self-actualization, and to the social requirement of answering one's calling in an earthly enterprise, career making has reached the surreal of producing and reproducing identity, status, and seemingly even immunity from the ultimate human fate, death (Baudrillard, 1988; Engvall, 2003; Rhode, 2006; Rossides, 1998; Weber, 1930). The academic career, in particular, ensures that an individual pursuing it is socialized in a field of the knowledge domain. One first learns to speak a specialized language known to the members of the field. One then formulates an agenda for advancement, presents one's ideas and findings, develops an image of oneself, and engenders an autobiography of specialties, titles, honors, and tenure which may be memorialized and followed by other academicians beyond one's physical existence.

The sequence makes an ideal career pathway. In reality, although hundreds of thousands of people aspire wholeheartedly and work painstakingly for an academic career, not everyone is able even to gain entry to academia. Among entrants, not everyone is fortunate enough to triumph through competition to win a place, obtain a sense of identity, and become a figure of importance in the academic community. Many aspirants are eliminated along the academic career pathway, even just at the beginning of formulating a research agenda or locating an academic niche. Thus, making a career in modern and postmodern academia may not only pave the way toward self-realization of individual potential and ambitions; it may also create a path for victimization and destruction of individuals (Clark,

2006; Elliott, 1996; Goldsmith, Komlos, & Gold, 2001; Grant & Sherrington, 2006; Rhode, 2006; Schuster & Finkelstein, 2006).

In a broader social context, career making derives from modern mass production and division of labor (Marx, 1967; Paechter, 2001; Popkewitz & Fendler, 1999; Slaughter & Rhoades, 2004; St. John & Parsons, 2004). Mass production necessitates a knowledge enterprise to continually prepare personnel and supply software. The knowledge enterprise proliferates rapidly over time. It becomes so complex that it develops a division of labor within its own sphere. The division of labor in the knowledge enterprise results in borders among disciplines, demarcations among fields in a discipline, and designations of specialties in a field. A single specialty in a field may still be too large for a person to master within his or her lifetime. To maintain a specialty, a field, a discipline, and further the knowledge enterprise, individual academicians have to stay on one after another as if they were making a career of their own. However, in the sense that the knowledge enterprise serves the needs of mass production, glorifies the history of human triumphs over nature, and supplies means for individual socialization, academic career making contributes to the production and maintenance of the capitalist social process. In other words, it generates authority, ideology, and the mainstream, which in turn can belittle, devaluate, and repress individuals and their intellectual initiative.

This volume connects career making to the general social context in which it takes place, career-making individuals to the large institutional establishment in which they operate, and specifically career academicians to the overall knowledge enterprise from which they draw their intellectual inspiration, on which they build their career achievements, and to which they contribute their personal talents. The main purpose is to explore what academic institutions, the knowledge enterprise, and the society as a whole can and ought to do to enhance productivity, facilitate performance, and improve experience of individual academicians in their career-making endeavor. Although various innovative ideas are presented to improve normal procedures or standard processes throughout academia, answers to this focal question often lie in different levels of organizational units involved in academic operation. That is, what should a department do for its faculty, a college for its departments, a university for its colleges, an association for its member organizations, or a government for its academic institutions, in the best interest of the latter? Similarly, although reformative measures are proposed to the attention of established entities or institutionalized systems, change within the existing situation or practice to a large degree depends upon how people in various social roles relate to each other, in attitude as well as in behavior, when they perform their specific job. In other words, what should a professor do for graduate students, a senior scholar for junior colleagues, a chair for faculty members, a dean for chairs, a university chancellor for deans, an editor for authors, or an association president for the general membership, from the due perspective of the latter?

The logic or legitimacy of examining this focal question and its organizational unit and social role is clear: a shining academician owes much to the support of his or her assistants, students, and followers, a rising university builds on the productivity of its individual divisions, and a thriving knowledge enterprise depends upon the success of individual career-making scholars. Beyond its own functionality and success, by division of labor, the higher level or the larger system has an inescapable responsibility to ensure that individual players or components therein grow, develop, and perform to the best of their potential.

In content, this volume consists of sixteen chapters. Chapter 1 identifies main pathways and stages in academic careers. Chapters 2–5 focuses on the career process, exploring major requirements that an academician has to work on and fulfill in his or her career-making endeavor. These requirements include educational preparation, job search, institutional placement, and professional networking. Chapters 6–15 centers on the career structure, examining essential elements that a scholar has to build and maintain in his or her career identity. These elements range from the academic degree, position, publication, teaching, presentation, service, grants, awards, and membership in academic associations, to tenure. The last chapter capitalizes on the curriculum vitae as a miniature of the academic personality that a career professional must present to the community of scholarship.

Each chapter divides into two sections: one on background and analysis and the other on innovation and reform. The first section examines and explains the chapter's focal issue, either a procedural milestone or a structural element in the academic career, in the larger historical, disciplinary, or social context for general information, understanding, and insights. The second section proposes innovative ideas and reformative measures surrounding the focal issue for effective and efficient management within a discipline, an institution, or a system. Each new idea or measure is proposed uniformly in three aspects: status quo, reform, and significance. Status quo reviews the existing practice or the current situation. Reform unveils what can and ought to be done on the matter in the perspective of careers and career-making academicians. Significance evaluates possible impacts should the proposed ideas or measures become reality. For example, Chapter 2 first analyzes educational programs as gatekeepers and track-setters in academic careers. It then proposes that graduate education be focused on training of essential knowledge and skills, cultivation of an academic way of life, and exposure to real-world academia. It also urges that graduate training be depersonalized between advisers and students.

With a clear focus on change, this volume overall attempts to serve three purposes for its readers: a forum for theoretical reflection, an inspiration for creative innovation, and a blueprint for institutional reform.

CHAPTER 1

THE ACADEMIC CAREER PATHWAY

An academic career pathway refers to the general career process that academic professionals in a society or historical era move through in their lifelong scholarly pursuits. It is specific to a society because scholars may follow different career paths in different social environments. It is specific to a historical era because academicians may take different career routes due to different historical forces. A typical career pathway in a particular society or era, however, is not necessarily universal for all academic practitioners therein. Obviously, some academicians may deviate from the general pathway by passing through its stages in different sequences or by dropping off in the beginning or the middle of the journey (Blaxter, Hughes, & Tight, 1998; Brown & Brooks, 1996; Gould, 1978; Grant & Sherrington, 2006; Heinz & Marshall, 2003; Hermanowicz 2002; Levinson, 1978; Piper, 1992; Rajagopal & Lin, 1996).

BACKGROUND AND ANALYSIS

In the context of modern and postmodern society, an academic career pathway generally consists of five stages: initiation, routinization, secularization, solidification, and graduation. Each stage involves specific tasks. It invokes peculiar false assumptions as well. At the stage of initiation, prospective academicians tackle five major tasks. The first is attaining proficiency and competency. Prospective academicians attend graduate school, learn the academic language, and command essential skills. The second task is learning norms and normative behavior. Prospective academicians follow requirements, familiarize themselves with customs, and internalize basic rules. The third task concerns identification and identity. Here, novices meet insiders, learn to identify and respect giants, and follow role models in the field. The fourth task concerns specialization and specialty. Academicians build motivation, develop interests, and decide on a focused area of inquiry. The last task involves adventure and experimentation. The academician conducts research, becomes familiar with presentation and publication, and moves through the larger professional waters in various academic media.

The false assumptions that academic beginners often make typically fall under five categories. First, "I can conquer the world." One is obsessed with grand ideas and ignores technical details. One is overjoyed by acquaintance with monumental achievement in scholarship but underestimates the meticulous effort involved in developing a masterpiece. One focuses on substance but fails to see the emotional sentiment involved in academic undertakings. Some representative acts are these: One openly criticizes a professor for misinterpreting a theory in class; one sends a manuscript to an editor in an attempt to overthrow a dominant paradigm. Second, "I am not fully responsible." One succumbs to the weak side of oneself. One is reluctant to put the whole of one's learning or the truth of one's position into scholarly presentation and publication. One condones one's own mistakes. A typical reasoning is: "I am a student, not a professor. It is no big deal if I misunderstand something, engage in unprofessional practice, or mess up a situation." Third, "It's still too early for me to try." One is fearful. One is self-inhibited. One defers written examinations, postpones final defenses, and bypasses opportunities for professional presentation and publication. For example, when some professors ask one to contribute a chapter to a volume they are editing, one turns it down by saying "I have not taken any course in that area yet. I am afraid I have to focus on my coursework now." Fourth, "I am not ready yet to enter the profession." One idealizes the romance of student life within the walls of the university while dramatizing the brutality of survival in the academic market. One registers for classes one after another and participates in aimless discussion in classroom settings. One is addicted to an entertaining yet unproductive type of intellectual exercise between university faculty and students and thus never graduates. A proof of the phenomenon is this: It takes more and more Ph.D. candidates longer and longer time to complete their training. Lastly, "I don't think I can make it there." One admires influential figures. One fears one's own mentors. One mystifies disciplinary theories and methods, overestimates the talent and effort required for quality work and significant achievements, and is blindly in awe of academic establishments. An illustration is: "I am an ordinary person. I don't think I am born to dream for those big things. I will be happy if I can just manage to survive with all these talented people."

Routinization is the stage when one settles into a tenure-track position in an institution. One of the major tasks one has to deal with is to get to know the job, the institution, the profession, and the disciplinary establishment. Specifically, one needs to learn rules, familiarize oneself with existing conventions, empathize with prevailing sentiments, and establish a network of interaction, reference, and support. Second is to build a teaching portfolio. One has to identify a set of courses one is good at teaching, prepare syllabi and course materials for each of those courses, set ground rules for conducting class, interacting with students, grading, and handling complaints, and cultivate a teaching style characteristic of one's own fluency and comfort. Third is to develop a research agenda. To start off, one needs to retreat from those grand ideas one embraces during graduate school or overcome those characteristic feelings of unpreparedness and unsureness one goes through as a student. One then must take the initiative to identify one's own strengths and weaknesses, delve into an area of specialty, program oneself into a research way of life, and place oneself, properly yet uniquely, in the whole knowledge enterprise. Fourth is to open and maintain a track of service. One needs to make oneself known and available for service related to one's expertise. Depending upon one's needs, interests, and visibility, one may actively seek opportunities for service or turn down various requests for service. Regardless of a personal situation, service is necessary and important in keeping oneself in balance between personal success and social responsibility in the phase of routinization. Fifth is to put the academic career in proper perspective with various commitments in life. Settling into a community, one naturally asks: Should I get married if I am single? Should I raise children if I am married? Should I purchase a home if I have a family? Should I develop some new interests in life? Or should I invest savings in bonds, mutual funds, or stocks? All these questions require thought and effort to answer. Along with academic concerns, these personal issues shape and reshape one's career in general and routinization in particular.

An academician becoming routinized should stay alert to the five common false assumptions many of his or her peers tend to make at this stage. One assumption is this: "My advisors and classmates are out there to support me." One keeps calling on one's graduate advisors, asks them not only for advice, but also for substantive assistance. One talks to former classmates about one's sufferings, and may even weep in front of them. One who acts in this fashion may unfairly drag someone in one's graduate training into one's routinization process. Another false assumption is "I saw that or I did that in graduate school, differently from what you guys do here." One tells one's students and colleagues, in classrooms and in department meetings, what one saw or did in graduate school, and implies what they do now and here is awkward, backward, or outright wrong. One who makes such comparisons may unnecessarily offend the old guard in one's college or university. Still another common assumption is "This is not what I expected." One struggles between the ideal and reality. One feels that one's students are under-prepared and ill-mannered. One laments that one's colleagues are cold-blooded and hostile. One resents that one's leaders are repressive and evil-minded. One complains or looks for an exit from one's situation. One who so reacts is likely to change jobs frequently. The fourth assumption is "I cannot do research because I am preoccupied with teaching and service." One is fearful of research. One spends time in the laboratory but never turns out anything. One collects data but never analyzes them. One juggles a lot of ideas but never puts anything on paper. One may do every little thing in teaching or service to avoid research. One may even lie to oneself: "I will get back to research as soon as I gain an upper hand on teaching and service." One who so excuses oneself may find it more difficult to pursue research in the later phase of one's career. The fifth common assumption is "I have to put a lot of things in life on hold so that I can get my career under control." One isolates oneself in one's office. One calls around, attends meetings, and chats with students and colleagues. One plays with words, numbers, and models. One follows most of one's activities and days in academic settings. When approached for life-related issues, one habitually responds with the simple answer "I have no time for those luxuries." One who so programs oneself may never find time for joy and happiness in life.

Secularization begins when one is tenured and becomes immersed in one's institutional as well as disciplinary establishments. At this stage, an academician identifies with prevailing norms and conventions, by practicing them, teaching them to one's students, and defending them when they are breached. In teaching, one rests with one's own methods, style, and reputation. One may be known for teaching a set of content courses and being casual, permissive, discursive, and boring or demanding, organized, inspiring, and helpful to students. With colleagues, one complainingly or jokingly talks about students being unprepared, uncooperative, disrespectful, or not as good as they used to be some time ago. Sitting on committees regarding students, one may argue for or against tough educational standards. One may torture or spoil an advisee with reasonable or unreasonable assignments. On the matter of research, one digs year after year in an area, by similar theoretical and methodological approaches, and with similar findings and publications. One reviews manuscripts in the area. One sits on editorial boards or rises to the association leadership in one's discipline. One is at ease with one's specialty, enjoys a certain level of visibility, and feels one is part of the knowledge enterprise. In service, one responds to calls for advice and expert opinion from the community, the government, and the media. One may take the initiative to organize a conference, run an association, edit a journal or book series, or engage in other academic undertakings. One makes money, gains respect, and extends influence. Finally, secularization makes one settled into a peculiar work routine and lifestyle. One may be known by janitors, security guards, secretaries, or neighbors for leaving the laboratory late every day, guzzling several cups of coffee after lunch, or taking walks in the neighborhood before midnight. Most important, one relates to people in other occupations in a way that typifies one's calling in academe. For instance, one may sound like a scholar even when talking about news and movies with next-door neighbors. Life activities and routines characteristic of academic efforts do not exist merely as side products. They serve as powerful reinforcements in scholarly endeavors. Developing a lifestyle compatible to academic endeavor, therefore, can be considered as one of the main tasks a secularizing academician works on in a scholarly career.

The most common false assumption held by a secularized academician is: "I know it all." One teaches classes off the top of one's head. One pages through new publications without serious reading. One writes papers following a set track of thought. One shakes one's head when seeing things out of the ordinary. To newcomers, one tends to assume "I am an insider." Under this assumption, one pours out stories, experiences, and versions of reality to the newer arrivals. One joins old colleagues to monitor, gossip about, manipulate, or even "torture" the newcomers. One labels them "naive," "inexperienced," or "unrealistic" when the newer arrivals experiment with something new or something one simply dislikes. One loses sight of the fact that these newcomers are the force of the future and the hope of one's institution. To students, one assumes the stance, "I am always right." With this assumption, one lectures students, orders them to conduct different exercises, or even forces them to attempt something out of their reach. One calls students "lazybones" or "uncarveable wood" if they do not live up to expectations. One fails to realize that one can be wrong and may learn from students. To people in other walks of life, one may be quick to assume "I am more educated, informed, and rational than all of you." With this assumption, one looks down upon common citizens as ignorant and gullible. One criticizes politicians as wicked and manipulative. One laments the media as biased and misleading. One is too presumptuous to appreciate the vividness of the larger social mosaic. The last common false assumption a secular academician is likely to make regards future and change: "I am not going to be different." One brags about one's years of service. One takes comfort in what one has accomplished in teaching, research, and service. One sticks to accustomed ways of thinking and acting. One resists change, innovation, and reform. One refuses to back down even in confronting mistakes made.

Solidification does not necessarily follow the stage of secularization for all career-making individuals. It builds upon or emerges from secularization among a small number of academicians. Sitting in full professorships, a great many faculty on university campuses feel they have arrived at their career destination. At most, they keep doing what they are familiar with doing, becoming ever more secular along their career pathway. A few, however, attempt to rise above their secular experiences. They reach the uncommon stage of solidification when they are successful. There are three paths toward solidification. One is through scholarly accomplishments. One makes extraordinary discoveries, puts forth revolutionary theories, develops unusual methods, produces masterpieces, or spearheads a new area of inquiry. One becomes the president of one's disciplinary association or is awarded highest honors in his or her discipline, such as the Nobel Prize. Another is by way of management. One is fortunate to be pushed, often through political maneuvering, into the chairmanship of one's department and the experience as chair makes one eligible to apply for a managerial position at the dean's level. The experience as dean sets a stage for a further ascendance to leadership at the university level. In one's second track of management after the first track of scholarship, one sharpens public speaking skills, strategizes human relations at different levels and in different settings, manipulates resources and opportunities, plays fundraising tactics, and relates properly to the larger political environment surrounding his or her job duty. As one becomes a career administrator, one gradually loses the drive and instinct for serious academic contributions. Still, another route toward solidification is through establishing a practice or service. One capitalizes on one's training, knowledge, or invention. One establishes a business or opens a practice. As a business owner, one may become more and more concerned with profit and eventually abandon one's aspiration for scholarly breakthroughs. Or as a practitioner, one may gather firsthand data from clients and develop a theory or a treatment of scientific importance. No matter what route one takes in one's academic career, one needs to make a significant effort to emerge from the mundane, the secular, or the transient to become solidified in the unusual, the exceptional, and the eternal.

A career academician who reaches the stage of solidification can also make and act under false assumptions. The two general assumptions shared by many solidified scholars are: "I am special" and "I represent it all." By the first assumption, one feels one is a genius, blessed with the special talent, skill, or opportunity to discover what others are not able to find, write about what others fail to see, control what others are incapable of handling, or profit from what others are unaware of. With the second assumption, one feels one is the sovereign of one's discipline, institution, or profession. One may declare that one's discipline is in a theoretical or methodological crisis, calling for a general reform or revolution. One may proclaim that one's institution must commit to a particular philosophy or standard, forcing all its members into a set track of thought or a fixed mode of behavior. Specific to different routes of solidification, one is likely to assume that "knowledge is power" if one gains influence through scholarship. As one is admired and honored for one's widely used theory or method, one may intuit that it is possible to conquer the whole world just by knowledge. Similarly, one is likely to assume that "power is everything" when one sits at the helm of an academic institution. And one is likely to assume that "money speaks" if one runs a knowledge-based corporation. In the first scenario, one sets rules, gives orders, and applies rewards and penalties. One sees clearly how one can manipulate the mass of secular academicians, even the stars of scholarship, by the power one holds. In the second scenario, one keeps a development team of scientists and engineers within one's company. One hires, fires, promotes, or demotes those scientists and engineers. One feels one can easily manipulate them, no matter how much knowledge they have, as long as one has money to employ them.

The last stage is graduation. Although some academicians vow that they will never graduate from scientific inquiry, others admit that they cannot wait to retreat back to the wishes of their childhood, the excitement of their hobby, or the comfort of their family life. As far as employment and job duty are concerned, graduation is indeed an inevitable and important phase of a complete academic career. The major tasks one is faced with at the stage of graduation include these: reviewing, winding-up, repositioning, adjusting, and slowing-down. Review involves both a retrospective examination of past work and an objective evaluation of current projects. In examining work throughout one's career, one sees ups and downs, gains and losses, pride and regret. The question is: Can one build upon one's achievements to move further or can one make up any of one's losses? By evaluating one's ongoing projects, one can responsibly decide what to terminate, what to hand over, what to leave behind, and what to carry on. Winding-up is based upon review. Using the time left on active duty, one wraps up an experiment, an analysis, or a manuscript. Most important, one may be able to clear a critical hurdle in the effort to establish a theory or method, unravel a puzzle or problem one has long dreamed of solving, or conclude a capstone project one has been pursuing for years. Repositioning is to evaluate oneself and identify a proper niche for oneself during retirement in the knowledge enterprise. Depending upon one's experience, reputation, network, energy level, and time commitment, one may deliver guest lectures from place to place, take short-term residency with a research center, participate in an issue-specific project, engage in writing, or volunteer in a service or educational organization. Adjustment is needed as any new line of activity in retirement requires a different approach, expectation, or perspective than one is used to through the pre-retirement career. There is a time of ease and joy when one acts upon a wealth of lifelong learning. There is a time of frustration and sadness when one is confronted with challenges previously unheard of. Finally, slowing-down is to admit the declining mental and physical power available for academic activities one is able to engage in as one draws close to the end of life. One keeps an eye on the academic world, reads scholarly articles, and may occasionally come up with some critical ideas. But overall, one knows that one is on the back stage of the knowledge enterprise, moving closer and closer to the absolute conclusion of one's academic career.

In a mood of graduation, a career academician can easily make false assumptions, specifically about his or her contribution, career, and discipline, and generally about life and science. Beginning with one's contributions, one may assume: "Nobody really understands what I put forth in my theory or method." With a feeling of betrayal, one may criticize the disciplinary establishment and admonish the mass of scholars for their inattention, obtuseness, and carelessness. Regarding one's career, one may feel: "I have nothing to be proud of." With a feeling of lack of self-worth in scholarship, one avoids talking about one's past work or the institution where one was employed, shows no motive to explore academic markets for research and teaching opportunities during retirement, and takes joy only in nonacademic hobbies or volunteering activities. With respect to one's discipline, one is likely to assume: "It's no longer my world." One has some ideas about one's discipline but buries them in one's mind, feeling that nobody would care to know about those ideas. On the matter of life, one may assume: "No life ever exists beyond my academic career." Under this assumption, one refuses to retire from academic work but continues a long habituated daily routine, with or without scholarly productivity. One retreats to life only when challenged by a disabling disease or other drastic event. Finally, a graduating academician may cap his or her scholarly career with some general thoughts about science and the knowledge enterprise. One may assume: "Science is a game," and complacently aligns oneself with the large army of smart players in academia. One may assume: "Science is the world of geniuses," and sentimentally characterizes oneself, along with the vast mass of ordinary academicians, as simple materials used by, or as little dwarfs in the service of, a few pioneers and leaders in the production of knowledge and domination.

INNOVATION AND REFORM

What can an institution do to facilitate its academic employees in their lifelong drive toward success? Is a university willing and ready to change itself or some of its standard practices so that it can fully embrace an innovative idea to the benefit of its faculty and their career movement (Acker, 2006; Arreola, 2006; Baez, 2002; Bright & Richards, 2001; Dickeson, 1999; Kaplowitz, 1986; Leaming, 2003; Licata & Morreale, 2007; Long, McGinnis, & Allison, 1993; Tierney & Bensimon, 1996; Wolverton & Gmelch, 2002; Zemsky, Wegner, & Massy, 2005)?

Reform 1: Establish a Career-Sensitive Reward System

Status Quo. The existing reward system builds upon the principle of seniority and operates under an assumption of demonstrated performance. It does not reserve sufficient room for potentiality and needs. Some simple yet ubiquitous ironies resultant from the system are these: You do not make enough money when you need it most; you make a considerable amount of money when you need it least; you are ignored when you need encouragement most; and you may be overwhelmed with honor, resources, and power when you do not need much external support.

Reform. Now these questions arise: Is it possible to reverse the prevailing pattern? What does it take to make salaries relatively even between earlier and later years, between promise and success? For instance, a university may study faculty salaries and identify an average yearly salary for a normally progressing faculty member over his or her whole employment career with the university. In reference to the average yearly salary, the university may set salaries for its entry-level and junior faculty high enough so that they can feel comfortable enough to start a family, raise children, or help to support their elderly parents. The level of increase may be adjusted in response to age progression, life events, and career mobility. Thus a faculty member receives a higher yearly salary, against the assumed total of a lifelong salary, in the heyday of his or her career when he or she is likely to have to support school-age children. He or she receives a lower yearly salary, against the assumed total of a lifelong salary, when he or she pays off a home loan, sees his or her adult children leave, and lives in relative health and affluence. A faculty member who leaves before the assumed duration of employment is technically required to pay back to the institution the overdrawn portion of his or her lifelong salary. Payback, however, would automatically become unnecessary when all academic institutions follow the same practice. That is, all academic employers even up compensations to academic employees so that individual salaries and benefits are sensibly and rationally distributed throughout employee career pathways in terms of both performance and need, both contribution and promise.

Significance. This evened compensation and reward system acknowledges the relatively equal importance of each academician in his or her job functioning. Indeed, an assistant professor does by no means perform less work than a full professor in teaching, research, and service. There is no justification that the former should be paid less, oftentimes much less, than the latter. An evened system remains basically blind to years of service, which in turn may facilitate job mobility and change of blood across academic institutions. In relation to the market, equitable compensation through career stages sends immediate stimulation to the economy as rightfully paid academicians in their early to middle careers are more likely to spend on housing, children's education, and other life necessities than their middle-to-late-career counterparts. As already known, highly compensated senior professionals can only turn their money to the government, charitable organizations, or trusted heirs after limited expenditure on their own. While money so transferred may end up in some good causes, it also inevitably leads to waste, corruption, and dependency. More generally, evened compensation and reward throughout the career pathway put into place a new philosophy of time, work, credit, and space. At present, employers are willing to pay more to seniors because they pay juniors only partially with a fixed packet of salary and benefits and owe juniors an assumed credit of service and loyalty due at higher levels. Juniors are willing to take less compensation because they expect to redeem their assumed credit of service and loyalty when they reach the senior stage. The new philosophy reverses this discourse of compensation and reward. An employee would no longer be paid partly with a fixed packet of salary and benefits and partly with a taken-for-granted credit of service or loyalty redeemable only in the future. Instead, an employment organization would be obliged to pay fully what one deserves here and now while it is freed from honoring any credit one earns there and then.

Reform 2: Set up a Career-Consistent Evaluation System

Status Quo. The current evaluation system is controlled by the old guard to monitor, manipulate, and even torture newcomers. Members of the old guard feel free to do almost what they want. The original rationale for such an evaluation system is that senior academicians have internalized academic norms and workmanship, they no longer need a tight net of external restraints and teachings in their scholarly endeavor, and they can productively use their autonomy and freedom for creative work. The reality, however, is that many academic seniors become political, abusive, and unproductive as they drift loose and remain aloof from accountability review. The likely outcome of any systematic study of scholarly productivity over individual career spans is that the majority of scholars complete most of their work in years when they are junior, relatively unknown, and subject to rigorous review and evaluation. In fact, as junior academicians strive for acceptance and recognition, they are more likely to do their best conscientiously and voluntarily. They will do the best they can in line with prevailing academic norms, standards, and practices.

Reform. The evaluation system, therefore, ought to be revamped to loosen control over newcomers so that they have sufficient freedom to explore different ideas, experiment with new methods, and charter academic careers that suit their individual talents and interests. For example, newly hired faculty members are not evaluated in the first year. Free from immediate scrutiny, they can take time to know their job, the institution, the community, and the discipline. During their probationary years, evaluation may take a sequential focus, examining only one aspect of the requirement for professional success each year: from teaching to research to service. The rationale is that probationary faculty members will be able to concentrate time and energy on developing abilities, establishing profiles, and building momentum in one area of their academic career at a time. When it takes a comprehensive approach where every aspect of a faculty member's performance is put under review at one time, evaluation can be done less frequently, such as once every two years instead of once every year.

To members of the old guard, post-tenure review should become more routine and meaningful. In terms of frequency, teaching can be evaluated every two years, research every three years, service every four years, and in the fifth year there will be a comprehensive assessment on all three aspects of the academic performance. Most important, evaluation is not just a "business as usual" procedure. A negative evaluation will result in both symbolic acts, such as warnings and reprimands, and substantive actions, including denial of service salary increases, denial of travel funds, and even decrease of steps in the same rank. Similarly, there will be appropriate rewards for positive performance.

Significance. The proposed reform challenges the existing power relations. It takes power from senior scholars and career administrators who tend to make rules and determine distribution of benefits and opportunities to their own advantage. It invests in junior academicians, rendering them freedom and choice that are necessary and critical in the early stage of their academic career. Productivity becomes a focus of attention. Performance takes center stage. Rewards and penalties are tied to evaluation results while the evaluation process itself is geared toward what an academician does or has done in scholarship rather than who he or she is in terms of age, sex, race, graduate school, mentor, rank, or years of service. The question now is this: Will members of the old guard be willing to give up power and control for the sake of scholarship in general and to the benefit of a successful academic career for the future generation in particular?

Reform 3: Improve Career-Counseling Services at the Employment Organization

Status Quo. Partly because scholarly undertaking is adventurous, creative, and unique, there is not much normal, routine, and standard advice or guidance available to career-making individuals in academia. Partly because a majority of scholars serve as university professors teaching students knowledge and skills for different practices, there is a conventional lack of direction and training for professors themselves to become better practitioners in the academic profession. Now in most academic institutions, a new faculty member is given a day of orientation just for a sense of welcome. A faculty manual is provided under the assumption that all faculty members already know the game and will follow necessary steps toward their expected destinations. Wherever there is a faculty union, it may offer strategies and tactics to fight against anything but seldom offers skills and tips to accomplish something. The Office of Faculty Affairs keeps records. The Faculty Senate debates issues. The Career Center offers assistance only to students. Faculty members can chat, complain, guess, and gossip with each other over serious concerns and matters in their academic career. But in most university and research settings there is no known place to which individual academicians can turn for serious advice, guidance, and support in their career-making endeavor.

Reform. While it is not feasible for an academic institution to offer residency or a period of intensive orientation for entry-level faculty members, it is possible to provide the faculty from junior to senior levels with meaningful career services on the basis of the human and nonhuman resources any typical university or research institute has under its organizational roof or indirect influence. Among faculty members themselves, a tradition of cooperative partnership can be formed and sustained between juniors and seniors in a university. A junior member of the faculty is formally or informally matched with a senior counterpart. Whereas the former learns from the latter in the latter's experience, skills, and connections which are critical to the early development of an academic career, the senior member can learn from the junior member in the areas of new knowledge, fresh training, bold dreams, and even wishful thinking that often prove inspirational to the later stages of a scholarly life. Organizationally, a university may set up offices or run programs to deliver various career-related services to the faculty. A center for instructional support can serve as a forum for the faculty to exchange ideas and experiences in teaching. An office of sponsored research can facilitate the faculty in their search and application for funding. And a writing-intensive program can assist the faculty in their publication efforts. In the area of indirect influence, some often ignored but potentially most helpful avenues can be explored. One of them is the utilization of voluntary organizations and services affiliated with academic institutions. For example, academic retirees and their respective associations can be encouraged to play an active role in career counseling, service, and support for the existing faculty. An office manned by retired professors, administrators, librarians, and even office staff may provide walk-in services for current faculty members. When necessary, a hotline attended by academic and administrative retirees may answer questions and offer tips for the faculty in the varying stages of their academic careers. Hours of service or operation can be determined by needs on campus.

Significance. Autonomy, self-confidence, and independence are critical in scholarly pursuits. So are referencing, mutual learning, and cooperation. With proposed change, people at different stages in their career pathway draw upon each other in their unique experience so that they can effectively tackle the task they each have to deal with on their own career-making journey. Generational gaps are bridged when older scholars learn about issues faced by their younger counterparts. Sectional misunderstandings are overcome when senior faculty members interested in management meet with their junior colleagues committed to scholarship. Academic institutions prosper when mutual understanding and support prevail among the faculty. The knowledge enterprise thrives when individual knowledge discoverers, producers, and distributors embrace each other across traditional divides, from age, gender, rank, and institutional affiliation to career stage, in purely innocent and cooperative spirits.

Reform 4: Improve Career-Counseling Services at the Disciplinary Association

Status Quo. A disciplinary association rises above individual universities and research institutes to represent a discipline in the academic community. By definition, it has a significant advantage to offer general career-counseling services to scholars from different institutions, big or small, elite or ordinary, comprehensive or special, national or local. At the present, however, most disciplinary associations do not seem to have capitalized on their unique positions in career counseling. There are sporadic events, such as grant-writing workshops, meet-the-editor sessions, and onsite interviews by employers, offered at the annual convention. There are irregular publications, such as employment bulletins, brochures on codes of conduct, and compilations of course syllabi, catalogued for distributional sales by the national office. But overall, neither systematic measure nor coherent coordination is taken by any single association to serve individual members under its disciplinary umbrella in their career-making endeavors.

Reform. Reform may begin with what many associations do currently with regard to career counseling. To make sporadic events regular features, an association can offer the following as a required part of the program at its annual convention: a series of meet-the-editor sessions in which each of the association-sponsored journal editors and some of the discipline-related journal editors are invited to talk about requirements for publication in their respective periodicals; a series of grant-writing workshops in which funding organizations, funding program officers, experienced grant reviewers, and successful grant writers are scheduled to offer information, perspective, and insight; and a series of career focus groups in which seasoned scholars are matched with newcomers to explore issues on research, teaching, service, promotion, and tenure. To make irregular publications standard, an association may provide the following as a taken-for-granted benefit of membership: an employment bulletin that carries all related job advertisements by different academic institutions; a newsletter that spreads news and tips on the profession; an inventory of forums, meetings, funds, awards, journals, and publishers that promote, communicate, and support research and scholarship in the discipline; and a generic career guidebook that describes and analyzes essential elements and processes in the academic life of the average membership.

Besides these two activities, a disciplinary association can take various other systematic measures in assisting its members through different stages of their academic career. For example, a career help-line attended by volunteers can be made available to the general membership. Members in various stages of the academic career may volunteer to be included in the service pool with their available hours and issues of specialty. Members who call in on various matters can be routed to specific volunteers according to their needs and preferences. The help-line may remain open a few hours a day through weekdays and/or over the weekend in response to membership demands. Another initiative a disciplinary association may take is to assist members to develop partnership or peer-coaching relationships among each other. The association matches one with another in terms of mutual preference, interest, and need. A teaching scholar may be lined up with a research academician, a female with a male, a junior with a senior, or a faculty member from a liberal arts college with a professor from a comprehensive university as peer coaches or partners in their respective career journey.

Significance. A disciplinary association with serious commitment to its members and their career development can effectively rally members under its roof. There will be not only a surge in general membership, but also an increase in member-to-member interaction, cohesion, and solidarity. Annual meetings can be more meaningful. Day-to-day operations can be more substantive. Overall association productivity and membership satisfaction will then rise to a higher level. Most important, the discipline itself grows and prospers as individual knowledge producing or distributing workers in its various areas and fields sail smoothly through their academic careers.

Reform 5: Systemize Career-Related Publications

Status Quo. Publication on academic careers is plentiful given the fact that there are multiple versions of biographies about famous discoverers, inventors, and scientists, series of faculty guidebooks or employee manuals, and volumes of issue-specific pamphlets or brochures by academic institutions, disciplinary associations, and publishing houses. It is scarce in the sense that none of these varying and often conflicting printing materials offers information general to the academic career regardless of institution or discipline nor advice specific to each of the major milestones in the career pathway.

Reform. Systemization of career-related publications begins with a clear classification of materials needed in career counseling and development. There is first a critical need for general encouragement and inspiration. Autobiographies and biographies should be systematically provided for general circulation about great scientific contributors, such as disciplinary founders, pioneers in a field, and monumental figures of an era. From year to year, Nobel Prize winners, awardees of highest honors in a discipline, and the president of the most prestigious association in a field ought to be featured in a full career-long story in the main publication forum of the field or discipline. For example, a feature article detailing his or her career, career milestones, and career achievements can appear in *The American Sociologist* or *Footnotes* upon inauguration of a new president of the American Sociological Association.

Besides inspirational publications, there is an urgent need for practical materials that offer specific advice and guidance. Career guidebooks can be separately devised for those who practice in engineering and natural sciences versus those who work in the humanities and social sciences, those in research organizations versus those in teaching institutions, and those in small liberal arts colleges versus those in large comprehensive universities. In the pathway of an academic career, senior scholars can benefit from positive reading tailored to their search for new direction and continuing development just as junior academicians learn from a faculty guidebook written for people in the earlier stages of their knowledge adventure. In other words, there should be career-counseling materials for both seasoned scholars and newcomers or beginners. In substance, academic guidebooks can cover everything pertaining to the scholarly life or delve into only one aspect of a career. For instance, there are books dedicated to teaching, research, and service, not only singly but also in combination. Demographically, women and minority scholars may face unique issues and problems in their academic career. As a result, there is a growing literature in academic guidance and career counseling for women and members of minorities.

Significance. A clear identification of needs for career-related publications offers guidance for academic associations to expand their influence and for publishers to increase their market share. Profit can come side by side with influence when an academic association launches a biographical series about leading scientists in the history of its specialized field or discipline all on its own from writing to editing to printing to distributing. Or influence can go hand in hand with profit when a commercial publisher becomes known and reputable in the publication of academic guidebooks or career-counseling materials for social scientists, junior faculty members, teaching scholars, or women academicians. On the part of career-making individuals, systemization of career-related publications makes it easier for them to find the kind of advice and assistance they need through different stages of their academic journey. There always will be something available in the library, at the bookstore, or over the internet whether they look for general inspiration as how to keep alive the spirit of scientific discovery and innovation, whether they search for specific direction in teaching, research, or service, and whether they struggle to tackle the secular matter of applying for a grant, securing a promotion, or obtaining tenure.

CHAPTER 2

EDUCATION AND TRAINING

The academic career begins with education. Education itself is a long process, constituting a significant part of the career pathway (Abel, 1984; Bowen & Rudenstine, 1992; Davis & Parker, 1997; Dore, 1976; Eurich, 1981; Golde & Walker, 2006; Maki & Borkowski, 2006; Paechter, 2001; Shaw, 2002c; Taylor, 2005; Tinkler & Jackson, 2004).

BACKGROUND AND ANALYSIS

The goal of education is to inculcate in prospective entrants basic values, common codes of conduct, established theories and methodologies, current debates, and recent developments of a discipline in particular and of the whole academic community in general. Compared to the time of Plato or to the Middle Ages when apprenticeship under a spiritual master for a few years was deemed enough to prepare a person for philosophical or theological undertakings, the education required for an academic career in the contemporary era can take as long as about one third of one's lifetime. First comes pre-college education from kindergarten to twelfth grade, a standard socialization process assumed for common citizens in modern society. Then comes a four-year undergraduate education, a general social requirement designed for middle-class employment and lifestyle under affluent capitalism. Next is a three-year master's level graduate education, where one either lays a foundation for one's academic pursuits or

In View of Academic Careers and Career-Making Scholars, pages 17–26
Copyright © 2008 by Information Age Publishing
All rights of reproduction in any form reserved.

prepares oneself for business management, technical or professional jobs, and other high-paying employment. Master's level education therefore serves only as a baseline for or a transition to the higher levels of training required for an academic career.

The standard for career academicians, for college and university professors, is doctoral education. Despite years of learning at pre-college, baccalaureate, and master's levels, doctoral students still spend an average of six years to complete their work for a degree of Doctor of Philosophy or Ph.D. With this degree, they merely meet a minimum requirement of qualification for teaching and research in academia. In fact, as the academic labor market remains a strong buyer's market, the minimum entry requirement with regard to education and training shifts to an even higher level. More and more teaching and research institutions now tend to recruit only those Ph.D. holders who have a few years of postdoctoral training and work experiences in other similar organizations.

In the process of academic career making, education plays the dual role of both gatekeeper and track-setter. As gatekeeper, education screens in only those who are able to survive its lengthy and pedantic procedure. An enrollee has to take many examinations and contests to prove that he or she has mastered all necessary knowledge and skills for academic undertakings in a specific discipline. In addition, one has to submit to a myriad of exercises and challenges to demonstrate that one has internalized all appropriate rules, codes, and distinctions for professional practice in the community of scholarship. It is known that students drop out of the educational process when they fail in major examinations in an academic subject. It is, however, not so publicized that students are forced out of educational programs because they are not willing to kowtow to their advisors or because they are determined to challenge an academic authority with regard to a substantive fallacy or an unprofessional practice. There are no sufficient conditions in knowledge acquisition and behavioral maturation. A career-making scholar can never proclaim that he or she has learned enough in or beyond school. Instead, one has to always connect oneself to the educational system for continuing learning and resocialization throughout one's academic career.

As track-setter, education predesignates what field or subject one is to delve into, what perspective or orientation one is to take, and what finding or product one is to turn out in one's academic career. It also preassigns where in the academic world one is to play one's role and build one's influence. Specifically, the institution from which one graduates and in which one finds one's graduate advisor and classmates predetermines what network one enters and how removed one is from the core of the academic community. A graduate under the apprenticeship of a prominent scholar from a leading department in an elite university has a totally different network waiting for him or her than one graduated from an institution deemed mediocre.

The faculty directory, which conventionally includes information about a faculty's graduate school and academic interests, showcases how graduate school sorts out academic hopefuls, feeding them into different institutions in higher education. In California, for example, graduates from elite institutions, such as Harvard, MIT, and Princeton, fill positions in elite schools, such as Stanford and Caltech, University of California (UC) campuses, and sometimes the California State University (CSU) system. Graduates from leading UC campuses, such as Berkeley and UCLA, feed less prominent UC campuses, the CSU system, and sometimes community colleges. Graduates from UC campuses dominate the CSU system and major community colleges. It is rare that graduates from a less prominent UC campus take positions in leading UC institutions, much less in elite schools within the state.

One argument for the track-setting influence of graduate education is that graduates from top programs have undergone more rigorous training in fundamental skills and knowledge in a discipline and therefore possess a greater potential for significant contributions to the academic enterprise. There is, however, support for the opposite of this argument. That is, top graduate programs do not necessarily produce only high-quality students while lower-ranking ones may be able to individualize programs for students and produce competent academic professionals. Institutionally, top programs are considered elite not so much because they produce first-rate students but rather because they have the best-known scholars on their faculty. These scholars are preoccupied with their own research and may be less likely to spend a lot of time with their students. The situation is further complicated by the number of students. Many top programs attract a large number of students in their graduate population. Another factor is that well known programs, as they stand securely at the top, may tend to care less about whether they turn out a few lesser-quality products among a large group of good ones. On the other hand, lesser-known programs are likely to be new and small; their faculty members are therefore highly motivated to prepare students with all necessary skills and knowledge for long-term growth in a discipline. Faculties may spend more time on graduate advisement. Each graduate student, among the few in the program, may receive a great amount of supervision and scrutiny throughout the educational process. As a result, graduates from some lower-ranking programs may, in fact, be better prepared for work and contribution in academia.

INNOVATION AND REFORM

Many measures can be taken to reform and improve educational structure and process (Brown & Schubert, 2000; Eggins, 2003; Eurich, 1981; Golde & Walker, 2006; Gornitzka, Kogan, & Amaral, 2007; Gossett & Bellas, 2002; Greenwood & Levin, 2001; Hines & Hartmark, 1980; Kerr, Gade, & Kawaoka, 1994; Maki & Borkowski, 2006; Noble, 1994; Shaw, 1999, 2001a, 2002a; Stephens, 1989; Tierney, 1991). As far as preparation of career scholars is concerned, acquisition of academic skills, development of academic ways of life, guided exposure to academia, depersonalization of graduate education, and institutional exchange are areas or issues where innovation and reform are most needed.

Reform 1: Strengthen Training in Academic Skills

Status Quo. Academic skills involve intellectual capabilities and technical competencies in reading, research design, laboratory experimentation, fieldwork, data processing and analysis, modeling and logical reasoning, presentation, and writing. They are relatively stable in content compared to the ever-changing substantive information and material in a discipline. They are essential and critical not only because they represent what a scholar knows about a specialty, but also because they predict what one can do in one's discipline. In the final analysis, it is what one can do, rather than what one may know, that determines whether one is successful in an academic career. While academic skills are taught, often implicitly, in content courses, they are not offered explicitly, emphatically, and straightforwardly anywhere throughout the existing educational system.

Reform. The situation demands innovation and reform in graduate curriculum. One measure is to offer concentrated or specialized laboratories, practicum, or workshops for each of the major skills required in a discipline. In the social sciences, for example, essential skills may boil down to specific abilities in data collection, data analysis, logical reasoning, reading, presentation, and writing. For data collection, there can be guided or unguided fieldwork, internships, observations, and ethnographical projects. For data analysis, there can be statistical laboratories and data-decoding exercises. For logical reasoning, there can be some open forums or contests where students take sides to debate on issues. For reading, there can be group projects in which participants are assigned to search for answers from different sources. For presentation, there can be weekly speech series through which graduate students share their novice research. Finally, for writing, there can be workshops wherein faculty and students tackle the challenge of written expression through academic outlets. All these skill-specific courses or activities can be provided as part of a graduate curriculum or incorporated in an overall graduate training program.

Significance. By taking skill-specific courses or exercises, students become demystified about the knowledge production process. They learn quickly how knowledge is produced and what it takes to become a productive worker in an academic field. Most important, with essential skills in hand, they will no longer feel overwhelmed in receiving information from subject to subject. Instead, they will become motivated to manipulate information and generate knowledge in the area of their interest and specialization.

Reform 2: Cultivate Academic Ways of Life

Status Quo. Academic ways of life build upon the fusion of academic aspirations, demands, and overtures on the one hand and real life commitments, necessities, and routines on the other. A balanced academic way of life enables one not only to draw upon life experience for academic creations, but also to inspire life with academic ideals. Most essentially, one thinks and behaves in everyday living in a way that facilitates his or her work in academic pursuits. As epitomized by a Chinese saying, one focuses one's mind on work so that one can always obtain twice the result with half of the effort. In graduate school, most students learn to cultivate their mind and develop their habits by emulating a favorite professor or venerating some great scholars. Learning is fragmented because face-to-face interaction with a life figure is usually situational and exposure to biographical writings is often sporadic.

Reform. To assist in the systematic socialization of prospective scholars into academic ways of life, two innovative ideas can be put into practice in graduate school. One is to offer an elective course on academic life. The course allows students to search and read biographical materials about five of their most revered scholars in a specific discipline or in general scholarship. Over the course of class discussion, students explore the way of life each of their chosen scholars led. In the end, they are asked to look into the future and develop descriptive projections of their own ways of life in academia. The other is to institute a host family program. The program would assign each graduate student to live with a faculty member and the member's family for a specific period of time. Under the live-in arrangement, participants observe and reflect upon how a real life academician commutes between work and home, balancing scholarly ambitions with life responsibilities. Depending upon resources and willingness from the faculty and students in a department, some watered-down versions may be implemented, including one-night sleeps-in, weekend excursions, and one-day walk-alongs. For example, a graduate student joins a faculty member and his or her family for a typical weekend experience. It may provide a snapshot of various issues related to life, work, and academic pursuits.

Significance. It is taken for granted that one studies to become a scholar. But the fact is that one lives to be a scientist or an engineer. Life matters. The way of life even determines whether one is innovative, productive, or not. A holistic approach to academic careers therefore should begin as early as with education. Students not only learn knowledge and skills to specialize in a field of scientific inquiry but also develop habits and a way of life to become a discoverer, a theorist, a methodologist, or any other specific role in scholarship. The earlier they know that it takes something more than study to succeed in science, the quicker they structure life and life engagements in the direction that suits their academic undertakings. The sooner they realize that it goes beyond work to be imaginative and creative in scholarly pursuits, the better they program themselves, how they think and act in everyday life, in a way that facilitates their quest for knowledge.

Reform 3: Provide Guided Exposures to Academia

Status Quo. Graduate education, as its stands now, seems to operate under either the assumption that school is school, and it teaches only academic contents or the assumption that students will automatically know how to practice in the professional role they expect for themselves once they have mastered substantive knowledge and skills. With regard to the doctoral education that prepares for career scholars, students are required to do only regular coursework from class to class, from seminar to seminar, or at a higher level from comprehensive examinations to theses to a dissertation. They are left totally alone or on their own with what they need to do in the role of a beginning academician.

Reform. As part of a complete academic career, doctoral training should and must include a guided exposure to academia in its whole package. Specifically, doctoral students ought to be encouraged, supported, coached, and rendered opportunities to explore academia on major activities a regular academician must perform in his or her professional life. For that purpose, a well-sequenced series of seminars on presenting, teaching, publishing, applying for grants, competing for awards, joining associations, hunting for jobs, and other scholarly undertakings can be offered in the formal training protocol or at least informally along with required coursework. Specific measures may also be implemented to assist students to teach, present, publish, and apply for grants. For example, senior doctoral students are matched with the faculty to co-teach an undergraduate class; faculty members are given tangible incentives to coauthor papers with graduate students for publication; and the chair of a graduate advisory committee is required to take the student to major academic conferences for formal presentation or on-site observation once a year. Another innovative idea concerns the structure and function of the doctoral advisory committee. Besides a one-purpose focus on the dissertation, can the committee take a multipurpose approach? Can it be set up earlier in graduate training in a way that each of its members is assigned to advise and guide the student in a particular area of his or her beginning academic endeavor? In other words, as soon as a student settles in the program, he or she will have a committee behind him or her, with one committee member, the chair perhaps, leading him or her on research, dissertation, and publication, one supervising him or her in teaching and scholarly presentation, one advising him or her on grant writing and funding application, and one directing him or her through job hunting and development of an academic way of life.

Significance. A guided exposure to academia turns doctoral students into beginning scholars. The educational system benefits from the initiative with a practical focus. Doctoral training is no longer education for the sake of education. Instead it is education for an academic career. Academia harvests from the initiative when prospective career academicians explore the landscape, experiment with various new ideas and methods, and turn out products that might first look immature or out of the norm yet substantively could be stimulating, instructive, or even inspirational. A few individuals can make a timely decision to withdraw from the academic pursuit when they see for themselves that the academic world is not the world of their unique talent or their general fortune. The majority, however, are likely to be more motivated, prepared, and determined in their later academic career journey when they integrate learning with practicing, dreaming with doing, and planning with experimenting through a guided exposure to academia earlier at their educational phase.

Reform 4: Depersonalize Graduate Education

Status Quo. Although knowledge is standardized for open circulation in contemporary academia, many individual practitioners still look for personal proclivities, secrets, or idiosyncrasies as ultimate assets, forces, or weapons toward success. Graduate education still features apprenticeship, mentorship, and age-old personal patronage. Whereas educators tend to influence students on a one-on-one basis, students scramble to foster personal relationships with each of their individual advisors. Focus is yet to be put on substance, that is, what an educator is capable of offering and what a student is able to learn about theories, methods, and applications in a discipline.

Reform. Depersonalization of graduate education calls for elimination of all unnecessary and burdensome attachments advisors tend to cement with students at a personal level, and vice versa. In the spirit of depersonalization, a number of innovative ideas can be put in practice. A graduate program can institute policies and procedures to limit the power of one chief advisor and to expand collective supervision by a representative five-member committee for a doctoral student and his or her dissertation research in particular or his or her graduate training in general. For instance, a committee chair would not necessarily put significantly more effort than other committee members in providing academic guidance to the student. The student could call any member of the committee into the chair's position at will. The student would not have to assemble a new committee should he or she adjust his or her substantive focus or change his or her chair. A graduate program may encourage or even require its students to take courses with different faculty members to diversify their general training experience or to prevent an early complete identification with particular instructors. More radically, graduate students may be persuaded or even mandated to change or reshuffle their advisory committee year by year so that they can witness varied guidance and supervision in their acquisition of essential knowledge and skills through major aspects of scholarship. The bottom line is this: Students do not have to do what a particular advisor wants them to do in the way that advisor prefers them to do. Instead, students should always pursue what interests them most, with standard advisement, guidance, and support in theory, methodology, application, and other substantive content from anyone in the graduate faculty.

Significance. Upon depersonalization, professors could phase out "my student," "my advisee," or "my protégé" from their vocabularies. Students could stop feeling fearful about and grateful to "my advisor," "my mentor," or "my sponsor" in their journey through graduate training. As both professor and student are freed from personal bondage and individual obligations inherent in it, each can dedicate more attention and effort to substance, its learning and production, in a discipline. A new system of beliefs, norms, and values will emerge when educators understand that if they want to leave any mark behind them, they should leave it on scholarship, rather than on a few individuals, in a discipline or for the whole knowledge enterprise. A new pattern of behavior will follow when students realize that if they set out to succeed in academia, they should build upon a solid foundation of knowledge and skills rather than the soft shoulders of a few personal contacts.

Reform 5: Provide Opportunities for Student Exchange and Transfer

Status Quo. Students are currently tied to their chosen graduate school. They are habituated to stay with their choice while graduate institutions are structured to prevent student exchange and transfer from one another. A student enters a graduate school, settles there, learns there, graduates there, and carries the reputation or brand of the school as if it were part of family background throughout his or her whole academic career. If a student does not fare well in his or her affiliation with a graduate school, he or she will feel bad there, fail there, and most likely end his or her academic aspiration altogether there.

Reform. Given the standardization of knowledge and skills in most disciplines, graduate curriculums can be designed and developed in a way that facilitates student exchange and transfer among academic institutions. With regard to student exchange, a graduate program may require all its students to have a minimum of one-semester and a maximum of one-year experience with other graduate schools in the form of coursework, teaching, and/or research assistantship. For example, a third-year graduate student from School A enters School B for one semester where he or she takes one or two courses while working with one or two professors on research projects in his or her preparation for formal dissertation work back in School A in the following semester. On the surface, it may appear difficult for both students and graduate schools to make arrangement for such an exchange. However, when exchange becomes a standard practice for all graduate schools, there then will be inner needs, outer demands, and inter-organizational mechanisms coming up for it across the educational landscape.

In the matter of student transfer, graduate schools can reconcile with one another to welcome transfer students at different stages of doctoral training. There are uniform requirements for first-year admission. In the same spirit, there can and should be standard procedures for second, third, fourth, or even later-year transfers. For example, a student who has taken all graduate courses in School A may directly sign up for comprehensive examinations in School B when he or she transfers there. A student who is at the stage of ABD, all but dissertation, in School B may directly register for dissertation research in School A when he or she arrives there as a transfer. Individual students may take necessary actions to bring themselves in line with other students at the same level if indeed there are holes or deficiencies in their training at a previous institution. However, they do not have to start all over again when they switch from one school to another. An easing of student transfer is obviously most needed between elite and non-elite programs. Before all qualified graduate schools adopt an all-way open and flexible transfer policy toward one another, elite schools may seek one-on-one alliance or partnership with non-elite schools so that they can readily receive bright and highly-motivated students from non-elite schools while allowing some of their lower echelons of students to go to a program that is more suited to those students' individual capabilities and desires.

Significance. The proposed reform does not necessarily call for change of standards and requirements set by each graduate school for its training program. It simply asks all academic institutions to be flexible, to properly recognize each other, and essentially to admit the transferability of standard knowledge and skills provided in the level of graduate education. With exchange, students benefit by diversifying their learning experience and expanding their professional contact. A graduate program gains from new perspectives as well as new needs brought by students from other schools. Through transfer, students will no longer feel entrenched in any particular program. A graduate institution will always have to be aware of its academic rigor, fairness, and integrity in facing a free flow of students. Between elite and non-elite schools, while no one needs to be stressed to death for the sake of elitism, every deserving student can make an attempt to be graduated with a brand name degree of their dream.

CHAPTER 3

JOB SEARCH AND CHANGE

Education is a necessary condition for making a career in academia. It follows an academician all the way along his or her career pathway. It is not, however, a sufficient condition. A prospective scholar who has fulfilled all educational requirements has yet to locate an academic institution in which he or she can earn a living and make connection to the established academic mainstream (Abel, 1984; Barnes, 2007; Bowen & Sosa, 1989; Catter, 1976; Clark & Centra, 1985; Dore, 1976; Formo & Reed, 1999; Heiberger & Vick, 2001; Shaw, 2000).

BACKGROUND AND ANALYSIS

The search for a job is part of an academic career because the position found places one in a work environment that may determine one's productivity, contributions, and quality of life. The search is not part of academic effort because it just meets a survival requirement. If he or she did not have to, no scholar would like to engage in a job search, a disturbing distraction from serious academic work.

In general, a job search provides one with the first opportunity to assess one's situation for a real-life academic adventure. After years of schooling, one has achieved something by obtaining a doctoral degree in a subject area. But most of one's properties are still ascribed: What age range one falls under, what racial and ethnic group one comes from, what gender category one belongs to, what school one graduates from, and whom one works with as mentor. The last two characteristics are partially achieved rather than ascribed because it takes efforts to enter any graduate school and a school of great prestige in particular. As wholly achieved properties, such as the dissertation, a number of articles in print or accepted for publication, and a few courses taught, are somewhat sketchy for beginning academicians, they may soon realize that it is important who you are or where you are from in the community of scholarship, just as it is important in the world of the mundane.

Specifically, one can learn a few lessons through a job search. First, one can immediately know whether one's advisors are genuinely supportive. Do they write glowing or business-as-usual recommendations? Do they give honest advice on where one should apply for one's first job? Do they send their letters of recommendation in a timely fashion? Do they warn that they can send only a few letters on one's behalf? Second, one can immediately observe the change in attitude and behavior by academic insiders. As student, one receives advice and encouragement from one's advisors and other seniors in the discipline. As soon as one's student chapter is closed, disciplinary insiders begin to look at one as a competitor. They no longer treat the candidate with condescension. They do not show kindness and support either. Third, one can have a critical taste of rejection from academia. One sends out a group of application letters with sincere hopes. One is soon pounded repeatedly by negative responses. One begins to understand that the academic world is not always a land of realizing dreams. Fourth, one learns to take a business approach toward the academic career. One is given a telephone interview, a campus visit, and a job offer. One manages one's impression, negotiates with job grantors, compromises on expectations, takes advantage of one's situations, and maximizes gains. Fifth, one develops a definite sense of reality about oneself regarding all of one's ascribed and achieved features. How much is one welcomed as a male or female, a gay or lesbian, a minority or majority member, a person of color or non-color, a native or nonnative speaker, and a person of young or middle age? How much is one appreciated as a graduate from an elite versus a non-elite school, a student of a renowned versus an ordinary scholar, and a junior academician of considerable versus minimal achievements? Finally, one learns to accept the fact that academic work is a profession and that academia is a marketplace. Throughout the entire job-search process, one walks out of one's idealized view of scholarship and academia, plunging into the reality of competition and struggle for survival. One begins to realize that engaging in academic work is not only to pursue a noble goal but also to secure a source of income. One begins to understand that in an academia where market forces reign, one fails or succeeds not only by one's own endeavor but also by unexpected luck or misfortune.

If first job placement hinges basically upon ascribed characteristics, later job change is to a large degree prompted by achieved properties. While everyone has to look for a first job, not a great many academicians ever change their jobs. There are several reasons for the general lack of job change among academic professionals. First, most scholars land tenure-track positions. It takes years of effort to be tenured with an institution. One loses one's years of service for tenure when one leaves the institution. One is not likely to regain full service credit for tenure upon joining a new institution. Second, most tenured scholars tend to stay with their guaranteed jobs because few academic institutions are willing to grant tenure to a once-tenured scholar from another institution. Who wants to exchange his or her tenured job for an untenured one? Which institution would follow its competitor's rules in offering someone tenure without applying its own standards for tenure? Third, academicians are judged primarily by scholarly contributions rather than years of service. Scholars who have been in long years of service are not necessarily strong "comeback kids" in the job market if they do not have adequate contributions on their records. One simply looks unworthy when one has a long history of service and a short list of achievements. Fourth, academic creativity and productivity are essentially uncertain and unpredictable. While an institution is interested in hiring a candidate because of his or her existing accomplishments, that candidate may not always feel so confident about his or her future efforts and fortunes in a new organizational environment. Finally, the academic profession is relatively guarded from market forces. Scholars who are devoted to their academic pursuits are likely to put up with difficulties and setbacks in mundane life. As a result, there are far more old-fashioned commitment and loyalty to employment than benefit-driven or gain-motivated job change and switch among academic professionals.

Despite a generally low level of change, academicians do look for and take up new jobs after their initial placement. There are typically three types of job change among career scholars. One takes place in the first several years among new entrants. New people may change their jobs relatively frequently because (a) they have difficulty in adapting to scholarly work in general and assimilating to an academic institution in particular; (b) they maintain contact with their advisors and feel free to ask them for letters of recommendation; (c) they have yet to realize the importance of time and tenure in academic life or simply wish to explore the world for a few years; (d) they switch from research-centered or elite to teaching-oriented or non-elite programs and vice versa as they know more about what they want to do and can do as career scholars; (e) They still look new and promising; and (f) hiring institutions tend to bet that first-time job defectors from another institution are more likely to stay with them than those brand-new graduates who have never had any formal employment experience. Another job change involves job opportunities related to academic employment. There are people who fall off the conventional academic track. They may conclude their premature scholarly career once and forever. They may land governmental, industrial, service, or counseling jobs related to their academic training and pursue freelance or applied research with or without formal connections to their discipline. There are people who move from applied fields to the academic mainstream. With inspiration from their practice-related jobs, they may become more productive scholars. There are people who move from affiliated research centers to established academic departments within an institution. With grant experiences from funded research, they may be better positioned to gain tenure and to serve the university community. There are also people who change their jobs because of marriage and family obligations. Still another job change falls upon those who have developed an attractive research record as well as an extensive scholarly network within and outside their discipline. They are enticed to join a department, lead a unit, or develop a program with higher salaries, more power, and richer resources. At the personal level, such job change signifies recognition, reward, and upward mobility in the academic career. Among institutions, it points to the competitive edge private, research, and elite universities often have over their public, teaching, and non-elite counterparts.

From a historical and systemic point of view, an academic job market takes form and sustains itself when educational institutions continually turn out qualified job seekers, existing job occupants frequently switch employment institutions, and academic employers routinely change their personnel. In the distant past, no job market existed when some reflective or investigative personalities self-taught to be academic masters and cultivated close apprentices to be their followers in a subject or institution. As universities were opened from place to place, there used to be a brief period of time when academic departments desperately hunted for eligible candidates to fill their faculty vacancies with bachelors, masters, or even no-degree practitioners. A similar situation may appear in new areas of inquiry where qualified scholars have yet to be trained by first-generation explorers. But the academic job market as a whole in the contemporary era has long and consistently featured a high supply of prepared applicants and a low availability of appropriate openings. Educational institutions are well established and prepared to produce doctoral graduates. No institution would volunteer to cut programs or eliminate itself because some of its graduates are not able to secure academic jobs. Some programs may even capitalize on the oversupply of academic candidates to expand and to maintain its scale. Doctoral degree holders then have to go overseas, enter nonacademic sectors, such as industry and government, or retreat to part-time teaching or postdoctoral research as they fail to crack open the front door to academia. There may be seasonal, periodic, regional, or discipline-specific loosening when the number of applicants comes more nearly into balance with the number of openings. Oversupply, however, will stay long and steady as a landmark feature in the academic job market. In a sense, it reflects how employment standards or educational levels move up in both academic and nonacademic sectors. The academic sector begins to retain only postdoctoral trainees for its own use while the nonacademic sector takes more and more doctoral graduates from it.

INNOVATION AND REFORM

Job search and change should not be only personal chores and exercises for individual scholars to draw upon their smartness and shrewdness. They are part of the social process in academia (Abel, 1984; Barnes, 2007; Becher, 1989; Catter, 1976; Cotten et al., 2001; Formo & Reed, 1999; Heiberger & Vick, 2001; Shaw, 2000). Innovation and reform take systemic efforts and will have consequences for overall academic dynamics.

Reform 1: Blind Review of Applications

Status Quo. Job applications are received and reviewed openly by the faculty in an academic department. Reviewers know directly or indirectly who job applicants are by name, gender, age, race, location, school of graduation, and other obviously ascribed or semi-ascribed characteristics. Faculty members, whether or not they sit on the recruitment committee, may unreasonably advocate or oppose an application upon calls from their former advisors or academic friends at large. They may also act with bias toward a candidate in terms of his or her racial, ethnic, religious, educational, or cultural affinity. The end result is that not all applicants are given equal consideration and treatment on the basis of their academic credentials, potential, and deservedness.

Reform. One innovative idea that could be put in practice is blind review. Like peer-review used widely in academic publications, review of job applications can be arranged without any reference to name, gender, age, educational background, and other ascribed or semi-ascribed characteristics. Procedurally, a recruiting agency, in its job advertisement, would advise prospective applicants to prepare their curriculum vitae and supporting materials in accordance with the proposed reform. For example, an applicant writes a cover letter with his or her name and contact information. In the curriculum vitae, one does not put down one's name. One lists the degrees held, but not the institution from which each was awarded. Regarding employment history, one may catalogue the number of years worked for an employer, but not the specific years from beginning to end. Among supporting materials, one removes one's name from all personal papers, syllabi, and publications with whiteout. The recruiting agency authorizes a non-review person to receive applications and gives each of them a reference number. Members of the review and selection committee are advised not to guess an applicant's identity nor to perform any search and research on an applicant beyond his or her submitted materials. They are required to focus only on accomplishments, experiences, and other achieved properties. The whole blind review procedure remains in force until a formal decision is made.

Significance. With the proposed reform, people will be hired, less and less because of whom they are and where they are from, but rather more and more because of what they have done and what they are capable of. Specifically, hiring institutions can minimize subjectivity and maximize objectivity in selecting most qualified personnel for their academic programs. Applicants can feel free from nonacademic obstacles, such as discrimination or unfair treatment. They can then put all their efforts into work, building a substantive record in their scholarly career and presenting a competitive case in their job search.

Reform 2: Eliminate Letters of Reference

Status Quo. Letters of reference are residues from apprenticeship. One works under a master, following the master's advice, order, and will. The master initiates one into the world of craftsmanship. Initiation not only ensures that only the master's favorite apprentices enter the practice, but also that the master himself maintains his authority and control in the community of craftsmen. In contemporary academia, knowledge is standardized and widely circulated. Nobody can ever claim absolute ownership of a particular skill, technique, method, model, or theory. But the age-old mentality for the senior to mentor, supervise, and control the junior still holds strong and steady. A letter of recommendation exemplifies how that mentality translates into practice in an institutionalized form. It is taken for granted to the extent that no one would ever ask why a letter of recommendation is necessary when a supposedly independent scholar looks for a job or a change of job in his or her career.

Reform. To keep pace with the modern and postmodern spirit of merit, autonomy, and individualism in scientific inquiry, letters of recommendation ought to be removed from the academic job scene. In other words, no letter of recommendation will ever be asked of any academic applicant to include as a required item in his or her complete job application. After all, what does a letter of recommendation offer? How much does a recruiting agency benefit from it? Does it offer anything that cannot be obtained from other channels, regarding personal character, academic achievements, or professional goals? Isn't it more effective and objective to learn about someone and his or her character, accomplishments, and aspirations through an interview, reading his or her publications, listening to his or her presentations, and other direct contacts? How seriously does an employer take a reference letter? Why does it have to be kept as a convention to burden every party involved? Would it not be nicer and neater if advisors were no longer burdened to write letters of recommendation for students from class to class, graduates were no longer burdened to solicit letters of recommendation from advisor to advisor, and employers were no longer burdened to review letters of recommendation from applicant to applicant?

Significance. Upon removal of recommendations as a required element in the academic job application process, members of the old guard would realize that the best way to keep their influence is not to control who goes where, but to substantiate their own substantive contributions in a content area. All academic participants can feel free to search for jobs wherever they want and change employment whenever they desire. Nobody has to worry about what others, either advisors or supervisors, think about him or her, and what they intend him or her to do. Free from manipulation in human relations, one can be more brave, open, creative, and productive in one's scholarly pursuits.

Reform 3: Academic Equalization

Status Quo. Tremendous gaps exist between private and public, between liberal arts and comprehensive, and between research and teaching institutions. A variety of perceptions and practices spread to sustain the gaps. For instance, many academic advisors use letters of reference to influence students in job choices. Faculty from higher-ranking universities often coerce their students into research institutions by threatening not to write a letter of recommendation or write a letter of non-support or even a letter of negative recommendation if students abandon their training in research and retreat in comfort to a teaching position. Faculty from lower-ranking schools sometimes discourage their students by not sending any letter of recommendation to any institution they themselves deem too high for their graduates to attempt.

Reform. The main idea of academic equalization is that elite schools recruit to their faculty graduates from none-elite schools for research experience while non-elite schools recruit to their academic staff graduates from elite schools for pedagogical growth. Blind review and elimination of reference letters can obviously facilitate academic equalization. With blind review, new entrants can be naturally distributed across academic institutions on the basis of their initial achievements. Graduates from non-elite schools may join elite departments if they demonstrate their capabilities and potentials. Graduates from elite schools are likely to land jobs in non-elite institutions if they fail to prove their worth and do not show promise.

Besides blind review and elimination of references, academic equalization calls for change in the mentalities of both institutions and individuals. At the present, most academic institutions reason that since they look for a lifetime employee to fill in a permanent position, they must make every effort to identify and hire an exact fit in terms of an individual's ascribed, semi-ascribed, and achieved characteristics. Similarly, most individuals calculate that because they are married to an institution for life, they must take every care to apply to and choose a place that best serves their needs and aspirations. To break the obsessive "fit" and "match" mentality underlying academic sectarianism, institutions should recognize that organizational diversity and vitality are best kept by people from both elite and non-elite schools, with strengths in both research and teaching, and in orientations of both analysis and application. Individuals should admit that they need a few years to explore and figure out what they are capable of accomplishing in their academic careers, that growth in both research and instruction is beneficial in the long run, and that things do not always turn out the way they hope for. Both institutions and individuals should understand that job change is normal and natural throughout the academic career. Only when they do not fixate on employment permanency, will they be able to free themselves from their rigid quest for exact fit and perfect match. Academic sectarianism will then lose ground, giving way to academic equalization.

Significance. Equalization does not challenge the distinction an academic institution holds for its scholarly productivity and contributions. Nor does it call for equal treatment of all regardless of individual creativity and merits. It simply targets the sectarian bias one group of academic institutions have against another. Most critically, it aims at the mentality of pedigree that is so deeply rooted in the mind of many ordinary academicians. With equalization in force, an academic institution welcomes new talents to expand and strengthen its program not because those new talents fit and match in terms of their ascribed or semi-ascribed qualities, but rather because they qualify and deserve by their accomplishments and efforts. A career-making academician does not have to shun some institutions while kowtowing to others simply because he or she is from a particular family, cultural, social, or educational background. As long as the candidate has substantive contributions to scholarship, he or she can apply anywhere and will receive fair consideration.

Reform 4: Eliminate Job Interviewing Services by Academic Associations

Status Quo. Some academic associations offer job-interviewing services at their annual conventions. Although these services vary by scale, form, and content, they are alike in procedure and operation. A common procedure is that prospective employers submit a comprehensive description specifying the requirements, responsibilities, and application process for their job; job applicants mail in a professional profile detailing their preparation, accomplishments, and preferences; employers are given access to the pool of interested job applicants and their application files while job applicants can view all participating employers and their job descriptions; and the association's employment service staff match employers with applicants, make schedules for them to meet for a formal or informal interview.

Reform. The service sounds great conceptually since it takes advantage of an academic association's annual convention to bring job seekers into contact with job granters. It does not serve any actual purpose, however, simply because the venue of an academic conference is not an appropriate place where either wholehearted job seeking or serious job granting can occur. For example, an employer manages to send one, two, or even a few larger members of its academic employees to conduct interviews at the conference. Those employees pass on their observations and interview notes to an official recruitment committee at home that, in all likelihood, consists of totally different people, upholds somewhat different standards, and operates under contrastingly different group dynamics. Each applicant spends time and a considerable amount of money as an unemployed or underemployed job hunter to attend an annual convention in order to have some interviews. The applicant has hope that each interview will yield a job offer, but may find in the end that he or she just played a game without any gain. Indeed, serious application review, interviewing, screening, and deliberation should take place only at the employment organization. The dynamics of collective consideration and decisions on hiring cannot be replaced or replicated elsewhere. Removal of job interviewing services at the annual convention of academic associations is in order.

Significance. Without any false sense of hope, job applicants can put all their effort into where it should go and avoid being fooled by useless game playing or being abused by any obviously belittling yet nonproductive procedure. An employer can then focus all necessary effort pertaining to hiring at its own site, ensuring the integrity of the process and the success of the task. Academic associations may also free themselves to fulfill some truly useful and beneficial functions for their general membership in job hunting, such as job announcements, information exchange, job-hunting seminars, and other employment services.

Reform 5: Standardize Advertisements for Job Openings in a Discipline

Status Quo. Job advertisements in a discipline are fragmented among different media outlets. An applicant has to visit different sources, from a local newspaper' advertisement section, a regional association's newsletter, a specialty association's website, and a national association's employment bulletin, to a few national publications in higher education, to find out who recruits for what in his or her job-hunting endeavor. Along with its fragmentation, job announcement is often barricaded behind the walls of some elitist bastion or within the boundary of each sectarian territory. For example, an elite school announces its faculty openings only to people and institutions on selected, sometimes exclusive, networks while a community college remains hesitant to publicize its available instructional positions in any medium that goes beyond the locality of the community it serves.

Reform. A disciplinary association can obviously serve as a prime site where all job openings in the discipline are listed in a special publication with such clear and indicative titles as *Employment Bulletin* and *Job Bank*. The job listing is published monthly and sent in a timely fashion to each academic department featuring the discipline. All individual members are also on the mailing list to receive the publication as soon as it comes out in print. Besides its paper version, the job listing can be made available on the worldwide web. When appropriate and necessary, the web version may enable visitors to access the whole inventory of job openings not only alphabetically by listing institution, but also categorically by location, type of institution, nature of work, application deadline, and other identifying variables. For example, an applicant interested in teaching at a community college in the South may input "domestic, south" for "location," "teaching" under "nature of work," and "community college" for "type of institution" when he or she searches the inventory on the web to find exactly what he or she is looking for.

The key feature of such a master list of job openings in a discipline is, of course, its completeness or all-inclusiveness. All available jobs, whether offered by conventional or non-conventional, elite or non-elite, public or private, and regional or national institutions, are included in the list.

Teaching positions are advertised along with research jobs. Hiring of temporary staff is announced amid searches for permanent employees. Openings in practice are listed side by side with vacancies in academia. For example, an opening for a part-time instructor at a local University of Phoenix campus is followed by a call for applications for a full-time faculty position at Princeton University in the same disciplinary association's employment bulletin. In other words, the known job listing of a discipline becomes the place where every possible employer goes to place its hiring announcement when it looks for an employee with training and background in the discipline.

Significance. A nondiscriminatory and all-inclusive listing of job openings in a discipline benefits both hiring institutions and job-seeking applicants. Employment organizations no longer have to advertise their job vacancies on different media outlets and can save cost and labor on recruitment. Candidates find all job advertisements from one place and will never worry about missing an opportunity for possible job placement. Most important, a complete job listing functions as an open market for job search and exchange in a discipline. Because it is widely known by all in the discipline, the listing itself can serve as a *de facto* insurance that every job candidate is informed of all possible opportunities in the open market and that every opening position is given the best possible test of competition by the largest possible pool of applications.

CHAPTER 4

ORGANIZATIONAL EMPLOYMENT

Institutional affiliation is another necessary condition for an academic career. Just as in education, where not everyone passes various hurdles to reach the doctorate, not every degree holder is able to locate and solidify an institutional base in the academic world (Altbach, Berdahl, & Gumport, 2005; Bianco-Mathis & Chalofsky, 1999; Bok, 2003; Clark & Lewis, 1985; Coiner & George, 1998; Gosling & Noordam, 2006; Greenwood & Levin, 2001; Newman, Couturier, & Scurry, 2004; Readings, 1996; Rhodes, 2001; Shattock, 2003; Toren & Moore, 1998; Weingartner, 1999; Wildavsky, 1989).

BACKGROUND AND ANALYSIS

Institutional affiliation remains at the center of an academic career. First, the institution provides a secular job by which a career-making academician earns an income to support himself or herself. In the era of social differentiation and organizational employment, it is rare for a scholar to be able to do serious academic work and build a respectable career by either taking a non-academic job or selling his or her academic products directly to a buying market. Social perception dictates that a career professional falls under the general division of labor and belongs to a systematic operation of the academic enterprise. Personal limitation does not allow for frequent switches among different states of mind and modes of activity. A career-making scholar relies upon an academic institution for his or her survival needs and for work in a specialized area of inquiry.

The fact that career-making professionals depend upon colleges or universities for employment income makes the quality of an academic career conditional on the level of support afforded by the institution. As it is known, faculty members in elite schools and leading research universities not only receive better salaries but also are better equipped for supplementary income through grants and consulting. Faculty members in less prestigious institutions, on the other hand, have to engage in off-semester teaching to increase their usually meager salary. The worst situation is that of postdoctoral scholars who receive only fellowships as their major source of income. To make ends meet, they either work on someone else's project or commute to different campuses for part-time teaching. Difference in the level of income often translates directly into qualitative difference in scholarly activity and output. Better-paid scholars have more time to do research, show higher productivity in publication, and enjoy more visibility in scholarly influence. In contrast, lower paid academic professionals spend more time on teaching, have less time for research, turn out fewer publications, and are hence more likely to fall into obscurity in the academic community.

Second, the institution provides an indispensable environment in which career-making academicians develop ideas, produce scholarly products, and prepare them for academic circulation. Academicians need to use books, journals, documents, and other academic materials in libraries, special collections, or archives; they need to work in laboratories if they practice in a discipline that depends upon experimental work; they need to attend professional seminars, disciplinary workshops, and thematic conferences; they need to consult or debate with colleagues, students, and other qualified participants; and they need to obtain secretarial or technical support and utilize computers, copying machines, and other modern research tools. In small or remote institutions, academicians may not find most of their needed references in a small library on campus or in the whole area. Interlibrary loans offer some relief but have various constraints. One has to file paperwork or pay money; one has to wait and can keep a loaned item for only a short period of time; and oftentimes by the time of the arrival of a requested item, one has already lost momentum for any serious use of the item in research. In institutions with a lack of academic stimulation, people may shun each other on scholarly matters; not many brown bag activities, seminars, speeches, or conferences are available on campus; and various constraints are instituted to limit access to information from the outside, to discourage contacts with colleagues in other institutions, and to limit attendance at professional conferences elsewhere. Obviously, career making depends upon institutional support; and support afforded by an institution varies according to its scale, mission, reputation, and resource. Differences in institutional support can translate directly into differences in scholarly productivity. It is a totally unfair game for a career-making scholar in a resource-impoverished, academically backward college or university to compete for academic recognition with his or her counterpart in a resource-rich, academically stimulating institution.

Third, the institution connects academic career aspirants to a disciplinary establishment in particular and the academic mainstream in general. It grants academicians legitimacy in conducting scholarly activities and assigns them specific tasks in research, service, and teaching. Just as education gives them stamps of proof for entry into the world of scholarship, institutional affiliation provides academicians with "drivers' licenses" to function in the modern academic enterprise. The academic enterprise is a well differentiated and well-organized operation. Questions lie under defined subjects. Subjects fall into recognized fields. Fields belong to established disciplines. Disciplines are institutionalized in academic organizations through centers, departments, and colleges. In order to raise meaningful questions, develop sensible solutions, and make recognizable breakthroughs in academic matters, individual scholars have to enter an academic organization, work in a specific division, and specialize in a particular domain of activity or territory of interest. In other words, academic tasks are socially defined, assigned, and executed through organizational establishments. No matter how many ideas, insights, and talents they have, individual academic aspirants may only fall into obscurity or deviance if they fail to place themselves properly in institutions in the academic enterprise.

The importance of institutional affiliation in keeping academicians in the academic current and mainstream was long witnessed even in the beginning of the modern academic era in the discipline that is least dependent upon institutions. In the early 1800s, philosopher Ludwig Feuerbach soon found himself dismissed from the academic currency after retreating into countryside living. In the ever-changing twenty-first century, how far can a philosopher go if he or she stays out of an academic institution without access to the literature, the logistical support, and the oftentimes institutionally or socially created and maintained debates on issues? It is needless to say a scientist who depends upon the library, the laboratory, the grant, and the community of science formed and supported within and among academic institutions.

Finally, the institution serves as a screening and sorting mechanism for social placement. Within the academic community, it determines how academic professionals develop their self-concept and self-image, how they are identified by other academic organizations and practitioners, and how they as well as their activity are coded into the knowledge enterprise. There obviously exists not only a system of knowledge in terms of subject, field, and discipline, but also a hierarchy of academic practitioners according to their position, seniority, and institutional affiliation. An academic institution grants positions, rewards, and honors to individuals who are affiliated with it. An individual and his or her academic products are then identified and labeled, in almost every occasion, by his or her affiliated institution as well as the position and honor he or she has earned from it. It is natural for editors, funding agencies, and other academic community members to use one's institutional affiliation as a primary basis to make decisions regarding one's fundamental interests: whether or not to give one's manuscript, research proposal, or speech serious consideration for publication or funding. On a regular university campus, students and the faculty keep rushing to seminars conducted by guest professors from Harvard, Oxford, Cambridge, and other well-known institutions even though they are often disappointed by the actual substance gained in such seminars. The academic brand names are just so eye-catching that they seem to work in the academic unconscious. At a typical academic journal, the editor has access to information on a manuscript's authors and their institutional affiliation, and makes the first decision whether to reject an article submitted without peer evaluation or to send it out for review. Who knows what difference institutional affiliation makes when a journal editor evaluates two similar articles, one by a senior professor of an Ivy League university and the other by a junior member of the faculty at a small liberal arts college or an urban comprehensive university whose primary mission is known to be undergraduate instruction?

Outside the academic circle, institutional affiliation provides an academic professional with social legitimacy, identity, status, and impression in interacting with friends, relatives, neighbors, and other members of a community. Social legitimacy concerns one's qualification to speak and publish in academia as well as one's deservedness of the kind of social expectation and respect accorded to the academic profession among all other different occupations in society. The fact that one works for a locally known academic institution as a researcher or professor automatically removes any reservation in the mind of local residents about one's legitimacy as an academic professional. Social identity concerns how one is identified in social communications. For example, one is called "Professor X" if one holds a professorial position in a university. Social status determines how much respect and what kind of treatment one receives from one's community and social network. Neighbors may address an academician with an honorific title when he or she exercises in the community park, dines in local restaurants, or shops in neighborhood stores. Friends and relatives may look up to an academician for advice and suggestions on matters of importance to them. Finally, social impression confers a general social image by which academicians are perceived and treated by others in the community. It is a generalized social property they develop and possess out of their legitimacy, identity, and status pertaining to their occupational pursuits.

INNOVATION AND REFORM

Academic institutions can be made better for many different needs and purposes (Alstete, 2000; Altbach, Berdahl, & Gumport, 2005; Baldwin & Chronister, 2001; Beckham, 1986; Bok, 2003; Clark & Lewis, 1985; Gosling & Noordam, 2006; Gossett & Bellas, 2002; Leaming, 2003; Lucas, 2000; Mortimer, Bagshaw, & Masland, 1985; Newman, Couturier, & Scurry, 2004; Rhodes, 2001; Shattock, 2003; Weingartner, 1999). As far as career academicians and their career-making efforts are concerned, five innovations can be considered for possible implementation.

Reform 1: Make Faculty Exchange a Standard Practice

Status Quo. Academic institutions have their own structure, process, climate, and culture. Some emphasize research, innovation, and intellectual growth. Some focus on teaching, learning, and collective sharing. An academic professional, after long affiliation and eventual identification with an institution, is often programmed into a specific way of thinking and acting which may not necessarily be beneficial to his or her overall career development. Since it is difficult for individuals to change jobs and to switch from one institution to another, it may only be feasible for institutions to exchange faculty and research staff with each other.

Reform. The main idea of faculty exchange is that individual scholars are afforded opportunities to change, to diversify their institutional experience amid a long affiliation with one institution. They would keep employment with their primary or home institution but would be able to stay for a year or more at another institution without losing any years of service credit. This innovation could be put into action by either institutions or individuals. Institutions could make discipline-to-discipline or department-to-department exchange of their faculty and academic staff on a short-term basis. For example, a research university could arrange to have its faculty work one year in a teaching university while receiving the same number of faculty to work on campus from its collaborative teaching counterpart. The exchanged faculty members work in the exchanged setting but continue to receive all salaries and benefits from their home institution. Individually, a faculty member from a liberal arts college might contact someone in a comprehensive university to exchange jobs for one year. During the exchange, each works in a new organizational environment but draws salary and benefits from the original employer. At the end of the exchange, each goes back to the original position without any disruption in years of service. Individual exchange can be coordinated and facilitated by a special office in each academic institution or by some national agencies specializing in faculty exchange.

Significance. Advantages of faculty exchange are obvious. Individuals gain exposure to new organizational environments. Research-oriented scholars sharpen their instructional skills and become effective professors by working in teaching institutions. Teaching-centered instructors broaden their research experience and become productive scholars by participating in serious projects in research universities. Each becomes a balanced academician with richer and more diverse experiences. Institutions benefit from new blood, new ideas, and new ways of working without invoking the costly process of employee hiring and training. The reform, if it gains popularity, might reduce or even eliminate gaps and barriers between elite and non-elite, research and teaching, national and regional, comprehensive and specialized institutions across the academic landscape.

Reform 2: Rotate for Academic Management

Status Quo. Most academic institutions model after governmental and industrial establishments in administration and management. They look for and cultivate career administrators or managers, although a significant number of these administrators or managers have academic backgrounds, to administer departments, colleges, and other units within their organization. The practice not only creates friction and gaps between front line academicians and their colleague-turned administrators, but also victimizes many potentially promising scholars by luring them away from serious academic pursuits into lifetime academic management. The lure is oftentimes powerful and irresistible because academic administration symbolizes success, including financial success, a version of success even more visible and valuable in the eyes of the general public. People in administrative positions wield power and influence, more than they would be able to gain from academic work. But from a purely technical point of view, scholars fail in their academic careers if they do not make any contributions to knowledge. They sacrifice themselves if they give up or compromise their academic endeavors because of administrative responsibilities.

Reform. The proposed reform is to make academic management a service and a responsibility to be shared by equally capable academicians themselves, rather than a power or a reward to be garnered and possessed by a minority over the majority. Most academicians are rational, well rounded, and therefore self-sufficient individuals. As they constitute the backbone of academic institutions, such as colleges, universities, and research institutes, they make those organizations ideal sites for institutional democracy and self-management. In a typical university, a department chair would rotate in a one-year term or a maximum of a two-year term among all eligible faculty members. Individual faculty members would be selected for service by lottery. Those who have functioned as chairs would not be allowed to serve any more until all eligible members have taken their turn. In a small and stable department, one might have to serve a few times during one's tenure within the department. In a large and changing department, one might never be able to serve as chair although one would always have a chance at each change of term to be chosen through random selection. The upper level of administration would follow the same procedure. College deans would rotate in a two-year term or a maximum of a three-year term among all eligible department chairs. The department whose chair is selected by lottery to serve as college dean would then conduct a new selection to choose a replacement. When a college dean serves out his or her term, he or she would automatically go back to his or her department to be a regular member of the faculty. At the university level, functional vice-presidents are filled by lottery for a three-year term or a maximum of a four-year term by existing college deans. The college whose dean takes turn as a functional vice-president would begin the process of selecting a new dean. A serving functional vice-president would go back to his or her home department at the end of term. Finally, a university president is chosen by lottery among functional vice-presidents to serve for a four-year term or a maximum of a five-year term. At the end of term, he or she, too, becomes a regular faculty member in his or her disciplinary department.

Significance. Under the proposed reform, there would be no costly search for academic administrators, from department chair to college dean to functional vice-president to university president. Administrative personnel come from and go back to the faculty. An institution would take in new blood only at the basic level. It develops and maintains its own management and leadership structure from bottom up, through a natural process, and on its own. There would be neither surprise nor disruption in institutional policy and practice. Conflict between upper and lower levels and among different functional divisions could be minimized. Most important, there would be no career academic administrators or managers but only career academicians. Individual academicians could always remain embedded in their scholarly pursuits and contributions. They would have the opportunity to engage in academic management and serve their fellow academicians with conscience and wisdom. But that would be only a small, necessary and inevitable though, part of their academic career.

Critiques of the proposed reform may arise in different forms. First, academic institutions are situated in larger legislative, political, economic, cultural, and social dynamics. They need to be led by career academic administrators or managers who are programmed to lobby, persuade, convince, and manipulate various parties and forces for funding and support. Second, there are individuals who have better vision, higher insight, stronger will, and greater skills in leading people and manipulating human processes. Third, academicians who are immersed in academic concerns and pursuits are less likely to be able and effective leaders. For each of these possible criticisms, there can be a theoretically sound counter argument. For instance, donations to and funding for an institution is essentially determined by the institution's own reputation and productivity. There is no magic leader who can raise money just by his or her personal charisma. Most academic institutions are well established and programmed to operate in self-sufficiency. Positions are well defined. Tasks are clearly laid out. It would not take much time and effort for an average academician to quickly enter an administrative role and perform those new tasks effectively and efficiently. Above all, the ultimate test is practice. It will never be known whether the proposed reform is feasible and beneficial if no institution cares or dares to ever experiment with it.

Reform 3: Create a Duty-Indicative Ranking System

Status Quo. In the United States and many other countries, a universal ranking system for academicians working in the colleges and universities includes three levels from assistant professor to associate professor to full professor. One is first hired as an assistant professor. After about five years of probationary service, one is granted tenure and promoted to associate professor. After sitting in the rank of associate professor for another five years or so, one becomes a full professor. The problem with this ranking system is that it ranks people but remains almost blind to what people do at each rank. In fact, as far as recognition and reward are concerned, the ranking system does exactly the opposite: One is put under assistant professorship when one works most creatively, diligently, and productively for tenure and promotion, and one is given full professorship when one slows down, seeks comfort and relaxation, or prepares for retirement in one's academic career.

Reform. An innovative idea for reform is to create a new ranking system from lecturer to professor and/or from researcher to professor to better align with what an academician does in work and deserves for rewards and recognition throughout his or her career. Lecturer or researcher constitutes the first level in the ranking system. One becomes a lecturer or researcher when one first enters an institution as a new Ph.D. In the role of lecturer, one carries a full teaching load and expects to develop adequate competency and proficiency in effective classroom instruction. Or as a researcher, one teaches only one course a semester and spends the majority of one's time on research, securing funding for research and publishing findings from research. The rank of lecturer or researcher lasts for ten years in the upward mobility scale. It may stay as a lifetime rank and title for some academicians if they choose to be a career teaching professional or research scholar or if they are unable to climb the ladder toward the higher rank of professorship. The proposed flexibility suits reality well because there are always needs for both classroom instruction and laboratory research in colleges and universities.

The second rank is professor. One is promoted to become a professor after ten years of service as a lecturer or researcher and upon successful fulfillment of essential requirements for professorship. The rank of professorship is in effect indefinitely, depending upon the individual who stays in the rank. One may keep one's professorship until retirement as long as one performs one's research, teaching, and service duty at a proficient and productive level expected of a professor. One may be assigned the lower rank of lecturer or researcher if one does not live up to the expectation of the professorial rank.

Significance. An academician can choose between two routes toward his or her career goal. One is through teaching, from lecturer to professor. The other is through research, from researcher to professor. One may aim high toward professorship or remain at ease with what one does, either teaching or research, in his or her entire career. Academic institutions, on the other hand, can recruit different talents to meet their different needs. A research university may make 70 percent of its positions available for the researcher-professor route and the other 30 percent of its openings for the lecturer-professor pathway. A teaching university may do the opposite, allowing its work to be performed by 70 percent of academic employees on the lecturer-professor track and 30 percent on the researcher-professor trajectory.

Reform 4: Separate Positions from Ranks

Status Quo. It is taken for granted that positions are inseparably tied to ranks. When one is in the rank of assistant professor, one is automatically seen as having the position as an assistant professor. One is called and compensated as an assistant professor even though one may do far more in scholarship than a full professor. In a similar fashion, one is naturally considered as holding the position of a full professor when one is promoted to the rank of full professorship. One is entitled to the level of recognition and reward accorded to a full professor regardless of what one does. In fact, some full professors may do much less in research, teaching, and service than their counterparts in assistant professorships. Indeed, there is a considerable gap between what one contributes in one's position and what one takes under one's rank in academic institutions.

Reform. One way to change the situation is to separate position from rank in the existing ranking system. Rank is redefined as comparable to the degree one holds upon successful conclusion of a doctoral training process. One advances to the rank of associate professorship when one has fulfilled all the requirements for the rank in the lower rank of assistant professor. Similarly, one proceeds to the rank of full professor when one passes the bar for the rank in the lower rank of associate professorship. Rank hence reflects what one did in the past or has accomplished in one's career. It serves as an indicator of honor and recognition. On the other hand, position represents what one does at the present. More pointedly, it determines how one is compensated for the job one is currently doing for an academic institution. For example, one may keep one's achieved rank of full professorship but is nevertheless paid at the position of assistant professor when one engages in classroom instruction without any contribution to scholarship. Or a full professor may be compensated at the level of associate professor when he or she requests a whole period of research from teaching, service, and other essential professorial responsibilities at the full rank. Separation of rank from position can be more easily implemented in the new ranking system proposed under Reform 3. While keeping his or her rank, a professor may simply work in the position of lecturer if he or she would like to teach classes primarily or in the position of researcher if he or she wants to put most of his or her time on research.

Significance. Separated from position, rank can serve as a simple indication of one's achievements in scholarship. It no longer will burden any academician because it does not automatically bring about more or less work to him or her in a position he or she holds in an institution. Individuals will feel free to take positions with an existing or a new academic employer at a level or in a position that fits their interests, preferences, focuses, energy levels, and other personal factors at a particular stage of their scholarly career. Nor will rank pressure any academic institution to recognize, reward, or honor an employee simply because that employee possesses a rank indicative of some deeds he or she performed in scholarship in the past or somewhere else. An academic employer supports one only in accordance with what one does in one's current position. Under the new system of rank-position separation, for example, a university or research institute would just state who did his or her Nobel Prize winning work when he or she held a particular position on its campus rather than unqualifiedly claiming how many Nobel laureates it has on its faculty as part of its scholarly distinction and prestige.

Reform 5: Stop Formation of a Part-Time Teaching Profession/a Floating Research Underclass

Status Quo. A part-time teaching profession is in the making as academic institutions turn out master-level as well as doctorate-level graduates blindly, to some degree irresponsibly, to the market while taking enjoyment in exploiting an oversupply of academic labor to save cost, to boost profit, and to keep their existing faculty policies. Part-time instructors teach courses for different departments in a comprehensive university or different colleges in a large area. They run from class to class or campus to campus just to earn a living. Some part-timers have a Ph.D. degree. They are resigned to part-time teaching because they cannot find permanent jobs in the academic market. Some part-timers hold a master's degree while remaining enrolled indefinitely in a doctorate program. They take part-time teaching in full gear when they see the poor prospect of formal employment for new Ph.D. graduates.

By a similar yet slightly different force, a floating research underclass is emerging in academia and its surrounding areas as well. Among members of this emergent floating research underclass, there are not only victims of academic overproduction in the domestic market, but also sacrifices by foreign institutions of higher learning across national borders. Most of these researchers have Ph.D. degrees or master's degrees at least. In colleges and universities, they work on projects controlled by the regular faculty as research assistants or postdoctoral scholars. While they may make substantive contributions to those projects, they are often paid as low as students and may not be allowed to take any credit in scholarly publications. For better pay or higher stability, some researchers float to the industry or the government where they can serve only as mere tools of changing commercial innovation or pure material for routine governmental management. The prospect for one to make any scholarly contribution on the basis of training remains even more remote outside academia.

Reform. To maintain the quality of college education, institutions of higher learning should keep an adequate full-time faculty force for classroom instruction and student mentoring. In universities with doctorate programs, part-time teaching should be reserved exclusively for graduate students who have passed comprehensive examinations and are registered formally for dissertation research. It should also be limited to what these doctoral students can handle under the condition that each all-but-dissertation student is allowed to teach a maximum of two courses a semester for a maximum of two years. In community colleges, educational requirements for the faculty should be lifted to a higher level, from the master's level to the doctoral level. All new hiring should then be Ph.D. holders. Universities that do not have doctoral programs should first have a full-time faculty capable of handling 90 percent of their whole teaching task. When they look for part-time instructors to meet the remaining 10 percent of their teaching tasks, they should eye only those working professionals who hold Ph.D. degrees and already have a full-time career job in the private or public sector. A part-time instructor should not be assigned more than one course a semester.

With regard to research, academic institutions should work together to provide adequate recognition and support for people who make due contributions to scholarship, most important, to refrain from exploiting trained researchers from overseas or new doctorates who do not fare well in the job market. By specific measures, research universities first ought to create and maintain an adequate number of positions for full-time researchers in their pursuit of knowledge. The current model of using a few faculty members to lead independent research teams composed of students and assistants must be reformed to suit a new reality of fast change, equal access, fair competition, and large process in scholarship. Second, research institutions must set some ground rules for using students, hiring research assistants, and keeping postdoctoral scholars. For example, research assistants are paid adequately for their time and effort, students are involved only as part of a clearly specified learning protocol, and postdoctoral training is limited to a two-year term upon receipt of a Ph.D. degree. The last measure is especially important in ridding of a prevailing practice in many academic institutions where foreign as well as domestically trained doctorates are exploited indefinitely as postdoctoral trainees with neither due recognition in scholarship nor due compensation for labor. In other words, an academic institution should recruit only new Ph.D.'s as postdoctoral trainees, can keep them in the status of traineeship for only two years, and must hire them as formal researchers with all due respects and benefits if it needs to employ them longer for its research mission.

Significance. The proposed reform for college instruction will certainly serve to protect the integrity of the teaching profession. Teaching from community college to liberal arts institution to urban comprehensive university will remain off limits to those who have only a master's degree. Setting the minimum educational requirement at the Ph.D. level for both full-time and part-time college instruction not only ensures the quality and sanctity of higher education, but also loosens the academic market for job placement by doctoral graduates. Indeed, a considerable number of unemployed or underemployed Ph.D. holders in the current market can be rightfully placed when all community colleges open the door to them and to them only. In research universities, doctoral students can be facilitated in their training since they are given only limited teaching assignments for a limited period of time. The quality of undergraduate instruction is ensured as only doctoral graduates who have made it to the stage of dissertation research are allowed in classroom teaching. In all other colleges and universities where no doctoral degree is conferred, full-time instruction by the regular faculty will be complemented, enriched, and diversified by part-time teaching when it is exclusively provided by doctorate-level working professionals who have a full-time career in various areas of practice.

Likewise, the proposed change for university research is intended to bring about fair treatment of field, laboratory, and project-based researchers who make due contributions to scholarship. As the age-old practice that a scholarly master uses apprentices for no compensation in his or her research agenda loses ground, there will be flatter and less hierarchical institutions for academicians to develop and grow in the general interest of knowledge. A new belief that every qualified researcher deserves proper recognition and support in his or her academic endeavor will soon take root. The landscape of scholarship will then see less entrenchment in particular paradigms but more competition among diverse forces when researchers are given the opportunity or empowered to work on equal footing across academic institutions.

CHAPTER 5

PROFESSIONAL NETWORK

Employment by a college, a university, or a research institute is a necessary, but not sufficient, condition for one's academic career. To accomplish what is expected of a scholarly life as career, one has to build a personal network for continual research funding and continual publication of research products (Bauer, 1999; Brodkey, 1987; Busch, 1986; Coser, Kadushin, & Powell, 1982; Darling, 2005; Digiusto, 1994; Fox, 1985; Kitchin & Fuller, 2005; Lewis, 1997; Locke, Spirduso, & Silverman, 2007; McGinty, 1999; Powell, 1985; Ries & Leukefeld, 1995; Shaw, 2002b).

BACKGROUND AND ANALYSIS

Network building begins with peers, classmates, colleagues, and former advisors. Although it is often phrased diplomatically as developing common interests, building common ground, and fostering professional congeniality, networking is actually a mode of social adaptation for academic professionals to explore and sometimes exploit human relationships for the benefits of their scholarly careers. Thus, many academicians develop their substantive interests in consideration of funding and publication possibilities. They may even shape and simplify their human contacts toward the "I-Funding-Publishing" triangle that is essential to the realization of their career aspirations.

Funding sources and publication outlets are numerous. Network building around research, finance, and publication takes delicate maneuvering through a complicated social process. For funding sources, there are private and public agencies, national and international organizations, programs oriented toward the practical or the theoretical, as well as various foundations with differing philosophies. While funding decisions are mostly based upon the scientific merit of proposals through peer review, career-making academicians who seek funding for their research cannot afford to underestimate, much less to ignore, the importance of human connections in the whole process. First, researchers need to foster a cooperative relationship with the office of sponsored research at their home institutions. The office may put their names on bulletin boards or add them to information networks so that they can routinely receive announcements and solicitations, electronically or by regular mail, from various funding sources. The office can assist researchers to pass through the human subjects review, develop a research budget, write up sections on institutional support and grant management, assemble proposal components, make copies of the final proposal, and send the complete application to a funding agency. During the execution of a funded project, the office can help researchers maintain routine contacts with the funding agency, manage the budget, and keep schedules for various milestones in the research progress.

Second, academic professionals who depend upon funding from sponsors outside the college or university for their research career need to cultivate a constructive relationship with their main funding sources. For large funding agencies, such as federal grants, they may have to smooth their relationships with a number of departments covering a time period from the receipt of applications, the review of proposals, and the management of project funds to the evaluation of research products. The most important relationship is with the program officer in the funding agency who usually coordinates different components pertaining to funding and funded research. An applicant can certainly benefit from the program officer's insights into the agency's funding priorities as well as the review panel's theoretical orientations and methodological preferences. Preparing an application with those constraints in mind, applicants can greatly improve the chance of being funded for their proposed research. A constructive relationship with the program officer and other stakeholders in the funding agency may even help researchers with special funds and emergency assistance when needed. Psychologically, such a relationship serves researchers as motivation to keep writing proposals and obtaining financial support for their research careers.

Third, academicians who build on funded research in their scholarly careers need to establish peer recognition and support for their research agenda. Funding proposals are reviewed and recommended for funding by a panel of scientific experts. Scientific experts are not heavenly figures. They are peers working in similar areas of specialty. Applicants who have established themselves in an area of research are normally in a better position to receive funding than those who are relatively unknown in the field. Besides scientific reputation, human relations also play a part. Applicants who have made themselves known through a wide net of personal contacts may have a better chance to be reviewed by peers who know them personally. Although it is difficult to verify whether reviewers consciously favor certain applicants, it is possible that they lower their commonsense suspicions regarding an applicant's qualifications to carry out a proposed research or give an applicant the benefit of the doubt in some weak spots identified in the proposal submitted, when they personally know the applicant. It ought to be pointed out that the rule of conflict of interest used by funding agencies in selecting reviewers does not usually prevent personal connections among academic professionals outside their institutional affiliations. It is quite possible that a set group of reviewers used by several major funding agencies in a field cross-review each other's grants, lend support to each other's research projects, and therefore perpetuate a research paradigm over a period of time. There might be no detectable coordination on the part of participating individuals. But the situation still qualifies as something approaching a conspiracy that showcases elitism and exclusionary practices in the world of funded research.

With regard to publication, journals, bulletins, magazines, newspapers, and newsletters as well as books, monographs, and edited volumes all serve as outlets for research. Different outlets publish different kinds of academic products, use different selection procedures and standards, circulate to different audiences, and enjoy different reputations in the eyes of academicians. Journals are the best known and most available records of ongoing research within a field. Journals publish research articles, field or laboratory work notes, and book reviews, use in-house editorial or outside peer reviews, cater to scholars in a specific field or discipline, and may be considered by concerned academic practitioners as top, middle, or low-ranking outlets for their scholarly products. Books may report specialized research, propose or elaborate theories, formulate or advocate positions, review major developments in a field or discipline, or present current knowledge for educational and other purposes. They may be printed by commercial publishing houses or university presses for academic professionals, college students, and a more general audience. Publishers may select book manuscripts using judgments by in-house editors or outside reviewers. Books published may receive different ratings depending upon the volume of sales, the number of reviews, and the judgment of reviewers in the academic media. The influence of a journal article or a book is often measured by the frequency of citations by other scholarly sources over a period of time.

While publication correlates mainly with the scientific merit of a scholarly product, some networking by an academic professional with editors, editorial staff, and publishers is also important. It provides the researcher with information, access, opportunity, and encouragement for publishing his or her academic contributions. Information about publications can be general and specific. General information includes what an academic professional knows about all possible publication outlets, their respective aim, content format, submission procedure, review process, readership, and reputation, in the field. It is simply a matter of identifying an appropriate publication outlet once a scholarly product is ready for publication. Time can be wasted if a product is sent to the wrong publication outlet as mere submission and review may take months to complete. Specific information refers to what an academic practitioner knows about a special issue edited by a journal on a specific topic, a monograph series launched by a publisher, and a thematic volume compiled by a fellow academician. These topic-specific issues, series, and volumes may serve as prime outlets for highly specialized products that would be normally rejected by the conventional academic media.

Access and opportunity determine much in a career academician's participation in publication activities controlled by his or her professional associations and employment institution. Journals are sponsored mainly by associations. Publishers usually line up with associations, conference organizers, and institutions on monographs and book series. Academic practitioners who serve on an association's publication committee, an association journal's editorial board, or a manuscript review committee for a publication sponsored by their home institution may be asked to edit a volume by a publisher, take charge of a special issue for a journal, or contribute an article to a book or journal, and therefore have a better chance to publish their own products or to just imprint their name on a publication. For example, in editing a volume of papers presented at a conference, an editor may not only include his or her own products by writing an introduction, some chapters, or a conclusion, but also claim his or her authorship, copyright, and royalty for the whole volume even though most of the articles in the volume were written by individual contributors. To avoid conflict of interest, some journal and series editors may choose to avoid publishing their own products in publications under their editorship. But the fact that they control a publication outlet may still render them better access and opportunity in the whole publication market for selling their own products. For example, editor A may publish editor B's products from his or her controlled publication in exchange for publishing his or her own products through editor B's outlet.

Encouragement is necessary and precious to every academician who strives to actualize himself or herself through publication. Publication, as painstaking it is, can easily lead to frustration, disappointment, and fatigue. From research design to data collection, from data analysis to theoretical exploration, from literature review to the development of an outline, from writing to editing, from submission to review, and from acceptance to publication, each part of the process usually takes months or even years to complete. For example, one may have to wait several months to see the results of peer reviews of one's paper and may have to experience one or two such lengthy reviews until one sees one's paper in print. Given the extraordinary patience and persistence required to deal with the tremendous uncertainty in publication, it is not difficult to see how being approached to write and edit a piece of work with a guarantee of publication could change the balance of the game. Indeed, many academicians publish books, book chapters, and journal articles often because of the earnest requests and gentle pressures from colleagues, collaborators, and scholarly friends made at conferences and through associations, projects, employment, and other conscious networking efforts.

Finally, specific relationships with the editor and editorial staff in a journal or publishing house may directly influence the outcome of a manuscript submitted for consideration. The editor makes decisions on whether to accept the manuscript for peer review, to whom to send it for evaluation, and how to interpret the comments by reviewers. In some cases, one may talk to the editor, explaining one's research rationale, suggesting a list of referees to avoid or to include in the review process, and arguing for a new round of reviews if the first round turns out to be negative. The editorial staff receive the manuscript, send it out for review, collect comments from reviewers, edit the manuscript, and prepare the final draft for publication. A smooth relationship with them can bring one multiple benefits. One may easily check the status of the manuscript, expedite the process of review, and give the best possible form to the final product prior to publication.

INNOVATION AND REFORM

On the matters of funding and publication, there are always problems and dissatisfaction. Donors and funding providers may feel they do not obtain what they were promised for their financial support while grantees and funding recipients complain that they are confronted with too many mandates and constraints by their sponsors in the way they conduct research, interpret findings, and present products. Editors and publishers may think they give too much leeway to authors and scholars in content, quality control, and scheduling of production while academic contributors grumble that they are cold-shouldered, pushed around, manipulated, and even abused by the publisher and printing establishment. There is obviously room for reform and change (Bresciani & Wolff, 2006; Darling, 2005; Kitchin & Fuller, 2005; Lindholm-Romantschuk, 1998; Locke, Spirduso, & Silverman, 2007; McGinty, 1999; Parsons, 1989; Powell, 1985; Savage, 2000).

Reform 1: Create a Network of Information on Funding

Status Quo. Like bartering between buyer and seller, funding for scientific research takes place to a large degree randomly when a financial sponsor finds a seemingly capable recipient who promises to carry out research in the area of mutual agreement. Sources of funding do not necessarily advertise their awards and grants as long as they receive a comfortably sufficient number of applications at each round of competition. Individuals who seek monetary support for their research do not necessarily feel burdened when they search from place to place for funding because they naturally assume that there is neither free meal nor easy meal anywhere, even in the noble business of knowledge production and distribution. Funding and its giving and receiving in and around academia are basically governed by the age-old rule of convenience, proximity, or simply who happens to know whom, what, and how.

Reform. An innovative idea for changing the status quo is to create a national registry of funding for scientific research and technological innovation. The registry begins with a legislative mandate that all funding providers formally register each of their awards and grants with regard to its amount, area of interest, duration, mode of competition, requirements for application, deadline, and other critical features. The registry maintains a website for public access. Individuals can search for awards and grants with all major variables, between public and private sponsors, between basic research and technological application, or by discipline, field, area, the amount of funding, the location of provider, and application deadline. The registry may also publish a general or discipline-by-discipline inventory of awards and grants on a weekly or monthly basis upon subscriptions by academic institutions, professional associations, governmental agencies, public libraries, corporate interests, and individual researchers.

Besides a comprehensive registry at the national level or before such a registry ever comes into service, individual organizations should gather and compile information about awards and grants as part of their routine operation. A disciplinary department can collect and receive systematic information for its faculty members about funding related to its serving discipline from local, regional, national, and international sources. A professional association may share specific news and announcements with its general membership about all known awards and grants pertaining to its serving profession. A research institute may even connect its scientific staff to particular mailing lists, email circulars, or electronic bulletins for funding according to each individual staff member's area of scholarship.

Significance. Spreading the word benefits both the giver and the receiver in academic funding. With a national registry, individual researchers just need to visit one common place to find all possible sources of funding in their quest for knowledge. Knowing major financial sponsors and having easy access to information about funding may also serve to motivate academicians in their scholarly careers for planning bigger adventures, attempting bolder projects, and hence translating more of their ideas and ideals into reality. On the part of funding providers, being known by the largest possible number of academic practitioners and being sought after by all seriously interested contestants for their awards and grants can only ensure that the precious economic support they render to knowledge fall in the hands of most deserving participants in scholarship. Thus, funding available for scientific research and technological innovation will be effectively and efficiently used when information about it is widely spread across academia.

Reform 2: Convert Funding upon Promise to Funding upon Outcome

Status Quo. Funding is currently given upon a grant writer's promise in the majority of cases. Applicants craft proposals. Proposals are reviewed for their potentials and promises. Awards are given before projects are carried out and outcomes are evaluated. Funding upon promise is justifiable in the sense that research is costly and calls for risk-taking, investment, and commitment from both providers and recipients. It raises questions as well because funding upon promise creates various problems for career scholars. First, scholars may be led primarily by sources of funding rather than by scholarly instincts and principles in research. Second, they may have to spend considerable time and effort on sharpening grant-writing skills rather than enhancing critical research workmanship. Third, some academicians may become career grant procurers rather than career scholars. They bring in funding, mobilize resources, control personnel, and decide who appears where in the final product although they themselves rarely engage in serious academic research.

Reform. An innovation that may bring about positive change is to shift funding upon promise more to funding upon outcome. Specifically, more funds are released as awards for previous or ongoing work. More funding agencies reposition themselves as recognizers and facilitators rather than sponsors and interveners. At an operational level, funding agencies set up a panel of judges to identify candidates for awards, just as they would have to assemble a review team to evaluate proposals for funding, on the basis of the agency's philosophy, priorities, and preferences. Candidates are selected for awards on the basis of their published work. They do not have to write and submit proposals. They do not have to prepare applications and materials. They are notified only when they are awarded. Awards are given with or without strings attached. Recipients can use their award in a way they prefer or in the way specified by the awarding agency, for continuing research or for personal improvement.

Significance.   Funding upon outcome, when it gains considerable presence in comparison to funding upon promise, can change the way career academicians conduct themselves in their scholarly pursuits. They may focus more on serious academic work and its general social consequence. They can become more motivated to continue a particular line of research when they are awarded funds and recognition. Funding agencies would find that they benefit from existing research rather than having to count on future studies. They would exert their influence by suggestion rather than by dictation. In other words, by awarding some research and some scholars, they make a powerful suggestion as to what is favored and valued. To scholars who do creative and exploratory work, suggestion may work more effectively than dictation. A majority of academicians do not necessarily do quality work when they are required or mandated to do something. They turn out quality products instead when they are enabled to do what they want to do in a way that feels comfortable to them.

As far as what funds and funding agencies may switch to the funding upon outcome model, a great many of them might opt for it. Funds within an institution can be more efficiently used for openly selective awards than for nominally competitive grants. Governmental agencies are as well poised to confer awards for one's scientific achievements as to sponsor research projects for one's scholarly promise. Private foundations and business corporations may also take a long-term perspective concerning some of their critical interests and promote those interests by disbursing funding for research and development through the award upon outcome model.

Reform 3: Create a Network of Information on Publishing

Status Quo.   The world of publishing seems to operate well upon market forces. Publishers print books and journals in response to demands from different academic disciplines or content areas. Book proposals are received, journal manuscripts are reviewed, and most publishing houses do not worry much about whether they have enough to print but rather whether they can sell all they have in print. In fact, a great many journals boast of a more than 75 percent rate of rejection as an indicator of their selectivity and prestige. Individual academicians do research, write articles or monographs, look for outlets, and may or may not find difficulty in sharing their work with the larger audience in academia. Indeed, every currently active scholar can instantly list a number of academic journals or presses to which he or she would submit his or her manuscript for publication consideration. Given this seemingly working situation, can anything be done to make it different or better?

Reform. One service that might connect individual scholars closely and clearly to the publishing establishment is to compile a worldwide list of academic journals as well as a global inventory of publishing houses. The worldwide list, as suggested by its name, should attempt to include all journals published in all languages for all possible content areas across academic disciplines. For each journal, there would be information about its aim and scope, editorial board, contents, styles, review process, submission requirements, and other important characteristics. The list is first of all accessible online. It may also carry a year-by-year paper version for academic libraries to collect in their reference section. As the list gains utility and visibility across the global community of scholarship, new or existing journals will volunteer to register with it to make it ever more complete and useful.

Similarly, a global inventory of publishing houses will offer systematic information about every press in the world with regard to its philosophy, areas of focus or specialty, forms of publication, geographical distribution, manuscript guidelines, review standards, and all other key features. Information can be accessed electronically in cyberspace. It may also be obtained in the form of an annually updated and printed compilation from major university or public libraries. In its initial versions, the inventory may not offer every critical piece of information about every publisher. However, as it grows gradually with recognition and distinction, the global inventory may eventually become the place where every new or existing publisher wants to register to make itself known to its target audience, both contributors and readers.

Significance. It obviously saves time and labor when individual academicians need to visit just one common place to find a suitable publication outlet for their work. While a majority of scholars normally assume they know where to publish it when they have finished their research report, they actually do not know every possible rightful place in the market that is available for their product. With a worldwide list of journals and a global directory of presses in hand, one indeed has a much higher chance to locate the kind of outlet with which one's contribution might best fit. On the other hand, publishers can use the worldwide list as well as the global inventory to reach their respective contributors in the most complete possible way. With a larger pool of submissions, selection can become more competitive and the quality of publication can rise to a higher level. The publication market overall will then operate on a new world dynamic. Not only will there be global publishers attempting to secure some local market shares, but also there will be community or institution-based presses struggling to fashion a global reach in their scope of business.

Reform 4: Create a Profession of Agents for Academic Publishing

Status Quo. Publishing of academic books, as it stands now, involves a great deal of hard labor on the part of scholars. Academic authors first have to develop a book proposal that normally includes an outline of content, a summary of main ideas or findings, a set of sample chapters, a comparison with competitions, and an assessment of market needs. Next, they send out their proposal to publishers for consideration. When they are rejected by one publisher, they will have to modify their proposal to accord with another publisher's requirements. The process can keep on going until they give up their hope on publication totally or when they are finally accepted for their book proposal. Once a proposal is accepted, the author will then be able to concentrate on research and writing for a period of time warranted by the contract. However, when one is finished with one's manuscript, one may have to spend time on preparation of a camera-ready copy as some publishers have shifted that laborious part of publishing to the academic authors as well.

Reform. There might be indeed a need for a new profession, a profession of book agents for academic publishing. The rationale is both simple and critical. That is, academic workers should be freed from the labor-intensive process of crafting and modifying book proposals, dealing with publishers, printing copies of manuscripts, and marketing books. They ought to be able to focus on research and writing so that they can make important contributions to scholarship and turn out the best possible academic products for consumption within and outside academia.

Operationally, book agents would serve as go-betweens from academic production to publication or from individual academicians to publishers. They would first receive complete manuscripts from scholars and researchers in academic institutions. They would then conduct market investigation on each manuscript with regard to its possible publication outlet, readership, competition, and significance. Once they have decided on a pool of most appropriate publishers for a manuscript, they would send the manuscript, along with any market-related supporting material they have prepared for it, to each of those publishers for publication consideration. As soon as they have successfully placed a manuscript, book agents would notify its author or authors. Or if they are unable to place a manuscript, they will inform its author or authors within a certain time frame. In the printing process, book agents can also coordinate authors with publishers on proofs and other matters concerning the substance of the book. To qualify as a book agent, one needs a bachelor's a degree, preferably a master's degree, in a content area. For instance, one specializes in placing books in biology and its surrounding areas because one has formal training in biology. One also needs adequate communications skills when one navigates between academic practitioners and publishers. As for compensation, book agents may collect a certain percentage of royalties from books they have successfully placed with publishers. They may collect a one-time reward from each publisher when they have successfully secured a book contract for the publisher's publication program. Or they may do both, but in a smaller amount on each. For example, a book agent receives a fixed payment from a publisher as soon as he or she has got an academic author sign on a book contract with the publisher. He or she will also receive directly from the publisher a percentage of the author's book royalty when the book is published.

Significance. A profession of independent book agents may not only benefit academicians but also serve the interest of publishers. Publishing houses can save cost by cutting their acquisition staff when book agents perform some of the functions that acquisition editors normally fulfill in their regular duty: gathering manuscripts from academic practitioners, screening them for overall fitness, and conducting basic market research in comparison to competitions. In technical aspect, a publisher would no longer worry about the gap it so often sees between a wonderful book proposal and a not so wonderful final manuscript as it reviews and acts upon only complete manuscripts collected by book agents from academic authors. Academic authors can obviously focus on what they are trained to do, research and scholarship, without wasting time and effort on the business chores of publishing. As the profession grows and matures, there will be experienced book agents who serve critically and indispensably in discovering scientific masterpieces or even contributing to the development of great scholars or thinkers in the knowledge enterprise.

Reform 5: Establish a Service-Oriented Publishing System

Status Quo. In the world of publication, presses, journals, monograph series, and other outlets still exist as authoritarian establishments to individual scholars who seek to share their research with the large audience within academia and beyond. There is little accountability for editors and publishers in their business dealings with authors and scholars. Academic journals do not have to follow any deadline in their critical responses to unsolicited contributors. For example, while they do not allow for multiple submissions of a manuscript by the author, many journal editors feel free and even shameless to excuse themselves for not acknowledging receipt of a manuscript in one to two weeks, not sending out a manuscript for review in three to four weeks, or not rendering the authors a decision in three to four months. It is not uncommon that authors and their contributions are held simple hostage without any action rendered for six months, one year, and even longer by scholarly journals or publishing houses.

Reform. Academic publishers must take institutional reform to change themselves from authoritarian establishments into service-oriented entities. Editors must follow a strict time line in their response to authors who have submitted manuscripts for possible publication. Or they must give up the customary demand that a scholarly manuscript cannot be submitted elsewhere while it is under consideration with a particular outlet. In the age of electronic communications, academic journals should take the initiative to accept online submission of manuscripts. By doing so, they not only relieve their potential contributors from copying, packaging, and mailing costs and chores, but also facilitate their own review and production processes. They can forward submissions to reviewers, gather reviewers' comments, and respond to authors, all within the sphere of cyberspace. There are no letters to write and print, no papers to pack and send, and no postage to buy and place on envelopes. Paper is saved. The environment is to some extent protected. For a few journals that require contributors to pay a fee at the time of submission, online communications may automatically eliminate the need for taking any money from authors. Submission fees should not be imposed upon contributors by any sensible reasoning. Collecting a fee for manuscript submission is probably one of the most awkward practices in the world of publication.

Significance. Under a service-oriented publication system, scholars who serve as editors or on editorial boards would perform their duty with conscience and sound judgment. They would not just sit there for honor and influence. They would voluntarily leave their post if they are not able to fulfill their scholarly obligations effectively and in a timely manner. Scholars who could serve as qualified reviewers would respond to requests within deadlines established by editors. Authors and contributors would work closely with editors to make necessary changes and revisions. As each party involved in the process acts upon their service duty and task with a sense of urgency and responsibility, the whole publication scene can take on a new look. Career scholars can then put more of their time and energy back into work and writing.

CHAPTER 6

THE DEGREE

The degree marks admission to the world of scholarship. With a doctoral degree, one conducts research, teaches classes, and participates in academic debates as if these activities were taken for granted. Without a proper degree, however, one probably has to put out a disclaimer whenever one sets out to do something within the academic circle. In the structure of an academic career, the degree is a cornerstone to determine the scale and the outlook of the building that sits on it (Abel, 1984; Bowen & Rudenstine, 1992; Bowen & Sosa, 1989; Cartter, 1976; Clark & Centra, 1985; Conley, 1997; Dore, 1976; Golde & Walker, 2006; Maki & Borkowski, 2006; Noble, 1994; Taylor, 2005).

BACKGROUND AND ANALYSIS

The degree is the end product of education. It carries all the information acquired through the educational process as well as all the commands held by the educational establishment.

The number of degrees shows the breadth of one's training and knowledge in academic subjects. In social presentation, one or more doctoral degrees, along with a few lower degrees, may create an impression that one is diversely trained in multiple areas. For example, one who holds a Ph.D. in electronic engineering and a Ph.D. in history may be considered as a prime candidate for research in the history of technology. One who holds a bachelor's degree in chemistry, a master's degree in physiology, and a Ph.D. in psychology may be regarded as a promising scholar in substance abuse research. As far as lifetime productivity is concerned, however, multiple degree holders may not necessarily be in an advantageous position. They spend more years in school. Knowledge and modes of inquiry they learn from different disciplines or levels may lead to contradiction and confusion in their research choices. Most important, in an era of specialization, a discipline is likely to be dominated by those who settle in the core of the discipline, rather than by those who wander into border areas with other disciplines.

The sequence of degrees from lower to higher levels demonstrates the depth of training and knowledge one has gone through in scholarship. There are all-in-one discipline degree holders. They take the same or similar subjects from undergraduate, to graduate, and to doctoral studies. They obtain their bachelor's, master's, and doctor's degrees in the same discipline. Over years of learning, they may gain a firm grounding in the theoretical and methodological approaches developed in the discipline. There are multiple-discipline degree owners. They take different disciplines, one in college, another in graduate school, and still another in doctoral level studies. The degrees they hold show the sequence in their educational effort. For example, one obtains a bachelor's degree in mathematics, a master's degree in business administration, and a doctor's degree in sociology. This sequence in education may likely qualify the candidate for teaching in a business school. Likewise, one who has a B.A. in philosophy, a J.D. in civil law, and a Ph.D. in political science may find placement in a law school. It is obvious that a cross-discipline educational sequence not only widens one's exposure to scholarship, but also deepens one's involvement in it.

The degree concludes education and neutralizes high with low performers in the educational process. One may not do well in a multitude of courses, retake major examinations, and struggle all the way in graduate school. But as long as one holds the degree in hand, the struggling achiever will be treated similarly to a stellar graduate in academic practice. As for productivity, high performance in school may not necessarily translate into more accomplishment in academic career. There are hundreds of cases where lackluster or rebellious students make brilliant or creative scholars. There are thousands of cases where model students fade into mediocrity later in their academic life. In fact, many successful scholars may well credit their career achievements to some unconventional ways of thinking they have developed from the time of being a student.

The degree serves as an identifier in professional networking. Within a department, having a Ph.D. from the same university may be the primary reason why a kinship relationship is forged between faculty members, a political faction is developed, or a kind of loose alliance on issues is maintained. At a college- or university-level gathering, graduation from the same institution may bring strangers into warm and meaningful conversations. After the conversation, some of them may continue in their informal or formal contact. Across an organization, a community, or a region, alumni from a university may gather in association-chapter meetings, exchanging ideas and offering mutual support in academic work. Another occasion in which the degree often figures in importance is the academic meeting. An accidental greeting or casual conversation at the reception, by the registration desk, or at the end of a session may lead to in-depth relationships when the degree from the same institution happens to be mentioned as a reinforcing point. Some mentors may use a meeting to take former students to a dinner or to attend an academically oriented activity. There are national and international meetings where organizers reserve a night or hold a place just for alumni get-togethers. Some ties can therefore be forged and developed over individuals' academic career.

The degree also carries specific social expectations. At the time of job search, a graduate from an elite university may be pressured to apply only to research institutions even though the job candidate is a little unsure of his or her aptitude for research. Academic advisors may explicitly say that they send letters of recommendation only when their graduates apply to universities that emphasize research. On the other hand, a graduate from a less elite university may be forced to apply only to institutions where the teaching load is heavier and research is less emphasized even though the candidate is prepared for and enthusiastic about serious research. Research universities in the market are likely to suggest, if only implicitly, that the candidate is not suitable simply because of his or her Alma Mater. Later in the career path, a degree holder is supposed to behave in a way expected by the university that conferred the degree. For example, a graduate from a little known university could create a surprise across a field if he or she makes an important breakthrough on a long unsolved problem. A degree holder from an ivy-league institution could be held in contempt if he or she turns out products deemed in low quality or below the normal expectation. To emphasize the differential value and expectation inherent in a degree, academicians normally include the name of the degree, the year in which it was obtained, and the institution that conferred it in their curriculum vitae. Institutions also selectively focus on those essential variables to present information about their academic staff in the organizational directory or at public briefings.

The degree itself is considered an achieved status. Just as professionals in law, business administration, social work, or nursing proudly put J.D., MBA, MSW, or R.N. after their name in official communications, academicians holding a doctor of philosophy (Ph.D.) in their discipline expect to be honorifically addressed as Dr. X in social interactions and be accorded proper treatment in academic dealings. Academic institutions also use the percentage of Ph.D.'s in their faculty or staff as an effective measure to attract students, to convince funding sources, or to demonstrate their adequacy and competency in the world of scholarship. The doctoral degree has long become an established indicator in official statistics compiled by the government and academic associations.

INNOVATION AND REFORM

Most institutions act upon common sense regarding academic degrees and degree holders. For the same degree, they probably give it a higher value or credit if it is conferred from a more elite university. Between one who has one Ph.D. in one discipline and one who holds two doctoral degrees in two different disciplines, they probably put more confidence as well as more investment in the latter in job assignment and resource allocation. The question then is this: Do facts bear out intuition or commonsense-based treatments (Bowen & Rudenstine, 1992; Clark & Centra, 1985; Golde & Walker, 2006; Goldsmith, Komlos, & Gold, 2001; Gosling & Noordam, 2006; Hermanowicz, 2002; Noble, 1994; Maki & Borkowski, 2006; Taylor, 2005)?

Reform 1: Track Job Placement at Disciplinary Associations by Ph.D. Conferring Institutions

Status Quo. There are no specific and solid data about Ph.D. recipients and their job placement. People assume that graduates from top departments in elite institutions join the faculty at first-rate schools whereas doctoral students from ordinary programs only attempt positions available in run of the mill institutions. Since it is not normal for a higher ranked university to take a new Ph.D. holder from a lower rated program, people naturally intuit that recipients of doctorates from more prestigious institutions have a better chance for job placement than their counterparts from less prestigious schools.

Reform. To clear the nebulous picture, disciplinary associations can take initiative to collect systematic data about job placement by Ph.D. recipients on a yearly basis. Procedurally, each disciplinary department reports by a certain time of the year its Ph.D. awardees and their individual job placements to the national association that officially represents the discipline. Upon compilation, categorization, and cross-tabulation of information from around the country, the national association issues a comprehensive job placement report on doctoral graduates in the discipline. From the report, people will know the number of new Ph.D.s conferred by the type, ranking, size, or location of conferring institutions, the percentage of doctoral graduates placed in academic positions by the type of job or the ranking of the institution in which jobs are offered, and other useful information such as years spent on doctoral training, the title of the dissertation, and whether the dissertation is to be partially published as journal articles or wholly printed as a research monograph. Furthermore, a national publication may build upon data from individual disciplinary associations to release a uniform job placement report for all Ph.D. recipients across all academic disciplines. For example, just as people turn to *U.S. News and World Report* for annual rankings of universities, academicians may refer to this authoritative source to find out whether Ph.D.-conferring institutions channel their graduates to specific destinations in academia, more pointedly, whether the job market does indeed favor graduates from higher-ranking institutions.

Significance. Information is power. With accurate information, people can overcome their natural inclinations prompted by intuition and make realistic choices in congruence to reality. For example, systematic data may support the belief that people with doctorates conferred by middle ranking institutions have the best prospect for job placement when some of them move up to higher-ranking universities, some of them slide down to lower-ranking organizations, and the majority of them fill jobs in similarly rated programs. This kind of information will certainly influence individuals in their decision on graduate school, coursework, and job search. Institutions may also make proper adjustments to their graduate program as well as to their hiring policies. Gradually elite schools will change attitude toward their non-elite counterparts when they have alumni from non-elite institutions working and doing well on their campuses. The entrenched mentality of pedigree will fade away. On the horizon will emerge a less hierarchical academia where scholars are judged primarily by what they do rather than by where they come from.

Reform 2: Track Job Performance at Employment by Ph.D. Conferring Institutions

Status Quo. Academic institutions overall tend to hire people from similar places or somewhere of a higher academic statue. This is especially true to recruitment of new Ph.D.'s to the faculty. For example, people in a research university may cheer on each other by saying "we have hired a young scholar from Harvard!" On the other hand, when a new hire is from a lower-ranking university, people may wonder if "we are not good enough for someone from a better place" or if "we are getting so bad to have to find someone from a lower-graded program." Ironically, although an institution may willingly bid a higher salary for someone from a prestigious department, it usually does not pay much attention to whether a higher-paid employee makes better delivery of performance on the job.

Reform. To be fair and rational, human resources offices in academic institutions should keep track of degrees, degree holders, and their job performance. These offices should answer questions such as these: Do the conferring institutions make any difference in the performance of the degree holders? Does a degree from a higher-ranking university lead to a higher level of performance than the same degree from a lower-ranking competitor? Is the number of doctoral degrees a significant factor in job performance? Does one who has two doctorates in two different disciplines necessarily perform more tasks and better than those who hold only one doctoral degree in one field? How is a doctoral degree with lower degrees in the same discipline to be compared to a doctoral degree with lower degrees in different disciplines? For example, A has a bachelor's degree in physiology, a master's degree in education, and a Ph.D. in psychology, whereas B has all his or her bachelor's, master's, and doctoral degrees concentrated in psychology. When A and B both work as faculty members in psychology, do they perform differently due to the different degree sequences in their respective education and training?

There are obvious difficulties in relating degree to performance in the real world setting. Technically, how is performance measured? How loosely or closely can performance be legitimately linked to the degree, the value or quality of the degree, the number of degrees, and the sequence of degrees? Sociologically, there is likely to be an inseparable interference in the form of a self-fulfilling prophecy. A Harvard graduate is entrusted to do a more important job. Because this graduate is given more attention, more resources, or higher expectation to do the job, he or she indeed turns out to be a better performer. Despite technical difficulties and possible contaminations, monitoring performance and career pathways by academic degree across the system and from year to year will definitely yield critical information for an institution on the matter of recruitment, promotion, and retention. In addition to institutional tracking, academic research can be designed and conducted to produce general knowledge about the effect of the degree on productivity and performance within a discipline as well as across the world of scholarship.

Significance. People live by myths in various areas of life. Pedigree is one of the age-old myths affecting academic practitioners in the community of scholarship. By tracking performance at employment, academicians will see directly whether there is any validity in their taken-for-granted belief that Ph.D.'s conferred by elite institutions tend to hold and produce better value than those awarded by universities deemed less prestigious. Once the myth is disproved by hard evidence, it will eventually lose its power in guiding people and their thoughts and actions.

Reform 3: Track Rank Advancement at Employment by Ph.D. Conferring Institutions

Status Quo. No matter how much effort it makes in drawing a seemingly promising applicant from an elite program, an academic employer normally does not spend much time or resources to follow an already hired employee to see whether this employee progresses from lower to higher ranks in accordance with what was contracted for at the time of employment. There are speculations, biases, and myths about academic employees with respect to whom they are, where they are from, and what they might be capable of accomplishing. But there is a phenomenal lack of factual evidence as to what individual members of the faculty holding Ph.D.'s from different programs actually do and have done in the position hired for. The question remains unanswered: Do Ph.D.'s from elite institutions progress faster and more productively in rank advancement as well as in general career movement than their counterparts from less prestigious academic organizations?

Reform. As in the area of job performance, both cross-sectional and longitudinal data can be collected about academic employees with regard to promotion and rank advancement. Among disciplinary departments, does it take longer for people in some disciplines to move up in rank than those in other disciplines? To what extent, does the Ph.D. conferring institution figure in the rate and speed of rank movement? In other words, do people who have graduated from higher-ranking departments tend to have a higher rate as well as a faster speed in upward mobility than those who come from less prestigious doctoral programs? Over time, a well categorized and maintained employee record can show what percentage of a cohort moves up to a higher rank and whether there is a significant difference in rank advancement between those who are graduated from elite programs and those who are hired from less prestigious schools. For example, an institution may find that among its fifty academic employees recruited in the year 1990, twenty-five have been promoted to full professorships and among those yet to be promoted to full professors, 60 percent hold Ph.D.'s conferred by elite programs compared to only 50 percent of doctoral awardees from elite schools in the total group of fifty. Or the institution may find that among the six endowed professorships held by the cohort of 1990, five are in the hands of those graduated from elite doctoral programs.

Significance. Fact is better than speculation. With department-by-department and year-by-year data on employee advancement through academic ranks, an institution can know how members of its faculty perform on their job, whether they make satisfactory progress in their academic career, what influence graduate training might continue to have on performance or rank advancement, and whether it needs to make any change in its hiring preference, personnel evaluation procedure, and general policy toward academic staff. For example, when it finds that faculty members recruited from elite graduate schools do not necessarily perform better or move up faster than those hired from less prestigious programs, an institution may then become more open-minded to applicants from different universities in the academic market.

Reform 4: Track Publications at Leading Outlets by Ph.D. Conferring Institutions

Status Quo. Most publication outlets require authors to include a brief biographical note while submitting manuscripts for publication consideration. There is, however, no standard format for such a required biographical note. An author may put down his or her academic interests, main publications, and current institutional affiliation in the biographical note. The author does not necessarily provide any information about whether he or she has a doctorate and where the doctorate was obtained.

Reform. Leading academic journals or publishers can compile and publish summary statistics regarding authors of printed articles or volumes for each year. With a standard format required of each article or book in print, information can be pointedly collected about authors with respect to their academic preparation, interests, achievements, and affiliation. For example, a generic biographical note may read like this: "John Doe received his or her Ph.D. from X University. Dr. Doe is interested in the study of Y and has published books, book chapters, and articles, including A and B, in that area. Dr. Doe is currently an assistant professor at Z University." With these key elements covered in a universal biographical note, a publisher can then have critical data about its authors for record-keeping, advertising, and other purposes. Each year, a journal may use its last issue to provide statistics about authors who have published articles in that year or in all those years since the journal's inauguration. A publisher may employ its annual catalog to publicize such information as well. From the statistics, people can clearly see who publishes in the journal or with the publisher by affiliated institution in such categories as research I university, research II university, and comprehensive university as well as by Ph.D. conferring institutions from elite to ordinary graduate schools or from higher ranking to lower ranking training programs.

Significance. It is a great irony that people often act upon intuition, commonsensical assumption, and hearsay even in areas where information can be accurately collected to provide reliable guidance for behavior. Under the proposed reform, publishers gather information about their authors without serious effort. They present the information handily to potential contributors who then can use it as an important reference to decide where they send their scholarly papers or scientific reports for possible publication. Transparency benefits both sides. On the part of publishers, letting people know the authors whose articles they have published is like creating a magnetic field for their most likely contributors. For individual academicians, knowing clearly where to send their manuscripts not only saves time and effort but also brings tangible benefits—acceptance, joy, and success. The overall result is an effective and efficient academic production that serves the general interest of knowledge in a specialized field.

Reform 5: Track Rank Distribution at Disciplinary Associations by Ph.D. Conferring Institutions

Status Quo. Statistics are now available on university professors, their ranks, institutional placements, and financial compensations. Information can also be found about the percentage of Ph.D.'s among the faculty at the college level, by rank, institution, or region. One thing missing, yet interesting to know in the compilation of academic employment data, is how academic practitioners spread across standard academic ranks by the year as well as the institution from which they receive their doctorate in a discipline.

Reform. Along with its effort in tracking job placement by new Ph.D.'s in the discipline it represents, major disciplinary associations can take initiative to compile and publish statistics about university professors and their rank distribution in a region or across the country by Ph.D.-conferring institutions as well as by the year in which they receive their doctorate. For example, using the prevailing rank system for the faculty at the college setting, how many assistant professors in the discipline are graduates from elite schools? How many associate professors hold Ph.D. degrees from lower ranking programs? Or how many full professors receive their doctorate from middle ranking departments? More important, how long does it take for an average doctoral recipient to progress from assistant to associate to full professorship? Does the Ph.D.-conferring institution make any difference in this progression? And what interactive effects do affiliated institution and Ph.D.-conferring school have on rank advancement? In other words, do doctoral graduates from elite schools fare better and hence experience faster upward mobility in elite academic organizations?

Significance. Scholarly active academicians remain connected mostly to their disciplinary associations. Information about job placement and rank advancement by Ph.D.-conferring institutions can therefore be most effectively communicated to its audience through disciplinary associations. Other associations, such as union-related and politically charged organizations, may already have data on academic employees, their material benefits, living conditions, and social impacts. But those data are largely consumed by the mass media and within academia, by only a small number of politically active academicians who have an interest in union activities or general social advocacy. For the majority of down-to-earth academic professionals, it is news about past training, present work, and future mobility or information on graduate school, employment institution, and career movement spread by disciplinary associations that offers immediate insights into everyday choices and decisions in scholarly endeavor.

CHAPTER 7

POSITION

Academicians earn positions through individual efforts. The position earned will in turn determine what academicians do and how much they do in their career-making endeavors. Academic beginners usually earn their position by the doctoral degree they achieve from the educational process. In their junior position, they may only do certain things and are likely to face various constraints even in their limited areas of work. Seasoned academicians, on the other hand, earn their positions either by years of service or by substantive contributions. In their senior positions, they may perform a variety of tasks and are likely to receive assistance in a wide range of functions. The unequal distribution of tasks and responsibilities leads directly to the unequal share of benefits and rewards, differentiating academicians into various stages and statuses in their career-making pathways (Alstete, 2000; Beckham, 1986; Bianco-Mathis & Chalofsky, 1999; Bright & Richards, 2001; Finkelstein, Seal, & Schuster, 1998; Gornitzka, Kogan, & Amaral, 2007; Leaming, 2003; Long, McGinnis, & Allison, 1993; Lucas, 2000; Schuster & Finkelstein, 2006; Tierney & Bensimon, 1996).

BACKGROUND AND ANALYSIS

There are different positions for academicians to acquire and take in various domains. Employment-related positions may include temporary versus permanent, part-time versus full-time, tenure-track versus tenured, probationary versus regular, and junior versus senior jobs or titles. Entering academicians may start with temporary and part-time jobs to accrue experience. When they land permanent, full-time jobs, they are likely to be in junior, probationary, or tenure-track positions. Seasoned scholars, on the other hand, are likely to be tenured in senior positions. Although they have full-time, permanent jobs, they may take part-time, temporary positions, such as consultants and visiting professors or researchers, to diversify their work and life experiences. Temporary, part-time positions, in this regard, have totally different outlooks and effects for entering and seasoned academicians. For the former, they are uncertain, exploitative, humiliating, and indicative of low status. For the latter, they are assuring, complementary, and status enhancing. In fact, they serve for many senior career scholars as an indicator of recognition, reputation, and influence.

Institution-granted positions clearly mark the rank, seniority, and status achieved by academicians in their career-making process. In universities, there are lecturers, senior lecturers, and professors or assistant, associate, and full professors. In research organizations, there are junior and senior associates, analysts, or scientists. These titles or positions have specific responsibilities and rewards associated with them. Academicians have to meet specific requirements or complete certain years of service with certain amount of work to move from lower to higher levels.

Association-designated positions come from professional associations to which career-making academicians belong by their subject interest, geographical location, individual background, or other characteristics. Associations are formed by practicing academicians to exchange ideas, advance common interests, and make a social impact. They serve members in their academic pursuits. They also provide members with opportunities to gain status. The presidency and vice presidency of associations are usually reserved for scholars of outstanding achievement. In addition, associations may use their newsletters, journals, and annual meetings to solemnly award members with such honorific titles as distinguished career contributor and scholar of the year. For many academicians, taking an official position or being recognized with a formal title by their association represents an important milestone in their academic careers.

Discipline-based positions may include various voluntary and honorary roles that support the life of a discipline. There are editors, associate editors, journal reviewers, and book reviewers who control and maintain the flow of information within the discipline. There are grant reviewers and project evaluators who decide the distribution of resources among practicing academicians in a field. There are conference organizers, session moderators, and panel discussants who perform on public stages in a subject area. There are also pioneers, founders, inventors, and discoverers whose names are affixed to a concept, theory, or method in a field and are celebrated, honored, and glorified from time to time in the discipline. Obviously, assuming a secular position as editor, reviewer, or organizer in a discipline enhances one's visibility, influence, and status. Being deified as a pioneer, founder, or classical figure may even extend one's academic career beyond the limit of one's lifetime to the status of a contributor to the evolving progression of human knowledge.

It ought to be pointed out that the position achieved in a particular domain not only determines the nature and scope of responsibilities and rewards one receives within that domain, but also affects the way one participates in the activities of other domains. For example, an academician who holds an assistant professorship in his or her college or university is not likely to assume the presidency in a well-recognized academic association or to be on the editorial board of an influential journal in a discipline. Also, there are overlaps and reinforcement effects among positions in different domains. Being recognized by an established academic association as a distinguished scholar may significantly reinforce one's professorship in one's home institution, bringing the honored individual tangible benefits from a one-time award to a permanent increase in salary.

INNOVATION AND REFORM

It is the academic institution that creates positions, assigns tasks to each position, and delivers rewards to individual position holders. There is no question that each institution should clearly and consistently define positions, specify concrete responsibilities attached to each position or rank, and set specific requirements needed for promotion from a lower to a higher rank. There is no question that a due process procedure ought to be instituted to ensure representation, openness, fairness, and the spirit of meritocracy. There is no question that administrative mandate and individual discretion should be kept minimal to avoid nepotism, favoritism, and factional entrenchment (Buller, 2006; Gornitzka, Kogan, & Amaral, 2007; Krahenbuhl, 2004; Leaming 2003; Schuster & Finkelstein, 2006; Tierney, 2004).

Reform 1: Create a Fast Track for Rank Advancement

Status Quo. Like any other bureaucratic organization, an academic institution is set up to accommodate normally performing individuals within its boundaries. Rules are made to benefit regular members. While one who lags behind may face collective push or pressure to catch up, one who outperforms on regular job duty is likely to encounter institutional pull or constraints to come back to the norm. Sometimes, institutional pull on outstanding performers back to the mean is so strong that it obliterates the spirit of meritocracy that is key to the vibrancy of the institution itself.

Reform. In addition to the regular track for rank advancement, an academic institution should make available to its members a fast track to move from lower to higher levels. Above and beyond the normal personnel process that is premised on years of service, balance of growth in different areas, and collective consensus, the fast track may focus on just one aspect of an individual's career achievement that is vital to the institution's mission. For example, if a university aims at research and scholarship as its fundamental goal, it may award a third-year assistant professor tenure, full professorship, and other appropriate honors when he or she makes a breathtaking discovery, solves a long-held mystery, put forth a revolutionary theory, or just publishes a series of influential articles at first-rate journals in a discipline.

Operationally, nominations or applications for fast track rank advancement can be submitted at any time of a calendar year. An ad hoc panel is assembled as soon as an application is deemed valid for formal consideration. The panel may consist of an expert from an external institution in the area of the applicant's specialty, a more senior member of the applicant's home department, a representative from the concerned department personnel committee, a representative from the concerned college personnel committee, and a member of the university personnel committee. To ensure prompt consideration, notifications and dispositions are officially required of an application within specific time limits. For example, an applicant is due to receive an acknowledgment of formal consideration in two weeks, a notification about formation of an ad hoc panel in six weeks, a recommendation from the panel in eight weeks, and a final decision from the university president in ten weeks.

Significance. Not many academic professionals are far ahead of their peers in scholarly achievements. However, promoting a few outstanding academicians in every cohort, every group, and every institution can significantly lift the spirit of imagination, creativity, competition, and meritocracy among ordinary career-making individuals in various academic settings. Whereas the regular track from assistant to associate to full professorship serves to normalize individual behavior, a fast track for rank advancement can elicit extraordinary and exceptional contributions from the faculty in a university. Whereas the normal personnel process keeps the status quo, an ad hoc employee review and evaluation procedure may bring about various inspirational practices in the management of a research institute. The overall effect will be more productive, stimulating, and vital institutions within academia.

Reform 2: Create Department, College, and University Professorships

Status Quo. There are endowed professorships created by private donations or memorial funds in some colleges and universities. Those endowed positions are contingent upon external sponsors and their specific interests, wishes, and investments. In the normal organizational design, no academic institution offers any built-in recognition, honor, or title at divisional or system levels to promote and preserve outstanding contributions within its structural hierarchy.

Reform. To incorporate institutional incentives for outstanding performance in the organizational setup, a college or university can create and maintain honor positions at different levels throughout its structural-functional system. Beginning with disciplinary units, each department has one department professor as the highest honorary title for which all full professors may compete within the department. Moving up the hierarchy, each college then has a few college professors for all department professors to apply throughout the college. At the system level, the university itself has a number of university professors for all of its college professors to vie across the campus. In other words, only one who has attained the status of department professorship is eligible for the competitive selection of college professors. And university professorships are open for competition only to those who already hold a college professorship. As an added rule, an individual can be in only one honorary role at any time. Once becoming a university professor, one automatically relinquishes one's honorary title as college professor. Similarly, one loses one's department professor when one rises to college professorship. Besides honor, department, college, and university professors may receive special bonuses outside regular salaries. As for duration, an honorary professorship at each level can be appointed for a specific period of time. For example, each department selects its department professor every five years. An honorary professorship may also be made a lifetime entitlement for extraordinary individuals. For example, a university awards one university professorship a year. The recipient keeps the honor as long as he or she remains employed at the university.

Significance. The honorary professorship at each unit will exemplify what people within that unit value and strive for in their academic career. In the normal promotion and retention process, people make reference to rules and requirements imposed by the administration. The contrast is vertical, one dimension only. For example, two persons who both pass through the process may be miles apart in their work but never care to match each other for scholarly contributions. With the proposed reform, there will be an additional dimension, a horizontal dimension, for people to compare and measure up. A person who has fulfilled all the basic requirements set by the university for a full professorship can then look at what his or her fellow professors have accomplished in scholarship. Upon any gap he or she has with his or her colleagues, the person is likely to find most powerful yet natural motivation to become the best possible, namely the unit professor, within a specific institutional context.

Reform 3: Use Ad Hoc Committees for Fast Track Rank Advancement, Endowment Positions, and Institutional Professorships

Status Quo. Since no fast track for rank advancement exists in the current system, a few exceptional individuals who wish to proceed through ranks earlier than the average years of service have to make a special appeal to the normal personnel procedure. Endowment positions, as they are to a large degree used as gifts of diplomacy or tokens of exchange by university executives to draw and receive financial, political, and other types of support from the outside, are often disposed of at the discretion of the administration. Unit professorships from the department to the college to the university are yet to be built into the institutional structure. In cases they are established and awarded, they are installed and supported similarly as endowed positions. There is no standard institutional mechanism for the faculty to contribute substantial input in the process.

Reform. The faculty is the core of any college or university in academia. Critical decisions regarding rewards, resources, and opportunities must lie in the faculty. The role of the administration needs to be limited to the matters of bureaucratic processing, formality, and record keeping. In this spirit of faculty governance, ad hoc committees composed of the faculty in the concerned area of specialty should be used to review, deliberate, and decide on cases for fast track rank advancement, endowment positions, and institutional professorships. As specified in the reform proposal for fast track rank advancement, a special panel can be assembled to handle each valid application for an endowed position as soon as it is received. The special panel may consist of an expert from the outside in the area for which the position is endowed, a faculty member in the unit where the endowed position is housed, a representative from the unit's personnel committee, and a representative from the university personnel review and policy board. Similarly, for the consideration of an institutional professorship, a faculty member of the concerned unit, a representative from the unit's personnel committee, a representative from the university's personnel board, and an expert from another institution in the same discipline may work together as an ad hoc committee. Ad hoc committees make recommendations to the head of a unit or the president of the university who then accepts or rejects those recommendations as administrative decisions of the institution.

Significance. Using ad hoc committees instead of regular personnel agencies at each level can overcome the business-as-usual conservatism that is so often held by those institutional setups. It takes power from the administration while boosting the influence of the faculty in decision-making on critical academic matters. Most important, ad hoc committees highlight the importance of fast track for rank advancement, endowed positions, and institutional professorships. Members of the committee will use their conscience and professional judgment to work on their case as they are in the limelight of a unit or the whole institution. An applicant will engage in serious self-evaluation before he or she puts himself or herself forward for formal consideration. The person who lands such a position through such a high-profile procedure will deservedly feel the honor that comes with the position.

Reform 4: Create a Flat Academic Management

Status Quo. Most colleges and universities, no matter how small or large, adopt a three-layer hierarchy in their structural setup. At the basic level, there are disciplinary departments or interdisciplinary centers. Disciplinary departments then form clusters in the name of school or college, usually by domain of human knowledge. For example, departments representing all the disciplines in the domain of the humanities join hands to make a college of the humanities. In the middle level of college, there are also professional schools, such as those for education, business, law, medicine, nursing, and social work. On the top is the university administration that normally consists of different functional units from academics to financing to student affairs.

Reform. Given the fact that students and the faculty specialize by discipline or an established interdisciplinary field, there is no need to pool departments into colleges or schools, creating a middle-level management in the university administration. A department, if it represents an independent discipline and draws a considerable number of students, can make its own decisions regarding class scheduling, student admission and graduation, faculty appointment and promotion, and distribution of funds in direct coordination with proper functional units at the university level. A department, if it crosses over with other departments in student learning and faculty specialization, should then merge with those closely related departments to make a new departmental entity. In other words, some professional schools can either convert into large disciplinary departments as a whole or split into a few independent departments in accordance with larger disciplinary changes in the knowledge enterprise. For example, a school of social work may stay together as a department of social work whereas a college of business administration may turn into a few stand-alone departments such as those for management information systems, financing, and marketing.

Significance. Removal of middle-level schools and colleges in the university saves cost and frees disciplinary departments from an unnecessary level of control. As power goes to the department, students and the faculty will have more autonomy in their learning and pursuit of scholarship. As for intra-university exchange, there will no longer be structural barriers. Vertically, departments deal directly with the university authority on every critical matter. Horizontally, people do not have to go through the bastion of school or college to reach their points of interest in any specific department. Students majored at department A can take classes offered by department B while faculty members may network with each other solely on the basis of their mutual interests rather than a secular consideration of which college who belongs.

Reform 5: Distinguish Service from Honor Positions at Academic Associations

Status Quo. Academic associations are supposedly places where scholars gather to exchange ideas and promote scholarship. However, as many associations attempt to make an impact on social issues, catch up with cultural currencies, or just remain politically correct in larger contexts, they sometimes allow their leading positions to be allocated in the name of equity and representation by gender, race, ethnic background, and other scholarship-irrelevant factors. As a result, some associations end up being led by persons who are not necessarily leading scholars in their field. Some association journals end up being controlled by persons who are not necessarily the most brilliant and productive scholars in their discipline.

Reform. There are usually two types of positions for members to compete, hold, and serve at academic associations. Type I positions are reserved for people who have distinguished themselves from the rest of the membership through scholarly achievement and excellence in the field to which the association is dedicated. The presidency of the association and the editorship of the association's prime journal are normally regarded as Type I positions. Type II positions are available for people who are willing to serve their association through hard labor and political maneuvering. The executive secretary, managing editors, and vice-presidents of the association or association journals are often considered as Type II positions. Keeping the distinction is obviously important because it reminds the general membership of a critical need to contain politicking in the association management and to restore scholarly symbolism in the association leadership, especially in the position of presidency. Indeed, if some association positions are meant to honor achievement, to symbolize excellence, and to signify direction, they should never be invaded and conquered by such secular forces as power, money, social activism, and political correctness.

Significance. Distinguishing service from honor positions at an academic association will help keep the sanctity of those symbols and titles that are essential to the scholarship of the field or discipline that the association is set up to represent and promote for the majority of the career practitioners. It will also serve to channel concern, interest, and energy for service, social advocacy, and political participation across the general membership since service positions are identified and made available for all individual members who are interested in contributing to their association through labor and volunteerism.

CHAPTER 8

PUBLICATION

Publication is the standard medium by which knowledge is recorded, transmitted, and shared throughout the academic community. To individual scholars, publication provides the basic and oftentimes the only channel through which to participate in scholarly activities and make contributions to the knowledge enterprise. It is difficult to imagine how a career-making academician could become established in a discipline if he or she is not able to develop and maintain a frequent dialogue with the discipline and the larger academic community through publication. If the degree held and the positions assigned are start-off capital, publications are final products in scholarly undertakings, signaling a scholar's substantive involvement in and ultimate worth to the academic enterprise (Barnard, 1990; Becker, 1998; Brodkey, 1987; Cantor, 1993; Carrigan, 1991; Cox & Cox, 2006; Digiusto, 1994; Flemons, 1998; Fox, 1985; Henson, 2004; Kitchin & Fuller, 2005; Lindholm-Romantschuk, 1998; MacDonald, 1994; McGinty, 1999; Parsons, 1989; Powell, 1985; Rosenwasser & Stephen, 1997; Shaw 2002b; Silverman, 2001).

BACKGROUND AND ANALYSIS

There are different levels of publication in the academic world and beyond. At the outset is the distinction between academic and non-academic publications. Non-academic publications may include commentaries, columns, and feature articles academicians write for newspapers, magazines, and other mass media. They may also include pamphlets, consumer guidebooks, and educational materials that academic professionals write for some practical purposes. They are non-academic because they do not present any new knowledge, target only a non-academic audience, and at most involve only the application of academic knowledge to a particular field in life.

Among academic products, a basic distinction is made between refereed and non-refereed publications. Although the distinction is used conventionally, it actually holds no absolute meaning. First, a manuscript always has to go through some review by the editor or an editorial board before its acceptance for publication. The editor, as the person trusted to control a publication outlet in academia, is likely to be an expert in a specific area. The editor's review of the manuscript serves as a peer review by default. Second, since peer review is stressed as a standard, most publication outlets tend to make claims about their adherence to the peer review procedure although in fact they may make their decisions by will or by convenience. Third, peer review is a procedure that can be used with a great deal of subjectivity by the editor. On the most possible objective side, an editor may choose reviewers only by the fit he or she sees between a manuscript's substance and a reviewer's demonstrated specialty. On the opposite side, an editor may use potentially friendly or hostile reviewers to accept or reject a manuscript about which he or she has already made a decision in his or her own review. Peer review, in this instance, may thus serve as a rubber stamp for the editor's own judgment.

With all these deviations and variations though, peer review is still the most widely used and recognized quality control procedure in academic production. Peer-reviewed publications, in general, bear a less personal mark from individual editors, editorial boards, or publishers, but have more substantive rigor to catch the attention of a wider academic audience. Major journals in established fields, disciplines, and interdisciplinary domains now adopt peer review as a normal publication procedure. So do most university presses and some serious commercial publishing houses. Products from these sources usually command more attention and respect from concerned scholars.

Among peer-reviewed publications, there are further differentiations in terms of coverage, importance, and influence. A specialty publication, such as journals in medieval religion, drug abuse, and molecular biology, may focus on a specific field and cater to scholars in that field and its related areas. A discipline publication, such as journals in sociology, chemistry, and philosophy, may cover a whole discipline and address all academic practitioners in the discipline. A publication covering a domain of human knowledge, such as a series, breakthroughs, or reviews in natural sciences, social sciences, or the humanities, the three domains of human knowledge, may synthesize knowledge in each domain and attend to the whole community of scholars in that domain. There are even publications that approach issues of interest to academicians of all disciplines and all domains of human knowledge. For each type of publication by topic and audience, there are also different classes or ratings by importance and influence. Discipline journals in sociology, for example, may divide into the prestigious, the important, and the ordinary. An entire group of articles published in ordinary journals may not garner as much influence as does one article appearing in a prestigious journal on the same topic in the same discipline.

Because of the value differentiation in publications, individual career-making academicians tend to frame their publication efforts as well as place their publication products in a hierarchical order. They work on academic publications regularly and respond to non-academic projects only occasionally or out of special invitations. They use refereed publication outlets mostly and turn to non-refereed sources only when the latter become the last resort as an outlet to put their ideas and findings in print. They focus on the publication outlets of their specialty but always aspire to reach a wider audience through the more general academic media. They aim high at the prestigious publication media but oftentimes may have to be content with less prestigious and more ordinary choices. Overall, individual academicians take pride if they publish widely in different classes of academic media through different publication outlets. They may also easily develop a sense of failure, inadequacy, and shame if they are not able to publish anything at all.

INNOVATION AND REFORM

Academic publications are controlled by both quality and market. On the side of quality, there are peer reviews, editorial boards or editorships composed of experts, publication endowments, and academic publishers subsidized by foundations or commercial publishing. Market forces influence readership. Association publications capitalize on association memberships, university presses build upon university reputations, and general academic publishers eye university libraries, public collections, educators, and academic practitioners for sales and distribution (Barnard, 1990; Becker, 1998; Brodkey, 1987; Cantor, 1993; Carrigan, 1991; Cox & Cox, 2006; Epstein, Kenway, & Boden, 2007; Flemons, 1998; Fox, 1985; Henson, 2004; Kitchin & Fuller, 2005; MacDonald, 1994; McGinty, 1999; Parsons, 1989; Silverman, 2001).

Reform 1: Establish a General Rating System for All Academic Publications

Status Quo. Although the market works normally with quality control, there are a great many assumptions as to the marketability as well as the quality of academic publications. Scholars act out of a general belief that they know where to look for trustworthy materials and what significance to attach to a piece of publication from a particular outlet. Academic organizations operate under a uniform assumption that they are on firm ground to determine what to purchase for their library collections and how much credit to assign to each of their members for specific publications in scholarly media. But in reality when pressed for serious empirical or rational justifications, no individual nor organization is able to say clearly and conclusively why they make certain choices or opt for certain decisions.

Reform. Regarding academic publications, there indeed should be some *U.S. News & World Report*-like ratings or J.D. Power and Associates-like rating organizations to guide scholars and scholarly institutions in their selection and judgment of scholarly work and products. First, there should be annual ratings for academic journals and academic publishing houses for the whole knowledge enterprise as well as across different academic domains, disciplines, fields, or specialties. Ratings may be based upon judgments of representative scholars, librarians, and educated citizens, in combination with professional opinions by selected experts. Criteria for ratings may include theoretical soundness, methodological rigor, empirical credibility, editorial process, general quality, coverage, readership, and overall influence. For example, the rating system may place top ten journals, whether it is Nature or Science, on the number one, number two, or number ten spot, and top ten academic publishers, whether it is Cambridge University Press or Elsevier Science, in the first, second, or tenth position, in general academia. The rating system then moves to academic domains, ranking major journals and publishers respectively for natural sciences, social sciences, and the humanities. Further, it provides ratings for publications in individual disciplines, from medicine, engineering, computer science, psychology, and political science, to social work.

Significance. With a universal rating system in place, every academic journal as well as every academic publisher knows where it stands in the market, what its competitors are, what it takes to move up in rating, what kind of contributors it can draw from, and what level of audience it may cater to. On the part of academicians, they will know, not intuitively by experience but accurately through data, to what journal or publishing house they should go for reliable information, rigorous analysis, or top-notch research, and what publication outlet they ought to seek to put their own work in print, in both idealistic and realistic measures. In search of a suitable outlet, for example, a scholar can use ratings available in a specialty, a field, a discipline, a domain, and even the whole knowledge enterprise as critical guides to identify and shortlist proper candidates for consideration and a final choice.

Reform 2: Conduct Regular Surveys of Concerned Publication Outlets at Disciplinary Associations

Status Quo. While almost every disciplinary organization sponsors one or a few academic journals, not many academic associations conduct rating surveys on all known publication outlets in the field or discipline that they represent and promote. Without solid information, individual academicians automatically turn to their association's flagship journal when they follow new research or when they hope to share their own contributions with a larger audience. As a result, they often miss important opportunities available in various other places to publish their work.

Reform. Disciplinary associations at national and international levels should conduct publication-ranking surveys and offer rating information to their membership on a regular basis. For instance, the American Psychological Association could collect standardized data from its members regarding all psychological journals published in the United States or more generally in English, as well as the major publishers involved in the publication of psychological work. Each year in a particular month, the association would publish the results in one of its journals or through its membership newsletter. The results might be as general as overall rankings for all psychology and psychology-related journals and publishers from top to bottom. It might also include information as detailed as ratings for specific categories, such as innovative ideas, emphasis on experimental design, clarity, and readability. Similarly, the International Sociological Association might rely upon its membership across the globe to collect information on sociology and sociology-related publications and publishers in an international scale. The information would then be analyzed and presented to the members in different countries as one of the standard membership benefits.

Significance. A rating survey on publication outlets falls rightfully in the sphere of a disciplinary association. The survey engages members in the association by soliciting information and ideas on a critically important issue from the general membership. It adds to the meaning and value of association participation and belongingness when the association provides members with useful guidance in publication through annually updated survey results. Indeed, association members and concerned scholars can benefit enormously for their academic career when they have exact rating numbers to compare and contrast different sources of information as well as various outlets of publication in their day-to-day scholarly choices and actions.

Reform 3: Sponsor Regular Publication Contests at Disciplinary Associations

Status Quo. A number of academic associations use their annual meetings to select and recognize the best research monograph published in the field of their respective representation during the past year or another specified time frame. There are, however, no systematic efforts to survey a whole academic area for most significant journal articles, research monographs, or textbooks yearly, for every five years, or for every decade. Nor are there many open competitions at academic associations to elicit best possible scientific essays and reports from individual practitioners.

Reform. To put publication at the center of their concern, all major academic associations should sponsor both open competitions for potential contributors and closed evaluations on existing publications. With regard to the former, announcements about paper contests can be made on association newsletters, journals, websites, and mail-in flyers. Specifications may include detailed directions or requirements on matters such as theme, theoretical analysis, methodological procedure, use of data, format, and submission. For example, a paper contest may invite innovative applications of a chosen theory or method, possible solutions to a known problem, or revolutionary ideas for the future from interested association members or the general public in academia. Judges are assembled from the related fields to review all submissions for the top five or ten entries. Winning essays are then published in a special issue to one of the association's flagship journals. As for the closed evaluations on existing publications, academic associations should run annual reviews and selections of best journals, best journal articles, best publishers, best research monographs, best textbooks, and other best categories concerning publication or publisher on their academic agenda. The competition may involve an association-wide nomination procedure. Objective standards can be established beforehand. Expert opinions can be incorporated later in the process when it is deemed necessary. An award ceremony can be conducted in the annual meeting site to maximize the academic symbolism inherent in the competition. For instance, the American Medical Association might use its annual convention to recognize the best publication or the best publisher in medicine or more specifically to acknowledge best publications and publishers in different forms for different branches of medical science.

Significance. By sponsoring an annual competition for best work published or unpublished, an academic association creates an active yet meaningful agenda for itself. Members, as they are involved in serious association activities and kept abreast of substantive academic matters, will develop a strong sense of connection to their discipline and profession. In particular relevance to academic careers and career achievements, individual academicians feel encouraged and excited in their quest for knowledge when they see their work given heightened attention by people working in the same area. An open competition for scientific essays can be especially encouraging and exciting to those who strive to establish themselves in an academic field.

Reform 4: Establish a Future-Oriented Journal for Each Discipline

Status Quo. There is a great irony in science and scholarship. On the one hand, science and scientific progress build upon imagination, creative ideas, innovative practices, and more dramatically defiance of the past, revolution against the present, or adventure into the future. On the other hand, scholarship and scholastic convention tend to become entrenched or fixated in data validity, paradigmatic compatibility, methodological reliability, experimental replicability, and procedural formality. New concepts, theories, and models that might usher in a new way of thinking, a new paradigm, or a new era are from time to time stifled in the cradle in the name of scientific rigor or scholarly standard.

Reform. There must be a free, open, and well-known forum to cultivate, express, entertain, promote, and protect premature, quasi-scientific, anti-scholastic, unconventional, or otherwise challenging and different ideas and practices in each and every scientific discipline. Establishing a future-oriented journal may well serve that purpose. Possible names for such a journal can be as eye-catching as *Beyond the Forefront, The Unsubstantiated, Quasi Science, Prescience (Pre-Physics, Pre-Chemistry, Pre-Sociology,* etc.), or *Emergent Science (Emergent Physics, Emergent Chemistry, Emergent Sociology,* etc.). The journal publishes imaginative ideas, unsubstantiated hypotheses, innovative experiments, unusual observations, or drastic proposals for disciplinary change. Individual articles should be brief and straightforward with their unique ideas or proposals. For easy access, they may all follow a standard format with four uniform sections from background, ideas, and implementation, to significance. To keep the journal's relevance and credibility as a scholarly forum, criteria for selection of submissions may include such general stipulations as "any idea conceived by a trained scholar in the discipline," "any practice developed by a capable practitioner in the field," or "any proposal fashioned by an average scholar who is adequately identified with the fundamental spirit or principle of the discipline."

Significance. Science is serious work on the basis of facts and evidence. The proposed forum, while serving to exercise empirical scientists and their positivistic mind, will not pose any challenge to the integrity of science. Although they might be steps into the future, contents published in the forum will not be pure fictions. Instead, they will only include imaginative ideas or future-oriented practices reflective of true scientific logic, principle, and reasoning. To individual academicians, the forum will benefit them by changing their angle of observation, strategy of inquiry, or way of thinking rather than by steering them from fact to fantasy, from logical calculation to marketeering speculation, or from science to myth.

Reform 5: Establish a Backward-Looking Journal for Each Discipline

Status Quo. Some journals offer annual reviews of research on specific theme topics or a whole field in one of their regular issues. Publishers may reprint a book or monograph when it fares well in the market. There is, however, no single established forum where academicians can find all best work that has passed the test of time in each and every scientific discipline.

Reform. A backward-looking journal may debut in all major fields or disciplines to meet needs by individual career practitioners for inspiration from the past. The journal may possibly take such identifying names as *Science in Review (Physics in Review, Chemistry in Review, Sociology in Review,* etc.), *the Proven, the Past, Beyond Time, or Sources of Inspiration.* In content, the journal collects best written, most cited, or most influential articles published in all academic journals in the discipline it serves, and may place selected articles under such sections as the last year, the past five years, the last decade, the past fifty years, or the last centennial. In addition, it may have sections for reviews of best books and memoirs of great contributors over similar periods of time. Book reviews may take a fixed format that includes a summary, comments on strengths and weaknesses, and specific indicators of demonstrated influence whereas personal memoirs may follow an established sequence from biographical data, career milestones, and major achievements, to disciplinary impacts. Selection of articles for inclusion, books for review, or figures for remembrance in each issue of the journal may be carried out at the discretion of a knowledgeable editorial board, with input from practitioners in the concerned discipline, or a combination of both. For example, scientist John Doe is featured in the last issue of the year at the urge of a large number of readers while the two articles chosen as representative work of the discipline in the year before are decided solely by the journal's own board of editors.

Significance. It is important to learn from the past in every human undertaking. For career-making scholars, work that has proven to be significant over time provides a profound source of inspiration for new discoveries, creations, and adventures. With a journal that exclusively features best contributions and great contributors in the past by different blocks of time for each major field or discipline, academicians find a basic yet stimulating reference to shape and reshape their own work. Amid their day-to-day laboring on specific academic duties, people will pause and ponder what they could and should do now to have some of their own career achievements selected years after in such a discipline-wide forum.

CHAPTER 9

TEACHING

Teaching is an assigned task involving a time schedule, a classroom setting, and a student audience. To academicians who work in the university, teaching may be the only responsibility in which they can directly see and feel immediate reactions from an external force or authority. Students make complaints when professors fail to show up in class. Administrators take actions when students complain. Because teaching is situational and involving, some academicians, especially those who are not able to properly perceive and pursue research, often mistake it as the only duty they can intelligently handle in their academic career (Bain, 2004; Baldwin & Chronister, 2001; Bianco-Mathis & Chalofsky, 1999; Fairweather, 1996; Kalman, 2007; Lattuca, 2001; Nilson, 2007; Shaw, 1999, 2001a,b, 2002a,c; Silverman, 2001; Sweet, 1998; Young & Shaw, 1999).

BACKGROUND AND ANALYSIS

Teaching, in essence, is a lively process of enlightening students with facts, ideas, logic, and reasoning, and, hopefully, changing those who are taught. But some outcomes of teaching can crystallize into measurable deeds in an academician's career. Statistically, for example, one can trace and record how many courses one has taught, what one teaches by subject, and where one teaches by institution; how many students one has taught in class, how many students one has advised in one-on-one settings, and what percentage of one's students graduate and further develop an academic or professional career; and what distribution one has in scores from blind student evaluations, how many times one is nominated for awards by students or peers, and how many awards in teaching one has actually received from recognized sources.

More substantively, a few academicians, upon establishing themselves as almost godly figures in a field or discipline, may be able to instantly turn their teaching into power and influence. Every word of theirs counts. Some of their faithful and thoughtful students carefully record their lectures, edit them into volumes, and publish them after the academicians' death. The practice started at the time when academic apprenticeship was a norm of training for new scholars. It continued over time but has become less and less common in modern and postmodern eras. With the reality that mass production has long replaced apprenticeship in education, academicians in contemporary time can expect to be recognized for teaching only after they have realistically established themselves through publication. In the most likely scenario, a well-known academician attracts students from different places to study under his or her mentorship; some of his or her students achieve considerable visibility in the academic community and are able to publicly credit their success in some degree to him or her as a source of inspiration in formal media; and toward the end of his or her life, if he or she continues producing creative ideas and insightful thoughts through teaching and if he or she is unable to organize those ideas and thoughts in publishable format by himself or herself, some of his or her students may take action in recording them and preparing them for possible publication at a later time. Being publicly acknowledged by famous students in formal media is certainly a record of accomplishment or a deed of success in teaching for an academician. It is a matter of achieved honor and privilege when his or her lectures are recorded, edited, and published by students before and after the end of his or her academic career.

To fully understand the significance of teaching in the career structure of an academician, however, it is necessary to go beyond individual deeds and records to see how teaching impacts knowledge, the knowledge enterprise, people, and the society. First, teaching spreads knowledge. Although it does not create knowledge, teaching cultivates prospective knowledge creators and prepares them for formal knowledge production. Effective teaching saves students time and energy. Students may, in turn, use saved time and energy for more creative work. Inspirational instructors expose problems, raise questions, suggest routes of exploration, and provide direction. Students may be encouraged and enlightened to discover new interests, acquire new attitudes, and explore new avenues for endeavor in the process of learning. In some sense, it is legitimate to claim that you create knowledge whenever you pass on knowledge.

Second, teaching changes people and their lives. Students come to school for a variety of purposes, depending upon their age, race, profession, and socioeconomic status. Young people attend school to prepare themselves for entry into the labor market. Mid-career professionals take content courses to update their knowledge and build credentials for upward mobility. Senior citizens participate in classroom activities to renew their connection to society and enrich their mind with information and technology. For immigrants and the new generation of many deprived social groups, education provides them means to overcome their circumstance and to enter a new way of life. Through teaching, academicians generally assist people to achieve their goals and realize their dreams. In particular cases, one may be able to personally relate to some students and see how one changes their life through advisement, classroom instruction, or role modeling.

Third, in the university setting, academicians obtain their compensations primarily from teaching. A professor is paid, literally, for teaching students. Without students, there is basically no need for professors and there are no sources of income for scholars working in universities. In the spirit of pragmatism, an academician should obviously approach teaching as a serious duty on a paying job. Every time one goes into the classroom, one should ask: What do I have to offer my students? Every time one receives a paycheck, one should ask: Do I deserve it?

Finally, teaching feeds back on research. Scholars often use their classes to test preliminary findings and ideas. They benefit from student reactions and critiques in the refinement of their work. It is common that professors conduct a seminar or graduate class as a testing ground for their experimentation, book contract, or other endeavor. There is also widespread use of student labor and talent in research projects presided over by professors. In a subtle way, students serve for many ivory-tower scholars as links and bridges to reality, the future, and life. It is only fair to say that teaching is two-way traffic: Academicians learn from students when they teach them.

INNOVATION AND REFORM

Teaching is an integral part of the academic profession. Poor performance by careless or incompetent professors, as sometimes satirically featured in novels, movies, and other literary media, can only tarnish the reputation and undermine the foundation of academe. To a university, teaching constitutes the core of its mission. No matter how established a university is in the world of scholarship, it will lose funding, suffer from negative publicity, and turn away prospective students if it focuses only on research and does not care to ensure the quality of teaching in its educational programs (Bain,

2004; Baldwin & Chronister, 2001; Fairweather, 1996; Grant & Sherrington, 2006; Kalman, 2007; Lattuca, 2001; Nilson, 2007; Shaw, 1999, 2001b, 2002a; Silverman, 2001; Sweet, 1998; Taylor, 2005; Young & Shaw, 1999).

Reform 1: Provide a Week-long Workshop on Teaching for New Faculty Members

Status Quo. While new hires in many other professions are given weeks of orientation or months of on-job training, first-time professors are often assigned to classroom teaching without any special directions. Knowing little about students on campus in particular and teaching in general, some fresh Ph.D.'s struggle hard in their newly attained professorial position to find balance between knowledge in the brain and teaching on the blackboard, between inspiring students and controlling a classroom crowd, and between dream and reality. Students suffer as well when they feel as if they are on a roller-coaster ride with inexperienced instructors.

Reform. While it is not feasible to give newly hired faculty members a long orientation, it is necessary and doable for a college or university to provide each annual cohort of entry-level instructors with a week-long workshop on teaching. At the workshop, would-be classroom teachers first learn about students, their preparation, attitudes, and expectations from student representatives, officials at the office of student affairs, and active instructional members of the faculty. They then become familiar with university rules and regulations regarding student learning and classroom teaching, class evaluation questions and procedures, prevailing academic standards and grading practices, and other institutional conventions. Third, they delve into common classroom problems and their possible solutions with seasoned teaching professors. Problems explored may range from disruptive behavior, controversial debate, and cheating, to grade grievance. Fourth, in the middle of all these informational sessions, workshop attendees may sit in some ongoing classes to see for themselves how experienced instructors manage classroom dynamics to benefit student learning. Lastly, to cap their week-long training, each participant in the workshop has the opportunity to teach real class for one session on campus. Reactions to the guest teaching may be collected instantly from students and other attendees in an open discussion immediately after the session.

Significance. Career academicians are self-sufficient individuals. Nevertheless, formal training in teaching will serve them well in gaining quick grounding in a new institution where they teach and participate as faculty members for a considerable time. At the workshop, they network with other members of their cohort and may find necessary mutual support for initial adjustment as well as later growth. Also critical is the fact that through the workshop they come to know all the points of contact within their employing college or university for various teaching-related issues. Symbolically, being welcomed with a teaching workshop gives new professors a strong sense of importance about teaching both in the university in which they work and in the academic career they make. Whether research is eventually more valued by their affiliated institution or throughout their career, it is always good to place teaching on track and have it under control at the earliest possible time.

Reform 2: Promote Peer Coaching

Status Quo. Joking about students and their under-preparation, laziness, or carelessness is part of the solidification ritual among college professors. While the ritual serves to keep the instructor's attention to students, it tends to shift the burden of effective learning away from teaching. Indeed, professors may find students interested, serious, and hardworking when they stop complaining about students and start focusing on how to improve teaching with one another.

Reform. Peer coaching is a program in active use through different professional settings. In college instruction, peer coaching can be especially pertinent and useful because of the level of freedom the faculty enjoy and cherish in their academic career. Coaches, as proposed herein, do not have to be seasoned classroom performers. They can be real peers who have similar levels of experience, are equally interested in teaching, or share the same concern for student learning. Peer coaches may pair with each other naturally when one asks the other or when two faculty members who know each other spontaneously feel the need or the practicality for a partnership in peer coaching. The college or university may facilitate the process by creating and maintaining a pool of volunteers so that interested participants can always find someone to work with in coaching each other's teaching. The partnership may last for only one semester or for as long as a few years. Throughout the process, peer coaches may review syllabi, examine course contents, set class objectives, visit classroom performances, exchange observations, offer critiques, and provide suggestions, all to the benefit of each other's teaching effectiveness. Participants may write formal reports about their observation or experience. But peer coaching, when it involves the college or university as an official sponsor, should not cast any shadow over the normal evaluation and personnel process. In other words, peer coaches are not official spies who gather information for influencing or making critical personnel decisions.

Significance. Peer coaching builds upon the strong sense of independence the college faculty hold in their academic life when it brings them together to work on teaching. Instead of succumbing to an external authority, college professors paired for peer coaching learn from colleagues who have similar credentials, interests, or penchants for self-sufficiency. Mutual learning will obviously enhance solidarity among the faculty. It may also lay the ground for the development of a collective mentality that would hold teaching in esteem as one of the most important professional responsibilities for career academicians.

Reform 3: Neutralize Peer Evaluations

Status Quo. Knowledge about the quality of instruction lies partly in the evaluation system for faculty teaching. The existing evaluation practice lacks rigor and objectivity in measuring the effect of instruction as well as in holding instructors accountable for their teaching. Peer evaluations by department chair and colleagues are done through individual visitation, and are subject to the influence of interpersonal relations, departmental politics, and personal preferences. For example, faculty members tend to cheer on each other in their teaching. A faculty member who prefers one teaching style may be categorically biased against another faculty member who is good at another instructional style.

Reform. There are many possible innovations for teaching evaluation. They may or may not work to reform the existing system. Regarding peer evaluation, one idea is to use a panel rather than different individuals to visit a class taught by the faculty member under evaluation. The panel could be composed of four persons, respectively representing administration, faculty, students, and parents or alumni. Depending upon the size of the university and the frequency of evaluation, a panel can be assembled annually for a term of one-year service in a departmental unit. For example, a discipline-specific department may assemble a panel of department chairperson, a generally elected representative by the department faculty, a representative sent by the student organization in the department, and a volunteer from concerned parents or alumni. The panel establishes areas of interest they look for in their visitation, from content, organization, clarity, instructor mannerisms, and ways of interaction with the class, to other possible issues. They visit half or one third of the faculty and their classes in a semester or quarter so that they can visit all of them in their term of service. The panel works with individual faculty to accommodate their preferences for the class and the time to be visited in the year. After a class visitation, the panel meets to make a collective decision on a faculty member's teaching. In addition to specific comments and suggestions, the panel may issue a general rating to the faculty member's teaching as "excellent," "average," or "in need of improvement."

Significance. A major advantage of the panel evaluation is that it offers a collective view of classroom performance by the faculty, balanced between students and instructors, administrators and non-administrative stakeholders, and between professors and non-professorial parties. The panel evaluation, compared to visits paid by recommending agencies prior to review for promotion and tenure, is free from personnel concerns and therefore can be objectively focused on teaching itself. In fact, when it becomes standardized from department to department across a campus, the panel evaluation may replace all ad hoc classroom visitations prompted by personnel processes. Personnel committees at different levels may just use annual panel evaluations in their consideration of retention and promotion for individual faculty members on campus.

Reform 4: Standardize Student Evaluations

Status Quo. Student evaluation is administered mostly by the faculty member who teaches the class. The procedure can be seriously contaminated by the unequal relationship between the faculty and students, especially before the faculty member makes his or her judgment of student performance. Most important, questions included in the student evaluation are usually written and selected by the faculty. They are often safe questions to guard the faculty against unfavorable student reactions. Obviously, if professors are serious about their teaching and a university is committed to its mission in education, innovative ideas and proposals need to be explored and entertained to see if teaching evaluation can be made more objective, substantive, and effective.

Reform. With respect to student evaluation, an innovative idea is to administer a standard questionnaire survey online for each class to all students enrolled in the class. The questionnaire may consist of entries agreed upon by a representative body of survey experts, faculty members, administrators, students, parents, and alumni. It may include a section of closed-ended questions for quantitative statistics and a section of open-ended questions for qualitative comments. Results for each class may be processed, presented, interpreted, and used through a procedure or in accordance with certain criteria agreed upon by the representative body. In a small-sized university that runs a cluster of similar programs, a standard survey instrument may be adopted for use across the whole system. In a large-scale institution of diverse programs, individual colleges or departments may have to assemble their own representative panel to decide on an evaluation instrument for use within their own college or department. As far as survey administration is concerned, a university would have to make a policy requiring all students to obtain their course grades online and fill out a class evaluation survey before they could ever access their grades for each class. In implementation, a university-wide computer program would have to be set up to allow students to obtain their grades online and complete a survey on each class before they can see their grades for that class. For example, grades are posted online sometime at the end of the semester, survey interviews are coded and attached to each class, and survey results are automatically tallied and presented when all survey questionnaires pertaining to a class are completed or when a system-imposed deadline is reached.

Significance. Under the proposed measure, the influence of the instructor and the grades he or she assigns is basically removed or at least minimized in the process of student evaluation. Although some students may take advantage of the new measure to seek revenge on instructors with whom they have had issues throughout the semester, the majority would be honest and trustworthy enough in the rendering of their judgment. After all, it is part of an instructor's responsibility to resolve any problem he or she might have with students in class before the problem lingers or mushrooms to affect student learning, student reaction, and teaching.

Reform 5: Regularize Institutional Teaching Awards

Status Quo. There are teaching awards given at different levels in different time frames. The problems are that award activities are not always in alignment with ongoing instructional processes and that selection of awards does not necessarily draw from the judgment of the largest possible pool of students. For example, a professor may obtain a teaching award simply because one of his or her favorite students nominates him or her for the award. Or a department may offer a few teaching awards in one year while it does not engage in any award-related promotion for teaching in the next few years.

Reform. To put teaching at the center of college and university, promotional activities should be conducted at the department, in the college, and throughout the university to recognize outstanding teaching performances and reward excellent teaching performers on a semester or quarterly basis. Information about teaching awards is spread from classroom to classroom. Judgment from students is gathered naturally through normal class evaluations and incorporated decidedly in the selection process. Different from the nomination process that can be easily manipulated by a few unwarrantedly active students, information collected from regular class evaluations is non-political, reflective of classroom experience, and hence most likely to screen in worthiest candidates for awards. Operationally, one way to carry out this proposal is simply to use highest points scored by the faculty on standardized student evaluations. In a department, one undergraduate teaching award is given every semester to whoever obtains the highest score in quantitative student evaluations among all undergraduate classes offered and evaluated in the semester. At the college level, a few teaching awards may be announced each year to those who have received a department teaching award more than once in the past three years. Campus-wide, teaching awards may go annually to faculty members who have received more than one college teaching award in the past five years.

Another way to execute the proposed idea is to include a special question in the end of the standard class evaluation questionnaire: "Would you nominate this instructor for a teaching award in the department that recognizes intellectual stimulation, innovative pedagogy, fairness in grading, and professionalism in relation to students?" The award at the department level falls automatically to whoever receives the highest percentage of nominations across all the undergraduate classes taught in the semester. For example, one earns a department's semester or quarterly teaching award because one has the highest percentage of students marking "yes" to that special nomination question in standard class evaluations among all eligible instructors whose undergraduate classes are included in the award consideration for the whole department. Teaching awards at the college and university levels may follow the same rule as suggested in the first measure of implementation.

Significance. A semester or quarterly teaching award given at the basic level as a disciplinary department can serve to galvanize students and the faculty about the importance of teaching. Students will not just gossip about professors privately and inconsequentially. They will actively compare professors in the discipline of their major and express their experience and feelings formally and vocally through normal class evaluations. The faculty will have to work with each student in their classes if they want to leave the best possible impressions on the general student population in the department. Courting a few favorite students will not likely change basic student reactions one receives through one's classroom performance, much less to bring about any surprised recognition and reward in teaching.

CHAPTER 10

PRESENTATION

Presentation is confined to a particular time and occasion. Its influence is usually limited to the audience who are present at the presentation. Also, because of the spontaneity of the information transmitted and various setting or time-specific constraints inherent in oral expression, presentation is not as detailed, accurate, and long-lasting as publication in the communication of academic materials. On the other hand, presentation is quick, simple, and direct in spreading new ideas and findings. More and more conference organizers invite academic and non-academic media to their meetings and publish conference abstracts or proceedings for larger circulation. Presentation can therefore become an effective means to report, publicize, and share most recent developments across an academic discipline (Cohen, 1997; Fenton, Bryman, Deacon, & Birmingham, 1997; Hyland, 2006; Professional Convention Management Association, 2006; Reinhart, 2002; Rendle-Short, 2006; Shaw, 2001b).

BACKGROUND AND ANALYSIS

In the individual profile of an academician, presentation may serve as a barometer of the level of activity in which he or she engages in his or her academic career. It may also provide a measure of visibility and influence in an academic field. Presentations can be tallied and compared by number. An academician who has made fifty presentations to academic gatherings may legitimately feel that he or she has better access to the academic world and higher visibility within it than someone who has made only five presentations. In quality, presentations may divide into different categories, forms, or levels by different standards. For instance, a presentation may be identified by the conference in which it was made: local, national, and international or field-specific, discipline-wide, and interdisciplinary conferences. It may be classified by the form in which it is made: informal roundtable, formal roundtable, poster, oral, or thematic. There are also differences in whether a presentation is invited or unsolicited, made to a small group panel or a thematic plenary session, and regarded as a regular or keynote speech. An academician who has made numerous unsolicited general presentations to various academic conferences may offer no comparison, in academic visibility and influence, to one who has made only a few invited keynote speeches at the annual conferences in one's discipline. As a rule of thumb, keynote speech and feature presentation to a plenary session at a major academic conference are reserved for only a few outstanding contributors who have established their positions in a discipline through publication.

To the general relationship an academician has with a discipline, presentations fulfill a number of major functions. First, the presentation takes one to a conference, a gathering of academic participants in a field or discipline. At the conference, one appears as a whole person, not just a name as one does in a piece of publication. One dresses in style or casually. One speaks with or without an accent. One listens carefully or with no regard to details. One smiles wholeheartedly or superficially. One makes gestures now and then, conveying one's intent and feelings in a sophisticated way. One asks questions thoughtfully and responds to queries quickly or pointedly. All these physical acts and features converge to create a public image of an academician. One may therefore make oneself known to be a person to befriend, a person to seek advice from, a person to collaborate with, or a person to distance from by other participants in the field or discipline with which one is associated.

One's presentation also can introduce what one is doing or about to do in research. Compared to publication, a presentation can be introductory rather than conclusive, preliminary rather than final, incomplete rather than complete, and informal rather than formal. An academician can use a presentation to make a public announcement or statement about what he or she is pursuing or intends to pursue in an area of inquiry. Interests and expectations may then be generated. Collaborators, partners, or competitors may be identified. Advice, critiques, and suggestions may be gathered. Publication outlets, communication channels, and possible audiences may be explored. With regard to a potential research paper, specifically, one may be able to collect useful comments from the audience so that one can substantively expand or deepen literature review, data analysis, theoretical discussion, or policy application in the main body of the paper. One may receive an invitation, by phone or in writing, from an editor so that one can contentedly and confidently prepare one's presented paper for publication consideration in a journal or in a monograph series.

Third, oral presentation supplements what one is able to convey through publication. Presentation is complementary to publication in a variety of ways. It highlights what will be or is in print. Reading a research monograph may take days. Perusing a scholarly article calls for hours of serious attention. Through presentation, however, an author may use the interactive setting to summarize main points or convey underlying assumptions in his or her work in a few minutes. With major highlights in mind, readers can easily walk through the whole text and gain a command of its content in detail. A presentation explains what is written on paper. In a scholarly piece, there are always descriptions, arguments, illustrations, formulas, figures, or lines of reasoning that are not immediately clear and understandable to readers. The author may have to resort to oral presentation to address queries and offer proper explanations. Thus oral presentation serves as a prelude to what is forthcoming in publication. An author may take a book tour in which an oral presentation arouses interest in the author's forthcoming work. Speaking to an academic conference, the author may simply direct the audience to one of his or her scheduled publications by saying "Please read my book, when it is out, if you would like to learn more about what I have said in my presentation today." Oral presentation offers closure to what remains on written record. After reading a piece of work, readers may be informed, convinced, and inspired or lost, unconvinced, and squelched. An author and his or her advocates may have to engage in public presentations to build on what the author has written and to transmit their conviction of its rightness to the audience. Also, there are people who take and retain information better when it comes in the form of oral presentation rather than in the form of writing. Even when they know and understand some ideas and reasoning well in written language, people are more likely to internalize and follow those ideas and reasoning in their own research and analysis when they receive reinforcement by hearing directly from the author.

Fourth, oral presentation highlights what one has done in scholarship. Publication is often scattered in pieces through different outlets. Although individual pieces add up in a scholar's rise to prominence, each piece itself may not give its author a particularly intense feeling of success, pride, and glory. Oral presentation, on the other hand, can be made to a large audience in a magnificent setting where the presenter can spectacularly highlight his or her position, status, and influence in a field or discipline. In academic gatherings, one may be invited to make an opening or concluding speech to a plenary session. One may be offered the opportunity to deliver a keynote presentation at a lunch or dinner banquet. One may be given the opportunity to offer a thematic exposition of one's contributions or career while receiving an award. As the sitting president of an academic association, one may even be entitled to provide a presidential address, conveying one's vision for an entire field or discipline. All these formal presentations are designed for presenters not only to communicate their achievements, contributions, thoughts, and visions, but also to receive cheers, recognition, honor, and admiration.

Finally, oral presentation celebrates the spirit of community in academic undertaking. Academicians, by training, are abstract, analytical, and logical specialists. They read articles, calculate numbers, make logical inferences, write books, and build models. They communicate with one another, mostly and essentially, through publication. From a purely utilitarian point of view, academicians do not have to spend time, energy, and resources on trips to academic conferences. They can just sit in front of computers, stay in libraries or laboratories, and cruise through electronic and published media, to achieve success in their academic endeavors. By birth, however, academicians are ordinary human beings with flesh and blood. They eat food, drink water, and engage in sex. They need interaction. They desire companionship. Each year, hundreds of thousands of academicians attend meetings and conventions in their field or discipline, for the most part, because they want to be acquainted with each other, to know and be known, to impress and be impressed, to please and be pleased. At the meetings, they shake hands, exchange words and nonverbal cues, give and receive greetings, give and hear presentations. They chat, walk, dance, laugh, eat, drink, and entertain, one on one, in groups, or jointly at large. The ultimate effect of all those activities is manifest and symbolic: to renew human ties and to keep a sense of community among fellow academic participants.

INNOVATION AND REFORM

Presentations are made to academic conferences. Academic conferences are organized mostly by professional and scholarly associations. To make presentation a quality form of communication among academic practitioners, conference organizers must balance standards of scholarship with monetary costs, audience turnout with media publicity, and the temporality of presentation with the retention or circulation of information. Here are some important ideas, not necessarily innovative, for improving academic conferences (Alley, 2007; Cohen, 1997; Fenton, Bryman, Deacon, & Birmingham, 1997; Haskell, 2000; Hyland, 2006; Professional Convention

Management Association, 2006; Reinhart, 2002; Rendle-Short, 2006; Shaw, 2002c).

Reform 1: Do Not Meet for the Sake of Meeting

Status Quo. Major academic associations hold annual meetings as a rule or a custom. They bring people together no matter whether they have anything substantive, unique, or special to offer at their once-a-year gathering. For large associations, a convention seems to work because something will happen when there is a sizable crowd. However, when all associations follow the convention to meet annually, many of them have to struggle to fill their program or to stretch their schedule of sessions and presentations with an insufficient number of submissions.

Reform. A simple measure to be taken by those associations that have difficulty to put together an annual meeting is not to meet for the sake of meeting. The suggested change of approach can be especially helpful to regional, sub-disciplinary, interdisciplinary, or field-specific associations that operate on a limited membership base. Instead of meeting once a year, they may choose to hold an all-member gathering flexibly, realistically, or on the basis of need as biannually, once every three years, or even once every five years. These associations then will have time and resources not only to prepare for better association-wide meetings, but also to work on more important issues, such as publication, provision of professional assistance, and social advocacy. Participants then will take each meeting more seriously when they have to wait for some time to share their ideas and findings face to face with colleagues in the field. Practically, if they can attend only one or two meetings a year, academicians can alternate nicely and neatly between general national or disciplinary conventions and their favorite regional or sub-disciplinary meetings. For example, participants will not miss their regional association's biannual meeting when they use the non-meeting year to present papers to the annual convention of their national disciplinary association.

Significance. Meeting fewer times can benefit many small-scale academic associations. The quality of each meeting will improve, not only in terms of submissions, but also in terms of participant-to-participant interactions. Following the conference program, speakers will find a large enough audience to share their research and ideas while attendees will see a wide enough variety of presentations to choose for their learning and inspiration. Most important, quality submissions set the stage for publication of conference proceedings whereas meaningful exchanges are likely to lead to collaboration among academicians working in the same field.

Reform 2: Strengthen Academic Standards

Status Quo. Most conference organizers follow their commonsense calculation that lower standards bring about larger participation. Desperate to meet some attendance quota or profit target, they sometimes only ask for a simple idea or a rough title from an interested participant to assign this person a place in the conference program. Indeed, a great many academic associations rarely bother attending to the fact that to maintain standards for annual associational conventions is to ensure quality participation by serious practitioners on a long-term basis.

Reform. Specific measures to keep quality and tighten standards for academic meetings may include a submission prerequisite, abstract review, abstract circulation, and a publication of proceedings. Beginning with submission, a conference organizer may require a completely written paper, a synopsis of content in five hundred words, or a letter of certification or recommendation by a senior association member for a submitted abstract. Presentation proposals can be reviewed by a specially assembled program committee or examined by a network of carefully selected experts who specialize in different fields or subjects within the academic scope of the conference. Abstract circulation may take the form of a booklet of abstracts to all registered participants or in the form of publication through a known data set. Circulation is important because a great majority of participants rely upon the conference not just to present their findings to whoever sits in their session but to spread their ideas to a larger audience. For example, the American Sociological Association publishes most of its annual conference abstracts in *Sociological Abstracts*, a data set that can be accessed by sociologists and other social scientists all over the world. Finally, publication of conference proceedings may serve as a powerful motivator to elicit participation. Academic practitioners are likely to make serious efforts to earn their spot in annual proceedings if papers included are carefully selected for scientific merit and if the proceedings have become an authority reference in their field or discipline.

Significance. People take it as a serious undertaking when they work hard to get into a conference program. At the conference, they would pay attention to what appears on the agenda and learn from what they hear. Attendance at individual sessions would then increase. So would the quality of exchange among conference participants. The facts that presentation abstracts would be in circulation to a larger audience beyond the conference and that a number of articles would be selected for print in the conference proceedings could further reinforce the effort each participant puts into the conference.

Reform 3: Diversify Conference Programs

Status Quo. Academic conferences focus primarily on oral presentations. Regular presenters are put into individual sessions where they share their ideas and findings under a loosely identified theme topic. Major speakers are scheduled to make their speeches in plenary sessions that most participants attend. Besides oral communications, there are usually book exhibits, poster sessions, student parties, general receptions, employment services, sightseeing tours, workshops, and business meetings. However, all these add-on activities depend upon whether conference organizers are ambitious, creative, energetic, or caring enough about what they do for all the participants who make serious efforts in coming to the meeting.

Reform. To better serve the community of scholars, academic conferences ought to work more on standardization of procedure and diversification of program. With regard to procedure, conference organizers should spread the word about their conferences as broadly as possible. Besides association journals, newsletters, and email circulars, conference announcements including submission requirements, registration information, and milestone dates can be made on both general and special media outlets. Receipt of submission is acknowledged. Acceptance or rejection is provided promptly, so is a preliminary program posted on an official website, both of which give participants sufficient time to make content as well as logistical preparations. At participants' preferences, registration can be done prior to or at the conference. The printed conference program is ready for pickup as soon as participants arrive at the conference site. If conference proceedings are compiled afterward, specific directions about submission, selection, publication, and overall time line will be included in the registration packet.

As for program, large-scale conferences may offer a wide range of contents and activities to engage and enrich participation. In addition to oral presentations on thematic issues in the full scope of a discipline or an interdisciplinary field the conference is supposed to cover, there can be workshops on grants and publications, discussion groups for department chairs and graduate coordinators, socializing gatherings for graduate students, alumni and alumnae, and retired scholars, and tours to historical sites, cultural points of interest, or conference-related manufacturing, engineering, experimental, service, or management facilities. Small-scale conferences may concentrate on one major activity at a time. For example, conference organizers host informational visits the year when the meeting takes place at a venue close to important sights. In the next meeting, the conference may just sponsor workshops on new theories, methods, models, or procedures developed recently in the field.

Significance. Academicians go to professional conferences with different expectations and purposes. When conferences are well organized with a clear procedure and a wide variety of program contents or activities, academic participants will likely hear what they need to hear, learn what they expect to learn, and connect to whom they intend to connect. Satisfaction on the part of conference participants bodes well for future attendance to similar academic gatherings. With loyalty and commitment by concerned practitioners, academic conventions will then become one of the focal points of interest for scholarly communications and exchanges.

Reform 4: Publish Conference Proceedings

Status Quo. Most academic conferences do what they mean to do, that is, to offer a time and venue for people working in the same discipline or field to meet, socialize, and share ideas and findings. Exchange takes place spontaneously. Nothing substantial and substantive is left and kept when the meeting is over. Back to their daily routines, academicians work on matters they deem serious, including teaching, grants, research projects, and publication, as if they had never attended a conference or as if they just had a party-like break.

Reform. Given the fact that publication serves as the most formal and influential form of scholarly communications, academic conferences should use association journals or line up with reputable publishers to publish conference proceedings. The conference proceedings can be selective, including only contributions considered to be most important or representative by a panel of scholarly judges. Immediately after the meeting, all presenters are urged to submit their full papers for consideration. The conference proceedings may also be all-inclusive, gathering each synopsis of presentations made at the meeting. The synopsis follows a strict format with a firm limit on length. For example, it may require such elements as assumption, hypothesis, method, evidence, theoretical argument, and implication in five hundred words. Whether selective or all-inclusive, the proceedings should be published once after each convention so that over time they remain as an institutional series for continuing reference in the field or discipline represented by the conference. For example, the American Psychological Association will have a volume of conference proceedings each year as it holds its membership-wide convention annually. From year to year, psychologists and related scholars can make reference to the annual proceedings in print for important developments when such proceedings are published continuously as a known series.

Significance. Publication of conference proceedings will make academic gatherings more meaningful and fruitful. With expectation to publish their research products beyond a spontaneous expression at the meeting, academicians will put more effort into their conference participation. They will have less of a sense of cynicism as is typically experienced by many conference participants toward business-as-usual academic meetings. Institutionally, conference proceedings have the potential to become an authoritative, even all-inclusive reference in a field or discipline when they appear continuously for each convention held by the disciplinary association.

Reform 5: Make Academic Conventions Not-For-Profit Events

Status Quo. The registration fee is prohibitively high for many potential participants at academic conferences. Some conference organizers may even be poised to profit in the name of scholarship. While it is understandable that conference planners need to balance revenues and costs, it is discouraging to prospective participants when a registration fee is set too high for them to be able to attend a conference. To academicians, It may even be dispiriting and alienating when conference organizers seem to be interested in only profit by collecting high registrations, charging publication fees, setting aside a block of hotel rooms, and arranging costly sightseeing tours for the participants.

Reform. There is obviously no magical number to suggest how much a conference organizer should reasonably charge for registration. The actual cost of a conference varies by location, facility, coverage, organization, and other factors. Registration should normally entitle all paid participants to a complete program, a general reception, and an opportunity to publish their peer-selected papers in the conference proceedings. In specific measures, conference hosts and organizers should first work on funding through public as well as private grants, endorsements, or sponsorships. They should work with airlines, hotels, travel agencies, and local governments to lower costs. With adequate funding from sources other than participants, conference organizers may even be able to provide incentives to induce participation. For example, they can offer discounts to participants who present papers at the meetings. They can give awards for best papers or best presentations in specific categories or settings. They can invite prominent scholars to speak at the conference. All these measures may generate a larger than expected audience to make the conference not only influential but also cost-effective. The guiding principle is this: Do not make academic conferences for-profit events.

Significance. At a general level, lessening monetary motives by conference organizers can attract larger crowds to scholarly gatherings. With a larger crowd, an academic conference may still be able to keep its financial balance by a lower charge on registration. An at-cost registration fee will serve not only to attract participation from a wide spectrum of practitioners within the intended scope of the conference, but also to maintain the general integrity of academic conferences in the eyes of the majority career-making academicians.

CHAPTER 11

SERVICE

There are essentially three dimensions in academic life: teaching, research, and service. The purpose of research is to generate and refine knowledge; the purpose of teaching to synthesize knowledge and pass it from generation to generation; and the purpose of service to relate knowledge to reality and apply it to improve the quality of life. In a sense, each dimension of academic life is equally important and valuable to human survival. However, there exists an institutional prescription of priority and limit for practicing academicians. Most institutions engage in research and/or teaching. Academicians working in those institutions naturally prioritize their activities in accordance with their institutional mission. Few institutions are set up as service organizations where working academicians take service as their overriding priority. As a result, there has formed a tradition among academicians that places service in a far less important position than teaching and/or research (Bianco-Mathis & Chalofsky, 1999; Dickeson, 1999; Fairweather, 1996; Goldsmith, Komlos, & Gold, 2001; Hamilton, 2002; Macfarlane, 2007; Tierney 2006).

BACKGROUND AND ANALYSIS

Service, as perceived and pursued by the majority of academicians in their institutional context, fulfills two important functions. One is citizenship. Academicians run committees, review papers and grants, organize meetings and discussion groups, voice concerns and opinions, and participate in various routine activities within their institution and discipline. By taking charge as responsible practitioners, they demonstrate the value of self-governance, promote the spirit of community, and maintain the life of their institution and discipline. In any typical university, there are committees, task forces, or policy groups at department, college, and university levels. Committees, task forces, or policy groups may deal with recruitment, performance evaluations, student awards, faculty incentives, academic grievances, educational resources, library acquisitions, technology, administration, community relations, and various other issues. Members of the faculty serve on committees, task forces, or policy groups, usually outside their teaching and research responsibilities, without any compensation in addition to their regular salaries. In all academic disciplines, there are manuscripts to be reviewed, grant proposals to be evaluated, conference programs to be assembled, meetings to be organized, newsletters to be circulated, journals to be edited, monographs to be published, associations to be maintained, and other academically related business matters to be attended to. Scholars spend a great deal of their time and energy on these service functions, often without monetary benefit and reward. There is no doubt that academic institutions, disciplinary associations, and the whole community of scholarship would cease operating should all their members shun voluntary good-citizenship service beyond regular paid job duties.

The other function is application. Academicians apply their knowledge and skills to the real world, offer advice, training, and direct assistance to people in need, and improve general spiritual and material conditions in the larger society. For instance, a medical scientist may run to the aid of an ailing neighbor. He or she may stop in traffic to attend the injured before the arrival of official rescuers. He or she may aid children in other countries in programs such as "Doctors without Borders." A criminologist may sit in a court hearing to offer expert witnesses. A psychologist may speak to the mass media about parenting and family life. A chemist may sit on the board of a local water treatment company to provide scientific advice. A civil engineer may testify in the city council about waste management across local districts. A sociologist may join a neighborhood committee to voice an opinion on various social issues. A social work scholar may volunteer in a public housing project for senior citizens to contribute observations and ideas to the management. In all these service activities, academicians may be paid for their time and effort, or they may not be given any compensation at all. They may be selected or invited because of their fame or specialty. They may step in out of their individual willingness. But one thing in common is that they apply knowledge to meet specific needs or solve practical problems in the real world. To the neighborhood, community, and society in which they live, academicians exemplify good citizenship when they apply their knowledge and skills to effect positive social change.

Taking a somewhat academically ethnocentric point of view, academicians may divide service into two categories: professional and community service. Professional service centers on academic activities that promote an academician's standing in his or her discipline. Specifically, it includes such activities as reviewing manuscripts, editing journals or monograph series, evaluating grants, organizing conference programs, leading panel discussions, presiding at meetings, editing newsletters, maintaining email networks, serving on association committees, and becoming association officers. Academicians work on professional service activities under certain circumstances. By reputation, they are invited to serve as editors or grant evaluators, or elected to become association presidents or vice-presidents. Out of individual willingness, they volunteer to be manuscript reviewers, session conveners or discussants, and association treasurers or secretaries. Within a personal network, they answer calls by former or current advisors, colleagues, or friends to sit on editorial boards or program committees, or serve in some assistant positions for disciplinary associations. Professional service benefits academicians in different ways. It assists academicians to progress in their home institutions. Most academic institutions take into account service contributions in personnel decisions. It provides academicians with a forum to express their ideas or a network to spread their influences. Editors and association presidents can use service positions to reinforce their already achieved influences by way of publication. Finally, service motivates academicians to stay on the academic track, making their due contributions to scholarship. Most academicians serve their discipline in awe of academic giants and their scholarship. In service positions, they observe and learn how the academic process takes place and how academic celebrities rise from the majority of ordinary academicians. They are therefore stimulated, even inspired to continue in their own academic endeavors.

Community service, on the other hand, may originate from an academician's professional affiliation or specialty but does not necessarily advance that individual in his or her professional development. As far as activities are concerned, community service can range from serving on a departmental scheduling committee, a college personnel committee, or a university committee for student complaints and grievances, and serving on an advisory board for a community organization, a private business, or a level of government, to appearing on a news report, a talk show, or a documentary to offer expert opinions. Academicians engage in community services for important reasons. First is to fulfill an institutional requirement. As a full-time faculty member of an institution, academicians are expected to perform community services at department, college, and university levels. Service may be assigned by institutional authorities or won through open competition. Because questions about service quality and the extent of service can be raised in the personnel process, academicians may have to actively seek service opportunities in addition to a passive acceptance of service assignments by their supervising figures. Second is to gain insight, solidify a position, and expand influence. In their home institution, academicians serve in order to obtain a general understanding of how their institutional system works and take specific opportunities to strengthen their position in the system. In their communal and social environment, academicians serve to extend their presence and influence from work to life, from organization to community, and from academia to the larger world. Third, and less important, is to make money and win fame. Academicians may be compensated for their services when they sit on the advisory board of a public or private agency or serve as expert witnesses in court proceedings. They may even become famous if they are frequently featured in the mass media on specific issues.

How does an academician codify service into his or her autobiography of career and career achievements? There are essentially two approaches: outcome-oriented and activity-based. In an outcome-oriented approach, an academician looks into the result of his or her service. The questions one asks about one's service are these: What marks do I leave, what impact do I have, or what difference do I make in the lives of the people I serve, the culture of the institution in which I work, and the scholarship of the discipline in which I specialize. However, since outcome is difficult to measure in the flux of change within an institution, community, or discipline, most academicians opt for an activity-based approach. They record all the services in which they engage in their career pathway and take pride in just being part of their community, institution, and discipline through service.

INNOVATION AND REFORM

Professional associations, colleges and universities, research institutes, and the whole academic establishment depend upon academicians and their volunteer services. Businesses, government agencies, and community organizations take every opportunity to tap academicians and their talents. As organizations are poised to select their favorite candidates for free contributions, they need to recognize and do something about the fair distribution of resources and opportunities among career-making academicians (Bennett, 2003; Bright & Richards, 2001; Darling, 2005; Dickeson, 1999; Fairweather, 1996; Goldsmith, Komlos, & Gold, 2001; Hamilton, 2002; Macfarlane, 2007; Tierney 2006).

Reform 1: Clarify Service

Status Quo. There is a rampant abuse of service in the academic community. Organizations use it widely to the extent of exploitation because service is free and can be tapped as a cost-saving measure. Individuals offer it willingly or wishfully, sometimes to the degree of self-harm, because service can be nominal and can be touted as good citizenship or even contributions to the profession. From time to time, there is no lack of academicians who manage to climb to the position of leadership, fame, and influence in their discipline or institution simply through the route of service.

Reform. What is voluntary service? What is regular work? Within service, what is substantive service? What is nominal service? What is substantial service? What is frivolous service? There is obviously a need to clarify service so that organizations do not relegate functional duties important to their mission to people willing to perform but really unqualified. In colleges and universities, recruitment, promotion, and retention are matters central to institutional reputation and to individual careers. Screening of applications in recruitment and evaluation of professional files in the retention, tenure, and promotion process should therefore be considered regular work, not voluntary service, by the faculty. Members of recruitment or personnel committees should be elected from the general membership of a concerned unit, rather than handpicked by the leader of the unit. Committee members, especially the chair, should be given some released time, when possible, from teaching and research so that they can concentrate on what they do in the committee. In disciplinary associations, journal editors, convention program chairs, and presidents wield a considerable amount of power and influence as to the direction associations take and how individual members move forward in their careers. These positions should all be filled through open competition or serious evaluation of candidates' academic credentials. A fixed salary, stipend, or honorarium should be given so that people who are selected to hold these positions have a strong sense of responsibility to do their job as regular work not as voluntary service. In a similar spirit, academic publishers should think about and perhaps change their longtime practice of counting on volunteer reviewers in their critical decision on manuscripts.

Significance. Clarification of service will assist academic organizations to determine priorities according to their fundamental mission. Operations that are key to achieving organizational goals must be given sufficient material resources and regularly employed personnel. Service by volunteers can be used only for secondary or supporting activities. Knowing what is regular work, what is voluntary service, what is paid for, or what is free contribution will also help individual academicians properly channel their time and energy through the academic career. People will then find less wishful thinking but more purposeful work, less sheer sacrifice but more self-knowledge and academic enhancement, less nominal satisfaction but more actual benefit.

Reform 2: Specify Service Qualifications

Status Quo. Many service positions are filled without serious consideration of volunteers' qualifications. As long as interested volunteers are current members, hold some degrees, reach certain ranks, or fit into specific stereotypes, they automatically gain access to service opportunities that may prove not only valuable to the advancement of individual careers but also vital to the growth of an academic field, discipline, or institution. It is not uncommon that a full professor sits on a university board simply because of rank, even though he or she does not have any substantive credential in the related area of service. It is no surprise, either, that an association member serves on a publication committee charged to make policies and guidelines for association journals just out of the member's active membership status, although that person does not have any experience in scholarly publication.

Reform. Qualifications should and can be specified for most service positions beyond a simple status or a nominal title. In a college or university, committees on teaching should be served by those faculty members who have proven excellence in classroom instruction or mentorship through awards, consistently positive student evaluations, stimulating lectures, or innovative pedagogies. A task force on technology would be most productive when each of its members works in the forefront of technology in his or her academic field. And a board on equity and fair treatment would benefit itself most if its individual members not only represent different groups by race, gender or other status, but also have specific cultural, social, or scholarly experiences in areas related to the functions of the board. Similarly, academic associations should fill their program committees with people who are active in scholarship, their publication committees with people who have published extensively in the field, or their outreach committees with people who have a track record in social advocacy. And scholarly journals and academic publishers should recruit into their pool of reviewers only those academicians who have published adequately, if not impressively, in specific areas of interest. It does not make any sense that a manuscript is accepted or rejected for publication by reviewers who themselves do not know what to research and how to write a scholarly article.

One concern about specification of service qualifications is that it may make it more difficult to recruit people into various academic services in need. The response is to break the negative cycle and create a positive cycle for service in academia. The negative cycle is that service positions are purloined by not so-qualified people, service is provided nominally and in substandard quality, people do not value and care about service, people shun service, and service positions have hence been filled by whoever is willing, available, or of a simple stereotype. The positive cycle, on the other hand, begins with specification of qualifications. When qualified academicians hold service positions, they are more likely to provide quality services; when quality services are offered, people are more likely to appreciate service and respect its providers; and when service is appreciated and its providers are respected, people are more likely to join or compete for service.

Significance. Specification of service qualifications will ensure that service opportunities fall into the hands of deserving individuals in a field or institution. There will be no chance for opportunists in serious scholarship who do not have much to offer yet still hope to appropriate fame or influence for themselves through nominal services to the academic community. Most important, quality services will be dispensed to the benefit of career academicians, academic fields, knowledge-producing or distributing institutions, and overall academia when qualified individuals offer the best of their training and experience in various self-governance positions.

Reform 3: Standardize Service Recruitment

Status Quo. Since it is voluntary and without monetary compensation or formal recognition, service does not carry the same rigor or seriousness in its selection of providers or contributors. Service positions in many academic organizations, from colleges or universities to disciplinary associations, from scholarly journals or publishing houses to private foundations or public funding agencies, are often filled by sheer convenience, out of individual willingness, or through personal connections. For example, a governmental agency selects actual reviewers without close scrutiny from a sign-in sheet it hands out at a scholarly meeting for people who are interested in joining in its pool of grant reviewers. Or an editor sends someone a manuscript for evaluation simply after he or she has a casual conversation with that person at an international conference.

Reform. Given the indispensability of service to both organizations and individuals, organizations should adopt standard procedures in recruiting and using academic volunteers. With regard to heavy-duty service, they should keep an open list and assign people to service positions not just using the first-come-first-serve principle, but taking serious consideration of specialty, qualification, and experience whenever possible. For instance, an editorial office would recruit into its pool of reviewers only those who have submitted their complete curriculum vitae and assign a qualified candidate to review of a specific manuscript strictly on the basis of his or her research and publication records. A disciplinary association's program committee for the next convention would not just consist of those who show up in the business planning meeting at the current convention site. Instead, it should include representatives of different regions, institutions, academic ranks, theoretical orientations, and methodological preferences beyond membership eligibility, basic scholarly qualifications, and personal willingness. On service concerning critically important issues, an organization should establish an open procedure not only to select the most qualified candidates, but also to ensure fair treatment to all who are interested in service. For example, personnel committees at department, college, and university levels would be filled by way of open competition. Association presidents and vice-presidents would take office after general election. Journal editors would assume their duty through regular job recruitment processes.

Significance. Standardization of service recruitment will ensure service openness, fairness, quality, and integrity. Academicians who are willing to serve their professional community have a fair chance to be considered and selected on the basis of their qualifications and experiences whereas academicians who are served can count on the wisdom, dedication, and contribution of most deserving individuals in their profession and organization. Quality service elicits respect from the concerned membership population. It can further stimulate interest from the academic public to offer better and more service for the greater benefit of scholarship.

Reform 4: Make Service an Open Process for the Academicians Served

Status Quo. There seems to be a general assumption in academia that academicians in each discipline or institution have received a standard education, do uniformly academic work, and share similar codes of conduct. It does not matter who takes what position in the service of a discipline or institution because like-minded academicians will do about the same things in various service roles and duties. On the other hand, it is always natural for the majority of ordinary academicians to often wonder who sit in those boards, committees, and task forces making rules and guidelines that dictate their everyday thoughts and behaviors.

Reform. To clear any confusion or doubt in the minds of those served, major service boards, committees, or task forces should make public who serves on their body, the length or status of term of each of their members, what credentials or qualifications each serving person possesses, and how anyone who is interested in serving the body may join it. In colleges and universities, service entities such as those on faculty affairs, student learning, campus resources, and administrative procedures obviously fall into this category of required openness and transparency. Filling those bodies by the will of an administrator, the connection of a never-retiring member, or the convenience of a secretary will severely compromise the quality of service each of them is supposed to offer to the faculty, students, and an entire campus. At disciplinary associations, the program committee for all-member conventions is customarily assembled at the discretion of the president. The president then should keep members informed of what agenda he or she would like to set for the association's convention and what kind of people he or she would trust to put in charge of implementing such an agenda under his or her term. Filling the program committee by convenience and running it behind closed doors can only leave the general membership to wonder whether the president has any direction at all for the association and its annual convention. Most important, academic journals should make their advisory or editorial board more open, active, and accessible to academicians who depend upon scholarly publications to obtain reliable information and to spread their research findings. Provision of a board member's name, degree, and institutional affiliation is simply not enough to give the journal's serving public sufficient confidence in the member's qualifications and abilities to screen in best possible academic products for use in academic careers.

Significance. It is only fair and just to make service an open process to the academicians served when service entities and their members make critical decisions on fundamental interests in academic careers. With openness and transparency, members will more likely resort to conscience, standards, and professionalism in the performance of their service duties. A service entity as a whole will more likely be considerate, effective, efficient, and responsive to its serving community.

Reform 5: Make Service an Equal Opportunity for the Serving Academicians

Status Quo. Most individuals serve on committees, organize meetings, and review manuscripts without any compensation. They perform their free service duties in the hope that these services may somehow assist them in their own career development. Indeed, service often translates into opportunity. Experiences in service sometimes turn into assets and resources for upward mobility. However, because organizations take service as voluntary contribution, they usually do not bother to make service positions available to every eligible candidate under the same rules they would abide by in formal job recruitment, regular work assignment, promotion, and other personnel processes.

Reform. Organizations benefit from individual services. Without voluntary services by the mass of practitioners, many academic organizations would simply become dysfunctional or cease to operate. Given the importance of service, stakeholders in academic organizations should resist any temptation to use their own acquaintances, colleagues, friends, or relatives when they are charged to fill service positions. The key is to look beyond individual convenience and self-comfort. In fact, once they go beyond their personal network, academic stakeholders will soon find themselves on a larger landscape for best possible selections. For instance, an editor may call people who are in his or her personal network to assemble an editorial board for a journal or book series. The editor can also put out public advertisements for editorial board members in major academic media concerning the journal or series. By the latter means, the editor may not only put together a board of dedicated and qualified people, but also add a group of new faces to his or her own professional network. Similarly, an association president may handily fill an annual meeting program committee with some of the names he or she personally knows in the profession. Although doing so may strengthen some personal ties, this association president can easily fail at the task of keeping balance and long-range perspectives on behalf of the association by not tapping into pools of new talent and younger members whose voices need to be heard at the annual convention.

Significance. Making service an equal opportunity will change organizations, organizational stakeholders, and their attitudes toward service. Assignment of service on the basis of personal favor or organizational discretion will gradually lose ground. Equity, fairness, and due process will eventually apply to voluntary service as to regular work. Open and equal access to service can obviously benefit academicians in their professional career whereas service by most qualified people in the field will likely improve academic institutions over time.

CHAPTER 12

GRANTS

Scientific research in the postmodern era is seldom an individual pursuit. Research on a single subject often involves investigators in different specialties over a long period of time. Cost for manpower, equipment, space, and operation easily goes beyond the regular budget of an academic institution. In order to carry out their planned research, academicians nowadays need to spend a great deal of time and energy to craft grant proposals seeking monetary support from various private foundations and public funding agencies (Bauer, 1999; Bolek et al., 1992; Locke, Spirduso, & Silverman, 2007; Ries & Leukefeld, 1995; St. John & Parsons, 2004; Savage, 2000; Shaw, 2002b; White, 1983).

BACKGROUND AND ANALYSIS

To individual academicians, a grant is in essence a means toward an end. The means is money. With money, they are able to assemble a research team, purchase equipment and materials, train staff, collect information, analyze data, present findings, write reports, and prepare publications. The end is the research product. It may vary in form, from invention, innovation, discovery, theory, model, methodology, and technical procedure, to a piece of writing in the academic media.

Obtaining a grant is now more and more considered as an achievement in itself. Researchers who obtain grants gain status and importance in the eyes of academicians. First, competition runs tight and intense in the quest for a grant. A normal grant application is in most cases a well-crafted scientific piece. It builds upon existing research and some specific pilot studies. It bears the name of its principal investigators and their close associates. In its main body, a grant includes literature review, theoretical arguments, methodological design, proposed research procedures, and expected outcomes on a specific topic. Literature review can be so extensive as to encompass all major contributions to the issue. Theoretical arguments have to be logically derived from prevailing models, paradigms, or explanations on the subject. The methodological design needs to be unique, conceivable, and executable. Proposed steps and actions may be as detailed as they would be in actuality. Outcomes can be imagined and speculated upon. But imagination is always guided by scientific analysis. To emerge from the competition as a winner, a grant as a whole must withstand serious scrutiny and meticulous critiques by experienced experts and scholars.

A grant makes it possible for a group of researchers to work cooperatively on a project, a valuable outcome in any institution of higher learning. It provides the principal investigator with an opportunity to demonstrate leadership in academic research. It promotes the spirit of community among career-making academicians. Most scientific projects are complex, calling for joint work by researchers from different disciplines or institutions. Some projects are multifaceted, creating needs for specialists in different categories, from theorists, logicians, statisticians, historians, computer programmers, methodologists, and experimenters, to writers. Some projects are scaled, generating demands for a number of researchers in similar capacities. Project scholars may work under one roof in a laboratory or at a research center. They may collaborate on a project over distance. But when they work as a team, they develop a collective conscience, group cohesion, and a communal spirit. They motivate one another. They overcome individual weaknesses. They demonstrate team strengths. They benefit from each other in both personal growth and joint projects. Cooperation also gives rise to leadership. On funded projects, principal investigators provide themes, establish agendas, decide on a division of labor, give directions, coordinate individual efforts, and assemble pieces of work into coherent products.

A grant is an indispensable resource in scientific research. It provides funding for manpower, equipment, and other costs involved in research. Scholarship in the contemporary era is no longer an individual endeavor. There might still be a few mathematicians or philosophers who claim that they need only pens and pieces of paper in their favored ivory tower to solve problems, identify formulas, or offer critical insights. Most scientists know they depend upon laboratories, instruments, and other material conditions to gather evidence, analyze data, develop hypotheses, test theories, modify methodologies, and improve models. A scientific laboratory takes millions of dollars to build. A precision instrument or rare reagent may require thousands of dollars to acquire. To obtain one piece of evidence, dozens of experiments may have to be conducted. A whole population may have to be sampled. To develop a feasible model from raw data, network computing may have to be used. To report and spread findings, researchers may deem it necessary to convene a conference for concerned scientists and stakeholders. A monograph may have to be commissioned with a reputable publishing house. All these efforts and activities need time, resources, investment, and commitment. Without funding, much research might never be executed. Without a grant, data might never be analyzed, a presentation might never be made, and publication might never be produced.

Grants are economic capital that empowers academicians in both their academic and secular positions. Academically, well-funded scholars can pursue their research agenda to the extent of their wishes, their wills, and even their dreams. They carry out projects actively, produce reports and publications frequently, participate in disciplinary associations actively, and experience upward mobility quickly. Besides academic visibility and influence, they may assume leadership roles fast and early, inside and outside their home institutions. In their secular aspect, grants enable scholars to make more money than their ordinary colleagues. If they work in universities, they can use grant funds to pay themselves for twelve full months instead of the nine months for which faculty members are usually paid. They can reimburse themselves for various research-related purchases and expenses. For example, they can change their computer and office equipment more frequently. They can afford to feel less uneasy about the cost of a trip to an international conference. In terms of human relations, grants give scholars more than what they may command with knowledge. With a grant, not only can a scholar advise fellow academicians, but he or she can also hire them and sometime influence them. The power inherent in a grant can obviously translate into control, influence, and a sense of accomplishment for academicians.

Finally, most academic institutions value grant and extramural support as critical indicators of their scholarly activity and institutional vitality. They take measures to accommodate, promote, and reward members who obtain funding from the outside. Indeed, when members bring in grants, an institution receives monetary resources to open programs, upgrade in-house hardware and software, hire employees, enroll students, and boost productivity. For example, a research center is established with federal grants on a university campus. The research center attracts scholars, provides students with research assistantship, and absorbs office staff. It conducts projects, sponsors meetings, and publishes research products. Beyond practical benefits, an institution gains status and stature when many of its members become active, visible, and influential in their respective fields. It may even be given different ratings by reference authorities in education and research in accordance with the total number of grants all of its members receive from public and private agencies. A grant brings to the public eye individual scholars. It also makes institutions famous and attractive.

How is obtaining a grant chronicled in an academician's career record of achievements? At the outset, there are numbers of grants in the academician's career pathway. The more grants an academician receives, the more distinguished his or her academic career looks. Grants can be differentiated by their sources as well: private versus public, local versus national, small versus large, and ordinary versus prestigious foundations or funding agencies. Being funded by a prestigious foundation may by itself carry a significant weight in the eyes of academicians. In compatibility with the prevailing view of commercialism in postmodern society, it now becomes more and more a convention that a grant is simply and directly measured by the amount of money received. Each grant is identified too often by its price tag. An academician can boast of funded research throughout his or her entire academic career by dollars in thousands, and sometimes even millions. While a larger amount of money tends to attract bigger attention, it does not necessarily entail more significant contributions to knowledge.

INNOVATION AND REFORM

A grant is a trust between providers and recipients. Funding providers offer financial resources for recipients to carry out scientific research in particular fields. Grant recipients promise to conduct agreed-upon studies and deliver expected research products as an obligation to their financial sponsors (Bauer, 1999; Locke, Spirduso, & Silverman, 2007; Ries & Leukefeld, 1995; St. John & Parsons, 2004; Savage, 2000; Shaw, 2002b; Slaughter & Rhoades, 2004; White, 1983).

Reform 1: Balance Grants with Awards

Status Quo. While grants have long existed as important funding mechanisms in science and education, there is always a discrepancy or mismatch between the expected, proposed, or promised and the realized, produced, or delivered. Granting agencies attempt to monitor the use of their funds and become dissatisfied when scientific output does not measure up to their financial contribution. Granted academicians scramble to meet targets and grow anxious when deviations or deadlines loom large on the horizon. As widely observed gaps frustrate both funding providers and recipients, people often wonder whether something can be done to change the way a grant is administered, funding is dispensed, and research is executed in scientific inquiry.

Reform. An innovative idea is for a significant number of funding providers to convert a significant number of grants into awards. To implement this innovation as a measure of reform, a number of concerns need to be addressed, one of which is the difference between grants and awards. Grants support research that is to be undertaken. Awards reward research that has been conducted. Whereas grants are given upon the promise of a scientific team and its proposed project, awards are determined on the basis of what proves to be true, effective, and significant concerning a subject in an area of research. The historical and contextual backgrounds in which grants have been given are very different from those for awards. Grants are given in the beginning of science to support a scarcity of scientists to explore a vast landscape of untouched issues and unsolved problems. Awards are conferred in a time when science has developed into a coherent system of knowledge by a full army of practitioners. Grants are released to expand and extend the forefront of scientific inquiry. Awards are bestowed to validate and consolidate the core of the knowledge enterprise. Grants act upon research and scholarship by some of the same mechanisms as do awards. Both grants and awards provide financial incentives and resources. They support research and promote scholarship. Grants provide material means. Grantees are obligated to use grants to explore new ideas, innovative methods, controversial issues, and yet-to-be-studied subjects. Awards offer monetary compensations. However, awardees are not mandated to use awards in any particular way. They may pay off debts from their established and recognized studies. They may initiate new lines of research, without the conditions and restraints they would normally face under a grant. Now is a good time to use more awards in the contemporary era. Science is established with rational divisions of labor between disciplines and interdisciplinary fields. Scientists are trained through standardized educational processes. Scientific studies are institutionalized across universities and research institutes. Research projects are conducted routinely by salaried personnel in scientific organizations. While the large body of scholars and academic institutions do not live on grants in scientific research, most of them can be motivated by awards for scholarly achievements and contributions. Finally, public agencies are most eligible for conversion from grant to award-given agencies. Public agencies draw their funds from taxpayers. They have every reason to use taxpayers' money cautiously and conservatively. Instead of promoting specific research in the form of grants, they should recognize general scholarship through awards. For example, the government should to a large degree retreat from administration of scientific grants and appropriate most of its science-support funds to award individuals as well as institutions for significant research achievements every year in all possible academic fields and disciplines. Disengaging from direct sponsorship of scientific research avoids controversy, uncertainty, waste, and breaking of promises that are so often associated with public grants. By recognizing proven contributions through awards, the government adds recognition and legitimacy to what is inherent in its authority. Private agencies, on the other hand, should be encouraged to play the major role in the delivery of grants. With different philosophies, missions, and interests, they may indeed cover the whole territory of science and scholarship for all necessary projects or lines of research under all possible theories, technologies, and methods.

Significance. Grants can be converted more and more into awards to reward existing research in the contemporary time as more and more scientific projects are carried out by trained staff scholars in academic institutions. If private funding providers have the motivation to support, through grants, research projects in the results of which they have a keen interest, public agencies have the obligation to recognize, in the form of awards, scientific studies that prove to be of significant importance to the general population.

Reform 2: Create a Common Grant Market

Status Quo. Grants are localized by specific fields, geographical areas, applicant or recipient characteristics, procedural requirements, or outcome mandates. Granting agencies target their intended audiences with bulk flyers, public announcements, snail mails, or electronic communications. Applicants act upon their individual information, knowledge, experience, or connection in their search for research funding. For example, from his racial background, John knows a grant that supports African American scholars studying economic segregation in urban settings; Sara learns from her research institute about a funding agency that sponsors experimental research into new treatment modules for drug addiction. There are no known places where grant providers place their calls for proposals and grant applicants screen for possible candidates to make their attempt at research support.

Reform. An innovative idea to change the situation is to create a common grant market for all career academicians. In practical steps, such a common market may begin with either individual academic disciplines or political jurisdictions. By political jurisdiction, a state or province may open a common grant market for scholars who live and work within its boundary. When each state or province has a working grant market, a country can then build a national marketplace for all private and public funding agencies to register, advertise, and place their grants. The common grant market can be physical, with facilities and personnel providing live assistance for both funding agencies and individual career-making academicians. It may also be virtual, with a website, a telecast system, or other cyberspace network delivering information about all kinds of grants to colleges, universities, research institutes, development firms, and other scientist- or engineer-hosting organizations around the country.

By academic discipline, a common grant market for a particular discipline may gather grant providers from different political jurisdictions, social backgrounds, or ideological orientations as long as they are interested in fostering scholarship in the discipline. Career academicians may also come with different languages, nationalities, or even research preferences as long as they are trained as professional scholars in the discipline. For example, a common grant market in physics may attract visits by both theoretical and experimental physicists, both English and non-English speaking scholars, or both European Union and non European Union citizens. Such a common grant market, especially when it is international, should accommodate any local, national, and global players who are interested in supporting academic research in the discipline of physics. A common grant market in a discipline can work within and outside jurisdictional borders; it can be both physical and virtual. Virtually, a common grant market for physics may debut as a multilingual website where physicists around the world can search all types of funding from all different sources for research in physical science.

Significance. With a common grant market in place for a discipline across jurisdictional borders or for a political jurisdiction across academic disciplines, granting agencies will not have to worry about whether their calls for proposals have reached every competent and deserving scholar in the intended field of their support. When there is a physical facility where the common grant market operates, major funding providers may dispatch their representatives to meet with interested applicants at different blocks of time over their individual funding seasons. For example, funding agency A may offer daily window services at the common grant market in the second week after its call for proposal is announced publicly. It may offer another weekly window service in the third week before the deadline it sets for submission of applications for its grant. Career academicians can rest assured that they will not miss any funding opportunity that is available in the area of their specialty. If they happen to live close enough to where the common market opens, they may talk directly to service representatives from some funding agencies to gain insight or dispel confusion over preparation of grant applications.

Reform 3: Establish a User-Friendly Grant System

Status Quo. In the era of commercialism, funding agencies automatically take an advantageous position in relation to individual academicians who look for grants to undertake their research. Guidelines, necessary or unnecessary, are set by grant providers on preparation, submission, and review of proposals. Mandates, reasonable or unreasonable, are imposed upon grant recipients over various substantive matters: from choosing of topics, use of human subjects, gathering of evidence, and analysis of data to presentation of findings.

Reform. To assist career scholars with their funded research, a user-friendly grant system can be established at the funding agency and beyond. First, each granting organization can use service representatives rather than program officers in its dealings with grant applicants and recipients. Grant service representatives sit in for window services at the common grant market, answer calls over the phone or via the internet, send out program information, offer specific reminders or status updates to grant applicants or recipients, and provide general assistance for the scholarly public. For example, a grant applicant can feel free to check with custom service agents the status of his or her proposal while a grant recipient may make a report about or request an extension for his or her funded grant any time by calling service representatives. Academic institutions could take over a wide range of grant application and fund management matters on behalf of their faculty and research staff. With professional custom services from a central office of sponsored research at each university, faculty members do not have to waste any time searching out information on grants, completing forms, making purchases, or preparing non-academic reports. Disciplinary associations may also aid in the grant-related support for their members. In fact, when there is a common grant market in the discipline it represents, a disciplinary association may become a focal point for a user-friendly grant system.

Significance. With a user-friendly grant system in place, career scholars take the center stage of funded research. They set their academic agenda, focus on their research, and do not have to waste time on non-scholarly matters pertaining to funding. Granting agencies, on the other hand, place their trust in trained academicians and retreat to the backseat in the knowledge enterprise. They deliver funds, provide service and support, and make their due effort to ensure that funding itself does not interfere in the sphere of academic affairs. A grant then becomes a simple means, rather than an intimidating power or a threatening mandate, for career scholars to utilize and benefit in their pursuit of knowledge.

Reform 4: Simplify Grant Processes

Status Quo. The grant process from receipt, review, and approval of proposals to the dispensing of funds, the monitoring of project activities, and site visits to midterm briefing, filing for extension, and the report of final findings is lengthy, complex, and burdensome. Requirements are often made upon grant applicants and recipients to satisfy funding providers' idiosyncrasy, bureaucratism, inefficiency, or simple unreasonableness. Academicians and their needs for research freedom, creativity, and productivity are ignored from time to time.

Reform. Various specific measures can be taken to simplify and straighten grant processes. In the phase of application, letters of intent required by some funding agencies should be removed because they do not serve any meaningful purpose other than placing strain on applicants and complicating the process. Electronic submission can be established as a norm since it saves time, money, and labor obviously. Review and approval of proposals for funding can be streamlined, following the peer review process used in scholarly publications, especially for small grants. In the phase of funding and monitoring, site visits by non-academic staff that serve to show off the power of funding agencies should be minimized. Accounting, management, and business matters should be kept separate from research activities, although principal investigators are entitled to their ultimate right to determine and approve personnel hiring, equipment purchases, travel, and other project-related expenditures. Lastly, reports and conclusion of a funded project should be focused on scientific accomplishment in the form of publication, patent registration, and other scholarly deeds. In the final analysis, a simple list of academic publications and recognitions that stem from funding is far more illustrative and substantive than a well-embellished volume detailing everything that is done with money.

Significance. A simplified grant process will make life easier and more productive for both granting agencies and academicians receiving grants. Granting agencies examine major facts and critical scientific findings that serve to enhance their funding mission. They will no longer be mired in attending meetings, reading documents, and other bureaucratic necessities as they tend to be with the requirements they habitually set on grant application and management. Since a simplified process is likely to attract more interest from the community of scholars for their grants, funding providers avail themselves of a larger academic landscape from which to identify and select most qualified applicants to execute research in the field of their intended support. Individual scholars can focus on the substance of research and the progress of their professional careers. There will be fewer of the diversions that so many grant recipients experience with their funded research. Never again will a scholar say, "Having a grant is like managing a business."

Reform 5: Strengthen Grant Reviews

Status Quo.   Review of grants is generally not as objective and strenuous as review of manuscripts for publication. Some grant providers make decisions purely at will and some use their in-house professional staff to do critically important screening work. Some rely upon a known pool of reviewers recruited from past grantees, willing individuals, and other non-representative sources from year to year. Some assemble a contingent of academic and non-academic evaluators by proximity, accessibility, convenience, and other random factors whenever they have grants to consider giving. In the process of review, applicants and their personal information are exposed to the review panel just as the scientific contents of applications are presented to the experts on the panel who assign scores to or make recommendations on proposals. It is difficult to know what contributes most to a positive or negative decision on a specific grant proposal: personal information about the applicant or the scientific merit of the proposal.

Reform.   To ensure that academic funding goes to most deserving scholars in their pursuit of knowledge, proper measures should be taken to strengthen grant reviews. There must be both preliminary review and post-review in the evaluation process. A preliminary review would look into the scholarly qualifications of applicants and their research team, the scientific merit of proposals, and the feasibility of proposed projects. Post-review would focus on the execution of proposals, the results of funded research, and the significance of major research findings. There must also be a division of labor in the conduct of review. An administrative or managerial review checks the accuracy of an applicant's personal information, uses established indices to verify an applicant's status, visibility, and influence, and may assign each applicant a general score of trustworthiness, dependability, or promise. An academic or substantive review examines the scientific quality and integrity of a proposal itself without any reference to the proposal's author or principal investigator. Evaluators are randomly selected scientific experts who specialize in the area of proposed research and may summarize their judgment on each proposal in quantitative scores from one to ten or by qualitative categories such as "acceptable," "unacceptable," or "revision and resubmission." A funding agency may utilize information from its post-review to determine whether a particular scholar and his or her research team will ever be funded again with its grant. As a matter of fact, when post-review is carried out fairly, objectively, and consistently from project to project and from institution to institution, its result may be shared as a critical reference across the community of academic grants. In other words, each scholar will have a kind of dependability or accountability rating score if he or she has ever used a grant in his or her research.

Significance. A strengthened preliminary evaluation process is more likely to screen out unqualified applicants from funding. When a grant-funded project is completed, post-award evaluation can determine to what extent the specific objectives of an academic grant are reached and realized. There will no longer be situations where granting agencies rush to dispense a set amount of funds it is scheduled to deliver in a calendar year without paying much attention to grant recipients' qualifications, dependability, and scientific promise. Nor will there be cases where individuals apply and obtain one grant after another without ever making significant contributions to scholarship. With a focus on knowledge, no serious scholar should ever become a grant dealer just for the sake of monetary gain.

CHAPTER 13

AWARDS

The distinction between an award and a grant is not always clear-cut in terms of promise and accomplishment. Although it is technically awarded to an academician for what he or she promises to do, a grant for promised research is in most cases based upon the principal investigator's demonstrated qualifications and achievements. An award is normally given to a scholar for what he or she has done. But it sometimes may be bestowed upon an academician to carry out a yet-to-be-fulfilled activity. For example, one receives a travel award to present one's accepted paper at a conference. In monetary terms as well as in some symbolic indications, the term award may be used interchangeably with grant. A travel award is called a travel grant while a research grant is designated as a research award (Clark, 2006; Editorial Board, 1993; English, 2005; Feldman, 2000; Rhode, 2006; Wasserman & McLean, 1978).

BACKGROUND AND ANALYSIS

There are various awards in the world of scholarship. Disciplinary associations sponsor awards for students and scholars within the discipline, field, or area of inquiry in which the awards are established. There may be awards for an excellent student paper, an outstanding publication, a professor of the year, or a distinguished career. Academic organizations make awards for faculty, researchers, and other scholarly staff on their premises.

A department may have awards for students in honor of some of its professors. A university may have annual awards for excellence in teaching, creativity, publication, and service. Government is undisputedly the most authoritative player in the delivery of scholarly awards. In a country, the head of state may designate presidential or royal scholars each year. In a province, the governor may from time to time hand out awards to different disciplinary scientists within his or her jurisdiction. Private businesses and foundations are also active in using awards to highlight scientific contributions and celebrate individual achievement in the areas of their concerns and interests. In terms of characteristic features, some awards are prestigious, institutionalized, historical, international, interdisciplinary, publicized, and large in monetary figures while others are less important, local, one-time, specific, less well known, and small in dollar amount. For example, an award for excellence in teaching by a student association may be given to a college professor when the association has a few hundred dollars available in a particular semester. The Nobel Prize, on the other hand, has become the highest honor most scientists in the world ever dream of in their academic career.

An academician obtains awards in different ways: by application, contest, or nomination. Award by application requires that one be willing to file an application, submit application documents by the deadline, and effectively demonstrate one's deservedness or worthiness for the award through submitted materials. For example, a university provides performance-based merit awards for full-time faculty. Interested faculty members need to document their contributions in teaching, research, and service for varying amounts of awards. A conference-organizing committee offers a number of travel awards for students and junior scholars. Interested attendees are required to include their full papers to be presented to the conference, their curriculum vitae, and letters of recommendation from senior scientists in their applications. Obviously, the key to obtaining an award by application is application. One has no way to obtain the award except through application. One's chance of winning the award is weakened if the application is not strong enough. The reward for a clean and solid application is that one receives the award without any further obligation once the award is made.

Award by contest usually focuses on a specific project, experiment, or activity in scientific inquiry or technological invention. Participants conduct a designated project varying from building a model, solving a problem, inventing a device, developing a theory, and refining a procedure, to writing an essay, on their own initiative, design, and cost. The majority of participants lose while a few win. But the larger the number of candidates who participate in the contest, the higher the quality of the products that emerge from the contest, and the more influence the contest holds in the circle of scholars. Significant breakthroughs, innovations, and developments may result from a contest. Major publications, even a masterpiece, may follow after a competition. In history, Jean-Jacques Rousseau made his debut through a famous essay he wrote for a contest. Award by contest caters mostly to students and junior scholars. Many academic associations sponsor paper, speech, and innovation or modification competitions in the fields or disciplines they represent. Candidates demonstrate their scholarly potential or special talents by performing a specified task in a short period of time. They receive an award if they win in a proper category in the competition. For example, when they compete by topic paper or thematic speech, candidates may be able to publish their winning paper in the sponsoring association's major journal or make their winning speech to the association's annual convention. In addition, they receive differential amounts of monetary awards according to their positions as first, second, or third place winners in the contest.

Award by nomination generally applies to distinguished performance or lifetime service in an institution, a field of study, or a whole discipline. Academic organizations use award by nomination to promote excellence and dedication in teaching, research, and service. Nomination may take place through a formal administrative procedure. For example, each department is allowed to nominate only one candidate for the college-wide selection while each college is given only one nomination for consideration at the university level. Because only one award is conferred for overall excellence by the university president, nomination at each level itself may be regarded as an honor. Disciplinary associations, in a similar fashion, sponsor an award by nomination to celebrate significant contributions to scholarship. Nominations may be carried out by the membership. For example, all association members are invited to submit their nominations for the two most influential publications in the past decade or the two most distinguished physicists, chemists, sociologists, or mathematicians in their time. Individual nominees are first generally recognized for their extraordinary achievements in teaching, research, or service within their home institution. Or they are well known for their significant contributions to scholarship in their discipline. Only when they command adequate visibility and a generally favorable reputation, can they be nominated by other academic participants or their scholarly peers for an award. Upon nomination, they may be asked to submit proper documentation for formal consideration by an expert panel. The award itself may be as general as a distinguished career award or as particular as an outstanding book award.

Most academic awards bring about dual benefits to their recipients. First is recognition. An award gives an academician a title to identify and honor him or her. For example, a merit award generates an image of outstanding performance. A grand winner of a worldwide competition in a discipline carries the pride of achievement and triumph. A distinguished career award gives one's academic life a special distinction. In scholarly as well as secular exchanges, the recipient of such an award commands attention and respect when introduced at a meeting. Second is compensation. Award recipients in most cases receive money or monetary benefits. For example, a well-known scholar may be reimbursed for registration, given a return air ticket and five-night accommodation at an international conference where he or she receives a book award of one thousand dollars from a disciplinary association. A student who wins an international competition for young scholars in his or her discipline may be paid fully for a week-long seminar at a world congress. The student may be issued a thousand-dollar check when he or she is formally honored at the congress. In addition, the department where the student works on his or her doctoral degree may give another thousand dollars as assistance for the trip because of the student's winning the award.

In recording awards received throughout his or her career, an academician may summarize them by totals, dollar amounts, or other quantitative measure. Qualitatively, one may group or divide awards by category, source, or significance. For instance, all travel awards fall in one group. Awards received from within the employment organization are distinctively separated from those received from outside. Awards are ranked by their academic significance. By chronological order, one may simply list all awards in natural occurrence. To combine natural sequence with academic significance, one may chronicle awards from the oldest to the latest while highlighting major ones in bold letters or with special symbols, in one's curriculum vitae.

INNOVATION AND REFORM

As always, the general picture of academic awards tilt favorably toward the established, the proven, the famous, and the old guard away from the unknown, the uninitiated, the undecided, and the novice. The reason is obvious. Elite institutions, armed with a bounty of endowments, are more likely to take up the most significant scientific projects for the most prominent awards. Eminent scholars, surrounded with followers and well wishers, are more likely to prove that they are most worthy of highest honors. However, history often shows that critical breakthroughs and innovations emerge from the new, the uncertain, the controversial, the unexplored, and the unproven on the side of newcomers (Clark, 2006; Editorial Board, 1993; English, 2005; Feldman, 2000; Heap, 2004; Rhode, 2006; Wasserman & McLean, 1978).

Reform 1: Establish and Expand Academic Awards for Students and Junior Scholars

Status Quo. Students and junior scholars are in the early stage of their academic career. Although they are actively learning, exploring, and experimenting in various academic fields, they seldom draw attention from institutional fund providers for their lack of mounting achievements or even convincing qualifications. As a great many students and junior scholars struggle hard on their own at a time when they need encouragement, motivation, and support most, the academic sponsoring agencies miss a large promising constituency or clientele from which they can likely make most of their monetary and other substantive investments.

Reform. To keep proper balance, institutional fund providers might consider expanding academic awards for students and junior scholars. A university and its various academic units may cultivate the competitive spirit among students by awards of various scales and differential significance. At the university level, there can be once-a-semester award contests for best engineering models, best scientific projects, or best theme topic essays among undergraduate or graduate students. There can be annual nomination awards for best undergraduate projects, best graduate theses, or best doctoral dissertations in the natural sciences, the humanities, or the social sciences. There can be application-based awards for diligence, persistence, collegiality, service, volunteering, significant improvement, or overall academic excellence. An academic association and its various sectional or regional branches may promote creativity and scholarship among junior scholars through awards for papers, projects, or speeches. Competition for the best paper may revolve around a critical topic on general scholarship. Projects may be as specific as building a model, changing a procedure, or conducting an experiment. A speech contest may center on a controversial issue and its solution through existing knowledge. Governmental agencies may establish a variety of awards in support of education and scholarship as well. For example, there might be awards for the best graduate students, the highest achieving Ph.D. conferees, best dissertations, or young scholars of the year in a county, in a state, or across the country.

Significance. Students and junior scholars are the future of academia. When they are given opportunities to compete for awards, earn credit, and establish recognition, they will develop an academic spirit of competitiveness, excellence, and merit early in their career and follow that spirit for the rest of their scholarly life. Expansion of academic awards to students and junior scholars are also likely to invite fresh ideas, creative activities, and adventurous undertakings in the pursuit of knowledge and shift due attention from older to newer generations of career academicians throughout the knowledge enterprise. The whole community of scholarship will then take on a new orientation that mediates well between the past and the future.

Reform 2: Create Special Awards for Creative Ideas and Revolutionary Breakthroughs

Status Quo. Most academic awards are set to reward and recognize conventional achievements or model scholars. Research issues must lie within the boundary of a defined discipline. Theories must have won widespread acceptance. Methods must have withstood series of challenges. Even awardees themselves must remain free from political, economic, or personal controversies. There will be heated debates if a prestigious award is ever given for a theory, a method, or a model that seems just unconventional to what is long established in a field. There will be enchanted gossip if a well-known honor is ever bestowed upon a scholar who seems just overly vocal in the mass media or indiscriminately active in personal affairs.

Reform. Given the conservative nature of the academic awarding system, there is an acute need to create special awards for critical ideas, innovative methods, revolutionary breakthroughs, and specific solutions. While institutional fund providers might dedicate some of their annual or routine award competitions to some critical, urgent, or prominent issues, they can always design and sponsor special or ad hoc awards for extraordinary or unique subjects. For instance, an association representing a discipline may establish an open award for the best essay of critique or the best experiment of confirmation when a theory is published. It may solicit through award competition ideas to change a known yet flawed theory, methods to modify an established yet ineffective procedure, or solutions to end a long-lasting puzzle. The association might invite public or private agencies for joint sponsorship. In fact, when themes, standards, and expert judgments are clearly laid out and securely provided by an association representing a discipline, commercial, service, and governmental agencies might want to contribute resources to a special award of their essential concern and interest.

Significance. In the actual dynamics of science, it is always the new, the unfamiliar, and the unconventional that changes the old, the familiar, and the conventional, and therefore expands the whole landscape of knowledge. Sponsoring special competitions and awards for creative ideas and revolutionary breakthroughs will provide necessary forums or opportunities for the new to meet the old, the unfamiliar to compare with the familiar, and the unconventional to challenge the conventional. No matter what follows, whether it is constructive dialogue, productive cooperation, or fierce confrontation, when two sides come to face each other, there will definitely be a higher level of activity and output in scholarly communications which in the end will only make the knowledge enterprise more diverse, dynamic, and prosperous.

Reform 3: Publicize and Promote Academic Awards

Status Quo. Aside from a few high profilers, a considerable number of academic awards often remain unknown, uninteresting, or unnoticeable to the average academicians concerned. It is not uncommon that information about an award is promptly circulated to a limited audience, selection is hastily conducted upon a small pool of entries, and an award ceremony is inconveniently arranged as if it were something that needs to be kept out of public attention. For example, in a liberal arts college, an institutionalized annual award for excellent publication may receive no submission in any particular year. The administration may always worry whether there is an adequate faculty turnout for its once-a-year award ceremony to honor outstanding performance in teaching, research, and service.

Reform. It is obvious that academic awards should be publicized and promoted among their target subjects as well as to the concerned public. Student awards should be made known to both students and the faculty. Faculty awards should not only draw interest from eligible faculty members, but also elicit participation from concerned students and administrators. Associations representing academic disciplines might use their seasonal newsletters, regular journals, and annual conventions to publicize and highlight their awards for students, young scholars, career achievements, publication, teaching, and service. They may send special flyers to their members for nomination and participation. When awards are selected, they may put the names of recipients on their websites or in their annual meeting programs. At the award ceremony, the media may be invited to report awardees and their contributions to a larger audience. Government may even use political power and institutional sanctity to emphasize the importance and prestige it grants to a scholarly award. For instance, the mayor, the governor, or the president hands out the award to its recipient or recipients in a special ceremony televised to the people within the city, the province, or the country. Depending upon the size of a political entity and the scale of the knowledge enterprise under its control, it is probably appropriate for a mayor to honor best students or best graduate theses, a governor to congratulate best young scholars or best academic publications, and a president to express appreciations for most distinguished career scientists or most significant scholarly contributions on a yearly basis. In general, the significance of a scholarly award must be recognized widely enough so that eligible candidates consciously try to secure it in their academic endeavors. The procedure of an academic award must be specified clearly enough so that interested candidates know exactly when, where, and how to prepare and send their nominations or applications in competition for it.

Significance. With adequate promotional efforts by award sponsors, students will know what awards are available within and outside the department, the college, and the university where they study. The faculty will be fully aware of all the major awards that are available across their discipline, institution, and academic associations. Career scholars, whether they are in the early or later stage of their academic journey, will actively seek various awards to publicize their research, win recognition, establish influence, and deepen their scholarship. Academic institutions, on the other hand, will constructively use every possible award to stimulate interest in scientific inquiry, encourage theoretical breakthroughs and methodological innovations, reward performance, and keep a general spirit of creativity, productivity, and meritocracy between students and the faculty they have under their organizational umbrella. Award will then become an important element to maintain individual morale, institutional vitality, and overall vibrancy in the knowledge enterprise.

Reform 4: Make Government an Authoritative Player in Academic Awards

Status Quo. In developed economies, the government is able to administer a considerable number of grants and contracts for scientific research and technological invention. The federal government of the United States, for example, promotes and advances scientific progress in the country by competitively awarding grants and cooperative agreements for research and education in the sciences, mathematics, engineering, and various other academic disciplines through such public agencies as the National Science Foundation, the National Institute of Health, and the National Institute of Justice. With regard to non-grant awards, however, the government seems to be extremely thrifty. Once a year, the head of a government may attend a ceremony to deliver some plaques of certification to recognize a few outstanding scientists, engineers, teaching scholars, and other academicians within its jurisdiction. But he or she seldom issues a bounty check for any individual scholar who has earned the honor of national, statewide, or other jurisdictional recognition.

Reform. In the era of science, the government should and must play its primary role in promoting scientific exploration, highlighting scientific achievements, and specifically, rewarding career scholars who make significant contributions to knowledge. There should be a much higher level of involvement by which the government commits itself to establishing awarding programs, sponsoring awarding activities, and publicizing awardees and their achievements in scholarship. It is not excessive if the head of a government has to host one awarding ceremony a week for accomplished academicians from discipline to discipline within his or her jurisdiction. For example, the president of a country may take the opportunity to deliver academic awards each month to outstanding individuals in scholarship, beginning January for natural sciences, February for engineering, March for social sciences, April for the humanities, subsequent months for special categories such as discovery, experimentation, theorization, revolutionary breakthrough, teaching, service, and general application, and December for overall excellence in the whole knowledge enterprise. Second, monetary compensation for awardees must be commensurate with the nominal recognition an academic award accords its recipients. The prestigious Nobel Prize gives its laureates in major academic disciplines the ultimate fame for scholarly achievements while in monetary terms it reaches the threshold of one million American dollars. Using the Nobel Prize as a reference, it is only reasonable for the head of a developed country, such as Australia, France, and the United States, to hand out a major award in science worth one hundred thousand dollars. Third, the government can play an instrumental role in gaining media exposure and general publicity for academic awardees before, during, and after the award ceremony attended by the head of the government. Pre-award advertisements can be placed on various media outlets. The award ceremony itself can be contracted to a major television network for one of its prime time spots. In-depth interviews with the awardees and feature stories of their academic highlights may appear widely across different media channels. Indeed, given the insurmountable importance of science, only highly achieving scientists deserve to be the greatest stars or the most venerable celebrities in the contemporary era. Finally, the government has the authority to keep a systematic record of academic awards and their recipients in various disciplines of science from year to year. National, provincial, or municipal archives, museums, or halls of fame can be opened to house award memorabilia and, most important, to detail scientific accomplishments behind each award. Students, academic professionals, and the general public can visit those records and constantly draw inspiration from great scientists as well as milestone achievements throughout the knowledge enterprise.

Significance. As the government becomes increasingly active in academic awards, it will gradually reduce its role in scholarly grants and contracts. Given the representative and hence neutral nature of government, it indeed should surrender to various private entities the business of promoting different research agendas of specific interests through grants and contracts and reserve to itself only the authority to recognize what has proven to be beneficial to society as a whole or significant to science in the long run. By awarding science and scientists, the government will gradually create a historical tradition, a cultural custom, and a social atmosphere of respecting science and honoring scientists throughout society, which is necessary for any country to experience lasting prosperity and sustaining progress in its evolutionary path.

Reform 5: Keep the Spirit of Competition, Meritocracy, and Excellence through Academic Awards

Status Quo. The purpose of an academic award is to stimulate interest, spread hope, and keep the spirit of competition, meritocracy, and excellence in the community of scholarship. However, since many academic awards are not open, competitive, visible, and rewarding enough, they often fail to serve their original purpose. Academicians concerned do not pay much attention to those awards while award sponsors scramble to fill application quotas, dispose of the funds they are charged to deliver, and conclude award activities as a matter of business. Some academicians may intentionally avoid or even look down upon certain awards when those awards are known to be nonobjective, non-academic, or purely political.

Reform. To restore the sanctity of academic awards, a number of measures need to be taken. The official sponsor of an academic award must be a credible and respectable agency in the eyes of average academicians. Besides the government, universities, research institutes, and established business organizations may qualify to play an active role in award activities. Small or emergent organizations may make monetary donations to an award. But for the sake of their cherished award and awardees, they may want to stand behind the government and other more recognizable entities in the public presentation of the award. A competitive selection process for an academic award must be maintained. It is better not to make any award at all than to dump an award into the backyard of a hastily or randomly chosen academician who does not appear to deserve it. Academic merit must remain at the center of any academic award. Even for the same level of achievement, one academician should not be selected for an academic award over another simply because of a closer connection to some stakeholders or due to a higher involvement in the local politics in his or her home institution or disciplinary association. The monetary reward of an academic award must be substantial to attract an adequate level of general interest in the award. It does not make any sense for someone to compete for an award if he or she has to spend more than the monetary amount of the expected award to prepare for and go through the competition itself. The nominal recognition of an academic award must be accorded with proper publicity in the mass media as well as in historical records. The awardees should be made known not only to the community of scholarship, but also to the general public. Overall, all these conditions need to be met if academic awards ever serve the purpose of keeping the spirit of competition, meritocracy, and excellence among career academicians.

Significance. Some may contend that academicians are self-centered and will never set aside their huge egos to willingly celebrate the achievements of their colleagues or fellows in the same institution, the same discipline, or even the same era unless those fellow academicians are indeed exceptional. However, in the normal academic world where the majority of academicians are comparable to one another in their effort and performance, it is still important to reward the outstanding. With the spirit of competition and meritocracy, people will likely strive for excellence in their work. Academic awards in various scales, contexts, and reputations will then be able to serve a goodwill purpose of keeping people in a community while differentiating them into individual performers, lifting the general morale while motivating personal attainment, and inspiring newcomers while encouraging existing members of the academe.

CHAPTER 14

ACADEMIC ASSOCIATIONS

Most academic associations are now open to people who apply and pay membership dues. Qualifications or achievements are no longer seriously questioned in the membership application. On the part of career-making academicians, however, membership in academic associations still gives them a sense of identity, belonging, and professional pride. It provides them a forum to communicate research, a network to gather feedback, and a community of nurturing for continuous academic pursuits. In fact, all essential elements of academic life, including presentation, service, and publication, are basically realized within the purview of academic associations (Cox, 2007; Dewsbury, 1996; Haskell, 2000; Professional Convention Management Association, 2006; Sachs, 1990; Weddle, 2007; Young, 1985).

BACKGROUND AND ANALYSIS

Academic associations are formed by members of various disciplines in the knowledge enterprise for their specific scholarly pursuits. But once they are established, they possess power to represent and influence individual academicians in a discipline or a field of study.

On the matter of representation, an academic association can serve as advocate, spokesperson, negotiator, and protector for the members of a profession or an area of inquiry. As advocate, it justifies the necessity of a knowledge branch in economic production and argues for social support in the form of funding and an adequate number of personnel. For instance, an association of chemical engineering may put out advertisements about the critical importance chemical engineers play in the production of consumer goods, urging young people to join the profession in their search for lifetime careers. As spokesperson, an academic association issues statements about its mission, its professional goals, and its policy positions on current events. An association for Middle East studies may condemn violence and propose peace as an alternative solution to conflict. It may back up its positions with research done within the sphere of scholarship it represents. As negotiator, an academic association may engage in explicit or implicit interactions with its neighboring disciplines over territorial claims. For instance, an association of anthropologists may claim its exclusive right to the study of an ethnic culture in a remote island whereas an association of sociologists maintains that its members are best equipped to study the island society. Negotiation may lead to cooperation and sharing of learning between the two disciplines. As protector, an academic association defends its members against cultural critique, political scrutiny, and institutional evaluation in their scholarly pursuits and career movements. For example, an association of teaching scholars may provide testimony about the academic value of pedagogical research when one of its members experiences trouble in his or her tenure or promotion review with publications on teaching and student learning. An academic association may also take part in political processes to secure benefits and safeguard rights for scholars and practitioners under its umbrella.

The effectiveness of representation by an academic association lies in the characteristics of its members. The number of members it includes under its organizational roof is important. The more members it represents, the more bargaining power it has in negotiation with other parts of society. The nature of the work in which members of an association engage is highly relevant. The more indispensable the work done by its members is to a society, the more importance an association may claim for itself in social interactions. Thus an association of medical scientists may exert more influence than an association of sociologists. The association of medical scientists may have to defer to an association of nuclear engineers in power at a time when the country is strategically committed to building an atomic bomb. The level of productivity of its members is also relevant. The more productive its members are in research, teaching, and service, the more visible an association is in a discipline and in the larger society. An association of criminal justice scholars may attract more attention than an association of social workers if members of the criminal justice association are more productive in their scholarly work. Political activism is from time to time critical. The more active some of its members are in political arenas, the more limelight an association may enjoy in social presentation. An association of political scientists may make the media, the government, corporate interests, or the populace take notice of it, not so much for the serious academic work its members do, but rather because of the numerous public demonstrations some of its members organize in confrontation with the political and economic establishments. Finally, some academic associations may apply the trick of "association" to communicate to the general public or boost their standing in the larger society. They may use celebrities in politics, the media, entertainment, or the business world to suggest that the discipline it represents can inspire one to become a successful person or that the profession it promotes can lead one to an illustrious career. For example, an association of psychologists may refer to some well-known persons in government, even though the latter just hold degrees in psychology or have long abandoned their practice in psychology.

An academic association can shape its members and their career-making efforts by various institutional means through which it communicates with its members. By the publication outlets it controls, an association can explicitly or implicitly push members into peculiar research paradigms or agendas. At one time, it may favor theory over application, quantitative research over qualitative study, or one area over other areas of inquiry. At another time, some sections or theoretical, methodological orientations may gain popularity under its auspices. By the presentation forums it runs, an academic association obviously determines what theme members follow in its annual convention, what issues they debate, and what topics, theories, and methods they may have to highlight or ignore in regional and sectional meetings. By the service opportunities it affords, an association may tax the reading capacity and the willingness to serve of a few old hands or political insiders with academic reviews, legislative testimonies, media interviews, convention organization, and association maintenance. Meanwhile, the majority of its members are left out of the loop. An academic association usually sponsors competitions, confers honors, and delivers awards. By singling out specific members and membership deeds for recognition, it influences the minds of its members as to what is important and valuable in a field of study. An academic association also creates among its members a general sentiment about their discipline, profession, competency, effectiveness, and social status. Whereas an association of scholars in the study of government may often feel uplifted by what they explore, an association of drug abuse researchers can sometimes feel tainted by the subject matter they study in their professional career.

The influence an association can have over its members depends upon its members and membership characteristics. In a discipline or a field of study, not all scholars or practitioners join the association that exists for them. Among those who do pay membership dues, not all of them present their research to the annual meeting, publish their products in association journals, cast ballots for association officers, and offer news for the association newsletter. A large number of association members are simply observers. They pay attention to what goes on in the association for their specific area of inquiry. They participate in substantive activities only when they are seriously interested. The number of products turned out by association publication outlets in a discipline depends on who control those publication outlets as editors, editorial board members, and reviewers. While an association may sponsor a flagship journal or monograph series in a field of study it represents, it does not have control over where people in the field publish. In fact, when association journals are dominated by a small group of members in one extreme theoretical or methodological orientation, the majority of the membership may come to regard these journals as remote sources of reference or outlets for publication. The people who become association leaders are individual members. They are elected into association leadership not always because of their widely acclaimed contributions; from time to time, people take office because of connection, ideology, and luck. When an association is controlled by a group of advocates who are viewed as extremists, that association may not necessarily represent the mainstream concerns and interests of the membership. Finally, the sheer size of the membership of an association may say it all: how seriously it is taken, whether it provides primary publications, and whether it represents prevailing interests and sentiments by or for scholars in a discipline or an area of inquiry. An association may possess only an empty name of representation if a large number of scholars it claims to represent do not belong to it and if it does not hold the hearts of most active and productive people in the discipline.

Although they are voluntary and have obvious limits in representation and influence, academic associations overall can shape academicians and their research interests over a career or life span. Out of ordinary associations, there are elite organizations. They offer membership as an honor to those who have demonstrated extraordinary worth to the knowledge enterprise. For instance, national academies of science, engineering, or medicine in many countries award their membership only for exceptional contributions. Membership in those exclusive organizations not only generates a pride of accomplishment and influence for a few outstanding performers, but also provides a source of inspiration and encouragement for many ordinary doers in their academic career.

INNOVATION AND REFORM

A dilemma facing most academic associations is representation. On the one hand, academic associations strive to inspire members and impress nonmembers with the best products they produce and the best scholars they represent. For that purpose, they sponsor journals and monograph series that publish only articles and books of the highest quality. They reserve association honors and the presidency for only the best scholars in the field. On the other hand, academic associations realize that most of their members are ordinary academicians. They come from different backgrounds in terms of gender, race, ethnicity, and training. They are subject to various limitations in funding, institutional support, and personal motivation. Not all of them are productive. Only a few are able to do outstanding work, reaching the highest points in their time. The dilemma specifically is this: Whom does an academic association represent if it highlights only a few elite achievers? And what does it stand for when it is dominated by political correctness, academic mediocrity, and the "principle of means" in the quest for knowledge (Cox, 2007; Dewsbury, 1996; Haskell, 2000; Professional Convention Management Association, 2006; Sachs, 1990; Weddle, 2007; Young, 1985)?

Reform 1: Be Service-Oriented

Status Quo. Although most academic associations have service for the membership on their mission statements, they become increasingly obtuse and ineffective in providing individual members with specific career-sensitive and -facilitative assistance. Like every other organization, an academic association tends to acquire bureaucratic inertia when it grows in size, routinizes its operation, and establishes its influence or visibility. As always, a bureaucratized association is likely to lean toward the elites, the unduly active, or the political trendy, and hence tilt away from the common needs of the general membership.

Reform. To keep its vitality, an academic association must stick to its roots as an interest group serving the needs of its members. Whatever it does must be for members and from members. From members, individual academicians need to communicate with each other, connect to their discipline and the general academe, and specifically need to attend school, find a job, secure funding for research, publish findings, teach classes, make academic presentations, and provide professional services. An academic association must therefore undertake necessary measures, including changes and reforms, to meet its members' basic as well as constantly evolving needs. While there is no question that an academic association should cover all possible areas where members need assistance, there is an obvious issue as to how an academic association can be innovative enough in using its limited resources to deliver most critical services. For example, should an academic association focus on serving members in their long-term career endeavors or scramble to answer calls by individual members from day to day? Should it embrace the whole membership or target underrepresented, marginalized, or emergent groups? Should it commit to provision of publication outlets, presentation forums, and networking support or retreat to dissemination of information through workshops on careers, web posting about research opportunities, or flyers on job placement or faculty exchange?

For members, academic associations should keep historical records so that members can trace changes within their discipline, make sensible comparisons to other professions, and catch major trends in academe. They should highlight extraordinary achievements and outstanding contributors from time to time so that ordinary members can feel proud, hopeful, and excited about their discipline. For example, a biographical series on prominent figures in the discipline can be published as a professional service to the membership. An academic association should also serve as an advocate on behalf of its practicing members in the larger society so that members are given proper recognition and compensation for their contribution to the knowledge enterprise.

Significance. Service is an important purpose of a professional association. With service at the center of its day-to-day operation, an academic association will maintain a better connection to its general membership. The matter of leadership and critical decision-making will be less likely to fall in the hands of a few self-privileged elites or unwarrantedly politicized elements. Also, when ordinary members benefit directly from various tangible services provided by their academic association, they are more likely to reciprocate by actively participating in association activities, volunteering time and labor, and making other necessary contributions. A positive relationship will then perpetuate itself, tying an academic association to its members as their home and rallying individual academicians to their association as its ultimate source of strength.

Reform 2: Be Knowledge-Driven

Status Quo. Knowledge lies at the core of each academic discipline. To represent a discipline, an academic association is supposed to build on knowledge, spread knowledge, and promote knowledge on behalf of knowledge producers. In reality, however, many academic associations seem to be failing in their commitment to knowledge. For example, in their dealings with the larger society, some associations engage unnecessarily in political activism, take undue part in social movements, or become helplessly involved in ideological controversies. There are even academic associations that unscrupulously profit from trendy social circumstances by offering training workshops or certifying degree programs without much substance in knowledge.

Reform. Just as it needs to embrace service in its mission to the membership, an academic association should focus on knowledge in its relationship to society. An academic association can provide knowledge and consultation to different social groups in the domain of knowledge it represents. For example, an association of nuclear physicists can do a better job in detailing the destructive nature of nuclear warfare than in organizing a protest for peace in the public place. An academic association can play a significant role in spreading disciplinary knowledge to the larger society. There is no doubt that regular warnings about certain foods or nonprescription drugs issued by a national association of medical sciences on the basis of serious research can be more powerful than multimillion-dollar commercials put out by manufacturers, distributors, and retailers about those products. An academic association should always act upon knowledge when it sets out to promote the discipline to the general public. A national association of philosophers makes itself credible when it demonstrates how philosophy informs, inspires, and enlightens people about logical analysis, critical thinking, and rational ways of life, rather than when it shows how many philosophers it has in their membership or how many philosophy departments there are across the country. Finally, academic associations should resist any temptation to cash in on the authority they have in scholarly representation or profit in the name of knowledge. There is obviously a widespread misuse of disciplinary authority and representation in social sciences and the humanities in higher education when unsubstantiated areas, fields, or disciplines open programs, centers, or departments, offering certificates or degrees to people who are intellectually unprepared for advancement and recognition.

Significance. With knowledge as its axis, an academic association will find its real strength in rallying members, sharpening its uniqueness in comparison to other professional organizations, promoting the discipline it represents, and making the best possible contribution to society. Specifically, members will focus on producing and spreading knowledge in the area of their specialty. They will not unnecessarily waste their time and energy on social activism or other politically motivated activities. The association itself will win respect and gain prestige across different social groups and strata as a neutral, objective, and principled entity on the basis of knowledge and for the sake of knowledge.

Reform 3: Represent the Ordinary

Status Quo. The ordinary are the majority to exist but not necessarily the majority to rule in most academic associations. For example, publication is one of the most important interests to association members. Currently, many academic associations subject their publications to a kind of quality control, style, standard, or scholarly orientation that often does not reflect the customary work of average members. The practice alienates ordinary members, pushing them away from associations in scholarly activities.

Reform. An obvious measure for change is to "deregulate" association publication outlets to meet the needs of the general membership. Specifically, all scholarly associations should expand, diversify, and popularize their publications so that the majority of association members can rely upon association journals and monograph series as primary outlets for their scholarly products. Style requirements ought to be relaxed so that significant academic content can make their debut without suffocation by matters of style. Unrealistic standards and unreasonable quality control should be lifted so that innovative, unconventional, and even revolutionary theories and methods can appear and be welcomed in the mainstream association media. Editors and editorial boards should rotate in a manageable frequency so that no single theoretical or methodological orientation dominates all others for an unfair amount of time. Thus association members, with normal training, capacity, and effort, should feel confident and comfortable to publish their scholarly contributions through association publication outlets.

While using the bulk of association outlets to support the majority of members in their publication efforts, an academic association may set aside two premier journals to highlight association contributions of the highest recognized quality. One would be a review journal. It would select for reviews and critiques most significant books published by members as well as nonmembers in the field of study. The other journal would be a collection journal of significant contributions. It would include most important articles scattered in regular association publications and other relevant journals in the past five years or so. Quality control in these two journals takes place automatically because it is obviously time, evidence, public opinion, and other open process factors that determine whether a particular piece is included.

Significance. When an association's publications become an outlet for average members to show products and exchange ideas, other arenas on the premium of the association will likely turn into stages or forums for the ordinary to voice concerns, participate in activities, and make an impact as well. The association will then be able to serve in the true representation of ordinary academic practitioners who work in a discipline with all their realistic circumstances, challenges, experiences, needs, and expectations. Just as in publication where quality control will no longer be an easy but cruel excuse to kill credible scholarly products, there will be no manmade barriers against the average, the ordinary, or the commoners by a few self-privileged insiders or elites in various other association activities.

Reform 4: Celebrate the Exceptional

Status Quo. Partly because of their professional modesty, partly because of their occupational distance from the media beltway, and partly because of their characteristic lack of political canniness, academicians fare poorly in highlighting their contributions to society, celebrating great achievers in their field, and promoting knowledge and scholarship as essential elements in human civilizations. While a few thinkers and scientists, such as Newton, Marx, Freud, and Einstein, have made to the hall of universal human giants through their individually appealing ideas or revolutionary findings, a great many outstanding contributors from discipline to discipline in science and knowledge production remain far below par in social recognition with accomplished individuals in various other human arenas from politics, business, and entertainments to sports.

Reform. A practical measure is to establish a hall of fame for the field of study an academic association represents. Academic associations must be explicit in their promotion and representation of high standards, high quality. Quality defines public image. Public image determines how effective a representation is in the eyes of the concerned public. There are various ways to emphasize standards and elicit quality. One effective way is to honor exceptional and great scholars whose work exemplifies quality, and to whom every academician can relate. Academic associations must also take a systematic and historical approach toward the discipline they represent. History undergirds reality. Reality conceives the future. There are different ways to record history and describe reality. One powerful way is to celebrate famous and influential individuals whose achievements epitomize the history of the discipline, and by whom most scholars can feel inspired and elevated. Furthermore, academic associations must assume their inalienable rights and responsibilities to record, retell, and replay the history of scholarship with respect to each field of inquiry they represent. Sports, entertainments, industries, and politics build museums and halls of fame to honor and worship their grand figures. Why do not academic associations also celebrate their great figures, their great minds? If they do not, who else will?

In implementation, an academic association may create a sequence for its members to attain the highest possible goals in the discipline. First, the association presidency should be reserved for high achieving members to compete for on a yearly basis. Second, the lifetime achievement award should be open for nomination and election once a year or once every few years among members with exceptional contributions. Third, on the basis of the association presidency and the lifetime achievement award, only a few great scholars might then enter the hall of fame in the discipline. To further highlight the distinction held by the hall of fame, selection would take place only once every five or ten years. It would involve an open and competitive process across the entire membership and beyond. For example, a panel of judges would first be authorized to nominate five candidates. One of those five individuals would then be voted into the hall of fame by all association members or all members with a number of selected nonmembers. The hall of fame itself could be physical or nonphysical. Physically, it might be placed in the association headquarter where people could view and examine all the "hall of fame" scholars, their wax figures, representative works, biographies or autobiographies, and personal memorabilia. In nonphysical form, an academic association might only maintain and publish records for every "hall of fame" scholar it honors. For example, it might publish a "hall of fame" biography for a scholar when he or she is selected. It might upgrade a special collection for all the "hall of fame" scholars every time a new "hall of fame" celebrity is added. The "hall of fame" publication might include life pictures, work samples, commentaries, and other honorific items.

Significance. By celebrating the exceptional within the discipline it represents, an academic association creates a general atmosphere of pride and inspiration among the ordinary it sets out to represent. When ordinary members feel lifted by great examples in their day-to-day experience, they are more likely to be active and productive through their academic careers. An active, productive membership will in turn provide the best possible background or context from which extraordinary scientific deeds appear and exceptional academic achievers emerge. A positive cycle will then set in the discipline for its dynamic functioning as part of the knowledge enterprise.

Reform 5: Balance Representation, Service, and Tradition with Excellence, Leadership, and Change

Status Quo. An ideal model for any academic association is to represent ordinary members while striving for scholarly excellence, to serve members in various career needs while providing general direction, and to keep the disciplinary heritage while embracing change and future. Gaps obviously exist and vary from association to association toward such an ideal balance. Whereas some associations create a great deal of membership alienation in the name of quality and excellence, others become lost in general direction and leadership when they attempt to meet diverse and divergent membership needs as a union might. There are academic associations that seem to have nothing to offer than worshiping some of their great founders in the long past. There are also associations that scramble to play different roles from service to representation to leadership but nevertheless end up achieving nothing significant in their institutional existence.

Reform. No single measure will make an academic association strike a perfect balance between representation and excellence, between service and leadership, and between tradition and change. A myriad of reforms are upon a great many associations toward the ultimate goal. As an illustration, an academic association might establish a few all-inclusive journals for average members to publish their regular work without unreasonable, unnecessarily restrictive, or knowingly discriminatory procedures in its effort to represent the majority membership. To highlight excellence, the association might sponsor a journal to carry and review most cited, most referenced, or otherwise most influential articles, books, or monographs that have passed the test of time sequentially as well as differentially in the last year, in the past five years, in the past decade, in the past fifty years, or in the last century. On the need for balance between service and leadership, an academic association can always put its ordinary members in the forefront of membership services, allowing them to serve one another in a variety of areas from career counseling, student mentoring, conference organization, manuscript review, and associational management to professional volunteering for larger society. The association presidency should instead be reserved exclusively for those members who excel through serious scholarly work. With genuine scholars in charge, an academic association says clearly to its membership that academic leadership is not through words or commands but rather through achievement, namely, exemplary contributions to knowledge. Lastly between tradition and future, an academic association may routinely confer distinguished career awards to recognize lifelong achievements while from time to time opening competitions and contests for newcomers to find opportunities, earn rewards, and establish visibility. Another measure to balance tradition with the future is to publish a journal for revolutionary ideas, yet-to-be-substantiated work, or even quasi-scientific hypotheses while keeping in print a biographical series of great contributors to celebrate the exceptional, to honor the past, and to inspire the future in the discipline.

Significance. The ordinary feeds the extraordinary. When an academic association serves well in representing average members and meeting their regular needs, there is then a higher likelihood that they will be creative, productive, and generative of excellent contributors from among them. Service signifies leadership. When an academic association provides various specific and tangible services to its members, it also offers a clear vision, a general guidance, and a definitive direction for quality scholarship. Tradition presages the future. Only when an academic association actively draws from its tradition, can it be prepared to embrace the most challenging opportunities in the future. Similarly, only when an academic association is to thrive in a promisingly prosperous future, can it constructively carry on its historical heritage from the past. In all, a balanced academic association will be able to fulfill its mission successfully.

CHAPTER 15

TENURE

The majority of academicians gather in colleges and universities. Colleges and universities award tenure to their full-time faculty. Tenure is originally designed to protect academic freedom. It now serves more and more as a means of protection against market dynamics. Faculty members are provided with job security in the mundane world where survival is important so that they can have peace of mind to pursue their somewhat non-secular academic interests. As far as their careers are concerned, tenure may represent a significant turning point for many academicians. One the one hand, it concludes an initial path of success and promise since tenure is awarded on the basis of substantial contributions in teaching, research, and service. On the other hand, it lays a solid foundation for continuous endeavor and excellence because tenure is given with the expectation of a long-term commitment to scholarship through teaching, publication, and service (Alstete, 2000; Baez, 2002; Chait, 2005; Finkin, 1996; Huer, 1991; Joughin, 1967; Leap, 1995; Meiners, 2004; Seldin, 2007; Shoenfeld & Magnan, 2004; Tierney & Bensimon, 1996).

BACKGROUND AND ANALYSIS

There is only one tenure to attempt or possess in an academician's employment career. Many academicians choose not to make mention of their tenure status in the public presentation of themselves. "Tenured" or "tenure-track" does not seem to appear on the business card, curriculum vitae, or self-introduction by academicians. However, in the back of their minds, academicians working within and outside universities care dearly about tenure. Before they obtain tenure, they fight for it as their ultimate goal. After they have tenure, they use it either as a foundation for an aggressive advance into research activities or as a safe haven from any serious scholarly pursuits. Academic clichés, such as "publication for tenure" and "teaching for tenure," offer testimony that tenure is a focal point and shapes behavior for many academicians in their career-making history.

There have been heated debates over tenure in recent years. Some argue for the elimination of tenure. Others fight for the continuation of tenure. Both sides carry a great deal of emotion in their efforts. Perhaps a systematic analysis of tenure in terms of its pros and cons can only come from a neutral, objective point of view. First of all, what is the benefit of tenure? On the part of academic institutions, tenure secures loyalty, commitment, and dedication from the faculty. It ensures that an institution maintains a stable, consistent, and uniform academic staff in its pursuit of excellence in general and specific scholarly orientations in particular. Universities are the most stable institutions in a market society. Part of university stability may be due to the fact that a university keeps a core faculty through the tenure system. A college may award tenure on the basis of teaching ability. A university that emphasizes research may award tenure only to those faculty members who have achieved certain levels of quality and productivity in scholarship. Tenure therefore becomes a mechanism of selection for the university to keep only those who share its academic mission and goals. Every time tenure is awarded to a candidate, the university awards itself an opportunity for renewal and reinforcement of the spirit of scholarship and excellence it holds.

On the part of individual academicians, tenure means job security and lifetime employment. A job provides income for a working scholar. Jobs offer a stage where career academicians seek self-actualization. Because no other job is more secure than that ensured by tenure, tenure becomes indisputably the most precious gift in the market economy. Tenure proponents also argue that tenure protects academic freedom. Before tenure, a scholar might have to publish articles and books that were politically acceptable in the climate of university, community, and state. Thus a professor who spoke for an unpopular point of view might have to yield to pressures from the political establishment as well as the university administration in fashioning scholarly work, dealing with students, and performing community service. Tenure advocates also argue that tenure ensures quality in scholarship. With tenure, one may be able to ignore external restraints, focus directly on what one is best at doing, and hence turn out the best products one can possibly produce. The underlying assumptions held by tenure supporters are obvious: Academicians are self-motivated, conscientious human beings; they will do best when they are assured of job security and academic freedom; and scholarly quality and productivity will be at the forefront when individual academicians are tenured.

On the other hand, what harmful effects does tenure bring to the knowledge enterprise? From an institutional point of view, tenure prevents a free, healthy flow of academic personnel from place to place across the market or through the community of scholarship. An institution owns a scholar once it grants him or her tenure. An institution may feel that it owns the best scholars possible in the world by its tenure system. But when it fills all its tenured positions, it loses motivation, space, and financial resources to take more creative, imaginative, and productive scholars constantly produced by the market. By owning a core of tenured scholars, an institution may also stagnate, be cut off from new ways of thinking, or be deadlocked into a seemingly active yet essentially useless pursuit. In terms of management, tenure prevents untenured academic staff from meaningfully participating in self-governance and other important decision-making processes in the university. It unjustifiably places power in the hands of tenured faculty. Tenured faculty members are not necessarily more productive and innovative in scholarship. But they are sometimes more vocal, resistant, and rebellious against new policy initiatives. In market conditions, a competitive institution must continuously take in new blood, embrace new challenges, and pursue new programs. With a large army of tenured faculty who navigate in comfort with their favored agenda and their preferred pace of work, an academic institution can soon become irrelevant in the competitive quest for knowledge.

Individually, tenure can make people relax, retreat, and rest. Before tenure, most scholars work hard. They pursue their research agenda rigorously, intensively, and persistently. They treat their students with care, patience, and respect. They respond to service seriously and effectively. After tenure, some academicians slow down and gradually retreat to the comfort of everyday life. In research, they do only what they know or do nothing because they are tired of what they do. In teaching, they may miss classes, muddle through classes, and treat students carelessly as juveniles or hostilely as enemies. In service, they may ignore calls, omit attendance at meetings, and make people wait. Tenure can corrupt people. Before tenure, the majority of scholars consciously and willingly yield to their senior colleagues in both academic and social interactions. They greet them, follow them, sometimes flatter them, and do things big and small to please them. Some may adopt members of the old guard as their protectors. A few may even bribe those in power with monetary, sexual, or social relational favors and benefits. After tenure, some academicians change. They become assertive, aggressive, and explosive, as if they want to regain what they have lost in the past as untenured servants. They begin to exploit social relations, demanding recognition and respect from newcomers. They may start to abuse their position, status, and privileges, enjoying favor and flattery from their untenured colleagues. They may even seek to manipulate academic and administrative processes, imposing their own will, their own version of reality upon those under their control. Tenure politicizes people. Before tenure, most academicians focus on their work. They listen to their leaders, follow rules, and defer to the political establishment. After tenure, some scholars start to diverge from work or research to which they were once committed. They voice concerns, make complaints, and speak out their dissatisfaction. They may openly politick with different factions and enjoy rebelling against management and the institutional establishment. Finally, tenure gives people a false sense of ultimate protection. The majority of scholars are competent, conscientious, and compassionate. They would do well without tenure. In other words, tenure serves for them no positive purpose. Rather, it has made them look weak, incompetent, vulnerable, and hence in need of protection in the eyes of other working professionals as well as the general public. There are hundreds of thousands of scientists and engineers who work in industry, commerce, and government. Embracing market dynamics, many of them spearhead scientific breakthroughs and technological innovations with a rigor no less than that of academicians under the protective roof of tenure. History reveals that protection often leads to individual incompetence and institutional stagnation. Reality demonstrates, again and again, that one does not need protection when one is competent, competitive, and effective in contrast to the market conditions in one's environment.

In all, tenure is a long-established tradition but faces historically challenging conditions. It is a widely followed convention in academia but meets serious doubt, criticism, and noncompliance in new market dynamics. Tenure will not go away soon simply because there are currents running against it. It will not remain the same either, simply because it is deeply rooted in academic establishments and institutional practices.

INNOVATION AND REFORM

Tenure appears and works in a time when scholars are rare, precious geniuses whom institutions scramble to own and support. In the era of mass production, scholars are trained in flocks and delivered to the labor market in crowds. There is no social legitimacy for them to claim entitlement to tenure protection. Institutions, on the other hand, are flooded with job-seeking academicians from season to season. There is no market rationale for them to keep a tenured army of the old guard and not to benefit from the constant supply of new talent. The tenure system is due for change (Alstete, 2000; Baez, 2002; Chait, 2005; Diamond, 2002; Finkin, 1996; Huer, 1991; Joughin 1967; Leap, 1995; Lewis, 1975; Licata & Morreale, 2007; Meiners, 2004; Tierney & Bensimon, 1996).

Reform 1: Separate Tenure from Rank

Status Quo. In places where rank moves from assistant to associate to full professorship, tenure is usually awarded at the same time when promotion in rank is granted. If an academician joins the faculty as an assistant professor, which remains standard in most cases, he or she is likely to receive tenure when he or she is promoted to the rank of associate professorship. Because of this practice of combining the granting of tenure with promotion to associate professor, a university may deny early promotion to anyone who otherwise deserves it through that person's extraordinary work. For example, the university may argue that tenure requires an intense scrutiny of five to six years on a candidate's performance and worth to the institution; that an early promotion in ranks preempts such a necessary scrutiny in a due time frame or obliges the institution to grant tenure later when the candidate overall may not be able to prove enough of his or her worth to the institution; and therefore that awarding of promotion should wait until granting of tenure is in order.

Reform. Tenure and rank should be separated because they are different in origin, meaning, and consequence. Institutions grant tenure to individual academicians because the latter have somehow through their talents, intentions, and deeds proved their indispensability, worth, and commitment to the former. With tenure, individual academicians have a guaranteed job and forum to exercise their rights to academic freedom. Rank, on the other hand, is based upon what one has done in his or her position. If one has done enough within a position of a lower rank and is capable of taking a position of a higher rank, one should be fairly and equitably promoted to the higher rank. With a proper rank, an academician has the necessary status and stature to engage in scholarly dealings within and outside his or her home institution. To separate tenure from rank, an institution does not need to do anything except change its ingrained mentality about the inseparability of tenure from rank. It awards promotion as it does routinely whenever an individual member of the faculty qualifies for a higher rank. In the meantime, the institution can firmly observe its preferred time of test on tenure. If it believes it takes five years to see the value of an individual academician to its mission, it can set the mandated time for tenure as five years. If it believes it takes longer, it may then set it for ten years, even fifteen years. Everyone has to wait for five years, ten years, or even fifteen years to obtain tenure regardless of the movement he or she has made in rank.

Significance. When tenure is separated from rank, an institution will obviously have the opportunity to take many more necessary reform measures toward tenure. Besides lengthening the time of test for tenure, the college or university may raise substantive requirements, limit the number of recipients each year, or gradually do away with the system altogether. Individual academicians do not have to prove their "indispensability" to an institution when they are ready to take positions at a higher level. They do not have to wait until the elapse of a manmade testing time for tenure to obtain their much deserved and needed promotion in rank. Most important, they do not have to feel they are falling into an institutional trap when they strive for recognition of status and rank for their activities in the scholarly world.

Reform 2: Make It a Standard: Ten Years for Tenure

Status Quo. There is no set time for the obtainment of tenure across academic institutions. If one lands a tenure-track assistant professorship job as a new Ph.D. recipient, one would normally have to spend five to six years to receive tenure. However, if one can demonstrate that one's teaching and scholarship are indispensable to the university, one might be able to obtain tenure earlier than the standard five to six years required of tenure-track assistant professors. There are also cases where one can pressure one's home institution to award early tenure and promotion when one secures a job offer from another institution or where one trades years of service elsewhere toward credit for early tenure and promotion. There are even cases where one receives early tenure and promotion by way of politicking, through exceptional scholarship, or out of one's demographic rarity.

Reform. If tenure means commitment, it should have a time dimension thereof for anyone who earns tenure to demonstrate his or her commitment to scholarship. If tenure means protection for academic freedom, it ought to be bestowed upon any serious scholar who does research, publishes academic work, and spreads knowledge, regardless of where he or she is, junior or senior, with or without institutional affiliation. If tenure means loyalty, it must not be awarded to those who contact other institutions and use some real or unreal promises from those other institutions to blackmail one's home organization.

Given the reality that tenure is something, but not all, about commitment to scholarship, protection for academic freedom, and loyalty to an institution, it is sensible to introduce a measure that makes a ten-year waiting period a universal standard for anyone to obtain tenure. The rationale of the measure is that one needs to spend a minimum of ten years or does not have to go beyond a maximum of ten years to demonstrate one's commitment to scholarship, worth of protection for academic freedom, or loyalty to a home institution. In consideration of various possible individual situations, the absolute ten-year waiting period should begin universally with the receipt of a doctoral degree in an academic discipline. In other words, one can start to earn one's service credit toward tenure as soon as one obtains one's Ph.D. Upon receipt of the Ph.D., one may continue on training as a postdoctoral scholar and then enter into a faculty position at a university, one may join one institution and later change to another, and one may take a full-time job at a college and stay with it continuously. Regardless of which situation one falls into, one accumulates one's year-by-year time of service for tenure as long as one engages in active academic work without any excursion into pure leisure or other non-academic activities. For example, one would receive tenure in three years in a new institution when he joins the institution after two years on a postdoctoral training program in a university and five years on a funded project at a research institute upon receipt of one's Ph.D.

Significance. The primary purpose of the proposed reform is to reconcile individual institutions with the entire academia. By recognizing valid service from institution to institution across the knowledge enterprise, tenure awarded by a particular institution will then carry the sense of protection for academic freedom that should have come originally from academia as a whole for each worthy practitioner. Commitment to scholarship will manifest itself not only by the kind of work one has done, but also through the amount of time one has spent, a standard ten-year testing period upon receipt of a doctoral degree. Also, loyalty will not have to lodge in a particular locale, but rather will need to extend to a consistent pattern of organizational sojourns in an individual academician's overall dedication and contribution to knowledge.

Reform 3: Strengthen Post-Tenure Review

Status Quo. If there is a considerable level of anxiety among tenure-track members of the faculty across colleges and universities, there is a conspicuous feeling of leisure on the part of the faculty who have received tenure. Under the current system, tenured professors, at both associate and full levels, are entitled to all privileges and rights in academic affairs and self-governance. Although most tenured professors at the associate level are seen working as diligently as they did previously in their drive for tenure, they can technically retreat to comfort if they choose not to attempt promotion in rank to the full professorship. With tenure, professors know that they will not lose anything if they do not have much to show in the business-as-usual post-tenure review that may occur as infrequently as once every five years.

Reform. A necessary measure to change the status quo is to strengthen post-tenure review. Post-tenure review should be conducted more frequently, perhaps every year on teaching, every two years on service, every three years on research and scholarship, and every four years for overall performance. Post-tenure review should also be made more substantive. The person under review must show considerable progress in teaching, research, and service for the period of a specified time. "No tangible progress" should not be accepted as "satisfactory" as it is under the current system. Proper alerts or warnings should be given following each post-tenure review. The faculty member reviewed will then have the opportunity to know where and how he or she needs to catch up within his or her academic work. Finally, penalty may be imposed when post-tenure review turns out to be repeatedly negative. For example, a faculty member could face a decrease in salary, a demotion in rank, or even a loss of tenure should he or she continuously fail to attend to proper alerts or warnings given to specific areas in teaching, research, service, or a combination thereof. Indeed, one would not deserve any protection of academic freedom for which tenure was originally conceived if one does not actively participate in academic dialogues through either scholarly publication or classroom instruction.

Significance. With a rigorous post-tenure review in place, awarding of tenure will no longer be a critical watershed in academia. An institution will not worry if it occasionally errs because it will find balance in review, evaluation, and action on individual employees between pre-tenure and post-tenure periods. Individual academicians will not have a false sense of protection nor will they act as if they were two different persons because they know they will need to do the best they can in their academic careers regardless of their tenure status.

Reform 4: Offer only a Limited Number of Tenure

Status Quo. Although tenure is an employment protection feature used only in academia, it actually does not mean more than what a "permanent" job category refers to in other professional settings. Also, when most, if not all, full-time faculty members of a college or university have tenure or are on track toward it, tenure will not seem to carry any special significance in a scholar's career. Most critically, a tenured professor would still lose his or her job should the institution that has granted him or her tenure close down; a tenured member of the faculty would still face termination or forced resignation should he or she dare to criticize national policies or rebel against established conventions on the basis of academic freedom; and given just these two scenarios, does a tenure-awarding academic organization offer more than what a "home" institution would do to its members in the time of need?

Reform. An innovative idea for reform is "limited tenure." The rationale behind "limited tenure" is that in the massive crowd of career academicians, there are a few unique, exceptional scholars. They have made so varied or so invaluable contributions to knowledge in general or to an institution in particular that they deserve the special recognition, status, and privilege that tenure would provide. From the perspective of an institution, it wants to own an individual scholar through tenure because the individual has proved to be such a worthy asset to it. In implementation, a "limited tenure" system would not award tenure to most academic employees. In a university, there might be some preset quotas for each discipline-based department. For example, only one tenured professorship would be allowed in any single discipline-based department. Once it was awarded, no more could be given. A qualified member of the faculty, no matter how deserving, would have to wait until the tenured professorship in the department or discipline is vacated by resignation, retirement, or death. Or there might be no preset quotas but only uniform, strict campus-wide requirements and standards for "limited tenure." For example, a representative committee might be set up to review and evaluate applications from around the university each year. Tenured professorships would be awarded in accordance with standards of quality, regardless of discipline, department, or college. As a result, one department might have no tenured professor while another department might harbor more than one.

Significance. When a thing is scarce, it is precious. Tenure will gain its distinction when only a limited number of professors are awarded it, those who have demonstrated their deservedness through excellent work in and longtime commitment to scholarship. The sense of protection tenure should have for its rightful owners will then become clear and strong. For example, the mass media as well as the public opinion are most likely to enlist their support should a distinctively tenured member of the faculty at a college or university lose his or her job simply because that individual has acted upon the right to academic freedom in criticizing tradition, status quo, or some established authorities.

Reform 5: Establish a Floating Tenure System across Academia

Status Quo. Under the existing tenure system, an academic institution confers tenure to the majority of its faculty as a long-honored convention.

It does not have a choice to ask itself if it really wants to protect, by tenure, a particular faculty member. At present, individual faculty members receive tenure when it comes at the authorized time. They reason that it does not hurt to obtain tenure when everyone else seems to have little trouble getting it. The overall situation is that individual academicians feel trapped by institutions because of tenure while institutions feel they are forced to extend tenure protection indiscriminately to anyone who happens to be on their faculty or academic staff.

Reform. An innovative idea to change the existing tenure system is "floating tenure." With "floating tenure," an institution can freely grant tenure to any scholar of its choice throughout academia. By conferring tenure upon a scholar, the institution makes a public statement that it wants to sponsor and support the scholar for the rest of his or her academic career. Tenure may bring the scholar to the institution to work for it; on the other hand, it may never draw any substantive attention from him or her. A scholar may receive tenure from multiple institutions. This person can choose to ignore all other tenure-offering institutions to work for only one institution. This person may also rotate among all those institutions where he or she holds tenure. To put "floating tenure" into practice, an institution needs to set up an expert panel to scout prospective scholars in disciplines of its concern. When tenure is decided on for candidates appropriate to the university's mission, stature, and reputation, the institution sends letters to individual recipients. There might also be commonly used media where announcements of tenure are published. Individual scholars might respond to tenure-offering institutions with letters of appreciation. If they want to move from their current institution, they might then work with the tenure-offering institution on details of relocation.

Significance. "Floating tenure" will create an open field of free choice for both individuals and institutions. Individual academicians would not necessarily rest with what their current employment organization expects of them. They would always have something higher and larger to strive for, above and beyond their home institution. By similar reasoning, an academic institution would not just work to keep its current faculty satisfied and committed. It would have an extra task or an additional agenda to attract and claim talented scholars from around academia. The new tenure system might indeed break various manmade barriers for a healthy flow of academic personnel throughout the knowledge enterprise.

CHAPTER 16

SCHOLARLY IDENTITY

What makes a scholar? What accomplishments or residues lie within an academic career? What image does a career-making academician attempt to build for himself or herself in his or her institution, discipline, society, and era? The curriculum vitae seemingly provide a condensed display, a crystallized reflection of an academician's career sequence and structure. Within the vitae, education and degrees usually appear in the forefront, indicating an academic aspirant's origin and background. Following this information are the jobs and positions held at employment organizations, signaling an academic participant's secular status and power. Publications, teaching, presentations, professional activities, and community service constitute the main body, representing an academic practitioner's substantive activities and contributions to the knowledge enterprise. Honors and awards cap the vitae at its conclusion, summarizing a career scholar's visibility, reputation, and influence in the world of scholarship. It is taken for granted in the academic circle that the best way to know a scholar is first to review the person's curriculum vitae.

In general, the degree, position, publication, teaching, presentation, service, grants, awards, association membership, and tenure are key elements in an academic career. Each element is important in its own right and takes a significant part, if not the whole, of a career-making process to develop, grow, and substantiate. In the meantime, these elements relate to each other in importance to form the structure of a career or a chronicle of achievements that builds an academician's self-identity and shapes future attitudes and behavior in his or her continuous career-making endeavor. For instance, publication by itself is a record to build for a lifetime. It relates to all other career components or in the mind of many scholars serves as a leading force to organize other aspects in the whole structure of academic life. A publication-centered career structure, once formed or in the process of formation, obviously affects how a scholar defines priorities, pursues research, engages in scholarly and non-scholarly activities, and maintains a public image throughout his or her career-making journey (Caughey, 2006; Cownie, 2004; Di Leo, 2003; Engvall, 2003; Garber, 2001; Lewis, 1975; Piper, 1992; Stinchcombe, 1999/2000; Talburt, 2000).

BACKGROUND AND ANALYSIS

Making an academic career involves developing a scholarly identity. In building one's scholarly identity, one meets specific requirements and fulfills general achievement standards in major categories, from education, institutional employment, teaching, and research, to service. For instance, research involves publications, grants, projects, and presentations. Teaching includes courses taught, pedagogical innovations, the number of students served, and the ways in which students will say they have been changed by the instructor's teaching. Although it presents only one aspect of a scholarly career, a particular category of scholarship may dominate the whole identity of an academician. In other words, a scholar can become so strong in one area of scholarship that accomplishments in that one area say everything about that person's scholarly identity.

The whole-part contrast relates directly to the compartmentalized versus multifaceted orientation in the construction of a scholarly identity. Under a multifaceted orientation, a scholar strives to cover every base of his or her academic career. One has a doctoral degree and feels one has fulfilled the licensing requirement for academic practice. One works in an academic institution, with proper access to scholarly stimulation, resources, and opportunities. In teaching, one constantly explores new ways of instruction and proves to be a dynamic and inspiring professor inside and outside the classroom. On the matter of research, one writes proposals, conducts funded projects, presents findings to professional audiences, and publishes articles and monographs through academic media. Besides teaching and research, one actively engages in service, from organizing conferences, editing journals, reviewing manuscripts, and serving on committees, to advocating for policy changes, within and outside one's institution, community, and discipline.

Scholarly Identity 175

Under a compartmentalized orientation, however, a scholar delves into one area and is not able to do much work in other areas. For instance, one has been teaching a fixed set of courses in a community college since receiving the doctoral degree. One seldom presents work to professional conferences and has never published anything in academic outlets. One goes home after teaching and is barely in the service of the discipline, institution, and community. Although claiming to be a teaching scholar, one does not have much to offer regarding pedagogy and general craftsmanship of instruction. In other scenarios, some scholars claim to be pure researchers. They are fully devoted to their own research, leaving little time for instruction and service. They miss class, go to class unprepared, or run class without clear objectives and agenda. Students cry for help to little avail. They never answer calls for service, hardly even show up in committee meetings, or keep only a nominal appearance on service occasions. There are also scholars who claim to be advocates, reformers, or service professionals. They engage in social movements, community activism, or expert testimonials in the media, the court, or the legislature. They do not offer much academic substance in classroom instruction nor have they published any considerable amount of serious, theoretically sound and empirically grounded, work in their discipline. They basically use their doctoral degree as a selling point for some of their personal and social ideologies.

Another important contrast in the building of a scholarly identity is individual expectation versus institutional demand. Individuals may choose teaching, research, or comprehensive universities. They may opt for governmental agencies or private industries. As far as academic aspirations are concerned, one may want to be a devoted instructor, an accomplished researcher, or a social activist. Personal aspirations are obviously moderated or constrained by individual perceptions, abilities, and resources. One who is fearful of research may find face-to-face interaction with students a justifiable escape from the usually lonely academic inquiry. One who cannot sit down long enough for serious reasoning and writing may feel one can only channel one's knowledge and training through service and social advocacy.

In the meantime, institutions where individuals work exist as powerful sources to shape and reshape individuals in their career design and development. A liberal arts college may only want its faculty to make students and their parents happy. It may not care much whether a faculty member publishes in academic media. A research-intensive institution may pressure its faculty to publish in leading academic outlets. It may turn a blind eye to how a faculty member performs in a classroom and whether numbers of students complain about him or her. A comprehensive university may expect its faculty to do a little something in all three areas: teaching, research, and service. In the end, it may only gather a collection of scholars who do not stand out in any one of the three areas. Industries and governments are known to restrict their employees from freely saying and writing about issues related to their work and specialties. They want their academically trained employees only to apply state-of-the-art theories, methods, or technologies to solve specific problems within their functional operation. As more and more individuals follow market forces to enter institutions outside their choice, institutional demands seem to become more and more imposing and dominating to override individual expectations in the development of a scholarly career and identity.

Still, another important contrast is idealized versus actualized identity. The contrast applies to both individuals and institutions. At the individual level, there are people who aim high and work hard but are not able to achieve even half of what they dream for. Although they remain unfulfilled, they still credit their high dreams and ideals to what they have actually attained. They believe they would not have reached where they are had they not been motivated by their lofty goals. On the other hand, there are people who are surprisingly successful even though they never give much thought to how high they want to reach in their academic career. They harvest their first gain by luck, under some patronage, or through hard work. They then seem to roll onto success with all forces coming to their aid.

At the institutional level, universities and research organizations put out faculty manuals, codes of conduct, or employee handbooks, specifying official requirements for tenure, promotion, or special awards. Strictly by written requirements, an institution should only garner a collection of geniuses, first-rate scholars, all-rounded high achievers, master teachers, or social engineers. In reality, however, gaps always exist between words and deeds. While an elite institution may house primarily high-achievers, in all likelihood, it will harbor some mediocrities as well. While a metropolitan university may dominantly draw classroom teachers, it may also include a few poor instructors as well as some productive scholars in its ranks. In a sense, written words from the employee guidebook are more about how an institution wants to be perceived by its employees and the general public than about reality. Once a public perception is formed about an institution, individuals often voluntarily choose to join or leave the institution. The institution, therefore, significantly spares itself the likely confrontational enforcement of personnel rules and regulations. For example, individuals would not apply for employment in a highly competitive university if they knew their career ideals did not measure up to the performance standards of the university. They would leave the university before the year of critical decision if they knew they would not survive or if they could not feel some sense of comfort, control, and dignity in the university of which they want to become a part.

INNOVATION AND REFORM

Institutions imitate one another in their structural design and personnel practices. In the game of imitation, the new, small, ordinary, and unknown look up to the old, large, prestigious, and renowned for inspiration and guidance. As a result, lower-ranking institutions may build upon models adopted by their higher-ranking counterparts. Teaching universities may attempt to put similar pressures, as research institutions, on their faculty for scholarly productivity while overwhelming them with a heavy teaching load and offering them fewer resources for research (Caughey, 2006; Cownie, 2004; Di Leo, 2003; Engvall, 2003; Garber, 2001; Ibarra, 2004; Piper, 1992; Talburt, 2000).

Reform 1: Clarify Standards

Status Quo. The pressure to follow the most notable applies not only to institutions, but also to individuals. In almost everything an academician does in his or her regular work, he or she clearly feels the force of an invisible hand that pushes or pulls him or her in line with what is most desirable, fashionable, or recognizable in the field. In teaching, there seems to be a master classroom performer for everyone to emulate. This master classroom teacher can turn his or her words into instant inspiration for students. In research, everyone seems to expect or to be expected to publish in a prime outlet although most people communicate their research in variously graded media. Fear prevails as ambiguous assumptions, perceptions, or expectations ride over clear objectives, standards, and guidelines.

Reform. Academic organizations should focus on their own mission, goals and objectives, resources, employee composition, and clientele. They should resist the temptation to follow what big players tend to do in academia. They should be unconcerned with what looks appropriate or correct on paper. Instead, they should be honest and straightforward about what they are and how much they want their academic employees to perform on the job. With minimal discrepancy between words and deeds, faculty members can contentedly follow official guidelines and keep their minds on what they are expected to do.

Specifically, a university may provide employee performance indicators appropriate to its mission for knowledge as well as its standing in academia. In teaching, a university may require members of the faculty to do a certain number of class evaluations each academic year and prescribes a range of scores within which student grading of an instructor's performance is deemed acceptable. On the matter of publication, quantitative yardsticks and measurements can be developed as guidelines for the faculty when they work toward promotion and tenure. For example, with reference to some widely recognized ratings of journals or publications in a discipline, a similar amount of credit may be assigned to one article published in the highest-ranking journal or to two articles published in second-tier outlets. The second author of a two-author article may claim only half of the credit for the article while a trailing fourth author of a four-author paper may take only one-fourth of the recognition for co-authorship of the work. There can be sensible formulas established for calculating academic credits for book chapters, books, and other forms of contributions as well.

Significance. By clarifying standards applicable in the real world, an academic institution will present to its academic employees a clear image of what it is, what it builds upon, and what it attempts to achieve. Individual academicians who work within the walls of the institution can then make their own goals, set their own agendas, and construct their own scholarly identity in accordance with proper contextual constraints and appropriate organizational restrictions. Thus neither institution nor individual will struggle between an invisible universal model into which they are supposed to fit and a tangible mundane identity they create and modify on an everyday basis.

Reform 2: Specify Expectations

Status Quo. While they may provide standards in abstract terms, such as commitment to scholarship, excellence in teaching, and dedication to service, a great many academic institutions are hesitant to prescribe specific expectations for their academic staff in day-to-day job functioning. The reason can be multiple: fear of legal challenge, concern over public image, or lack of efficiency and effectiveness in organizational management. For example, a university may not want to be criticized for babysitting its faculty or micromanaging academic processes. However, as no specific expectations are given, members of the faculty are left to figure out various issues and requirements on their own.

Reform. A needed reform in this aspect is for academic institutions to be straightforward. A liberal arts college can specify its expectations for the faculty as master classroom teachers who like working with students and who contribute to scholarship not necessarily through pure research but rather by various educational activities. Such clearly communicated expectations would by no means hurt the college's image as a qualified institution of higher learning. An urban comprehensive institution can openly expect its faculty to be effective teachers, contributing scholars, and participants in public service. A multifaceted expectation like this should not become ground for employee grievance or formal lawsuit in court. A research university can make a bold declaration to its faculty that it cares more about research than teaching, that it does not care much about service, or even that it cares only about pure scholarship. Such proclaimed expectations would only make the management work more effectively in dealing with students, parents, the faculty union, and the general public.

On the part of individual academicians, clear and honest specifications of job duties and position responsibilities by employment organizations may first sound local, restrictive, or even intimidating. But in the long run, specification can only help one understand one's institution, define one's priorities, channel one's effort, and develop one's scholarly identity. Attempting a little bit of everything in an urban comprehensive university may make one become nothing in the end, as pointed out satirically by some critics. But in most cases, a balance among teaching, research, and service does yield a viable identity in an academic career. Even when specifications push an individual academician in an opposite direction, it is still the specified expectation that makes the person what he or she is eventually. For instance, just as a specified expectation for excellence in teaching can be responsible for one to become a noticeable researcher, a clear demand on quality and productivity in scholarship may lie behind one's success as an inspiring classroom instructor.

Significance. With expectations specified for its faculty, an academic institution will automatically sharpen its own image of what it is in front of the public. The individual academician can then make an unambiguous choice as whether to enter the institution, what to do when becoming a member of the institution, and how to fulfill individual aspirations while meeting the institution's multifaceted demands. Most important, the academician will be able to make long-term career plans, set specific agendas in teaching, research, and service, and build a scholarly identity that is appropriate to the contextual dynamics of his or her home institution.

Reform 3: Provide Models

Status Quo. In their effort to build a scholarly identity, academicians look for examples they can follow and role models they can emulate. Unfortunately, examples are not often highlighted in institutional contexts. Role models are given only in abstract terms or from remote backgrounds. For instance, the principle of the mean prevailing in many organizational settings tends to keep people at a distance from their outperforming peers. Within a discipline, people feel more safe and comfortable in paying homage to founding fathers in the far past than showing due respect to those who are currently doing important work in the forefront of knowledge.

Reform. Using its organizational power as well as its collective wisdom, an academic institution can and should identify, celebrate, and promote outstanding individuals for the rest of its membership to follow and relate to. On a year-to-year basis, each academic unit may reward one of its members the lecturer of the year, the researcher of the year, the service professional of the year, or the faculty member of the year according to comparative performance records in teaching, research, service, or overall scholarship over the period of concern. The annual reward can go up to higher levels until the entire system, whether it is a university, a multi-campus consortium, or a statewide network. Then, for every five or ten years, a distinguished professorship or a career of academic distinction may be bestowed upon an individual from unit to unit or across the institution as a whole. As the models so selected come from where ordinary academicians work and live, they can be convincingly and contagiously influential in their specific settings.

Similarly, disciplinary associations can lead the way in providing tangible examples and real-live role models for career-making academicians working in the field they are supposed to represent and promote. Besides honoring the memory of a few founding fathers and pioneers who loom abstract, ghostly, and remote in history, an academic association can and should find, present, and recognize individuals who are making critical contributions to knowledge here and now. The competitively elected presidents of the association should exemplify the best of scholarship in the current time. There also ought to be an open selection of best educators, best practitioners, or best researchers for the membership to look up to from time to time. There also should be an agreed-upon collection of best monographs, best applications, best experiments, or most cited articles for people to make reference to every year or for a sensible period of time. Live examples can be more inspiring and stimulating than historical figures because people can directly see the impact of leading scholars upon the field or in their own work.

Significance. As it is put in a Chinese saying, the power of example is unlimited. By providing models through rewards and ceremonial activities, an academic institution speaks loud and clear about its mission, long-term goals, short-term objectives, and, more specifically, what kind of faculty it desires, what type of scholarship it favors, and what specific actions or achievements it expects of its employees over their regular work. Instead of bearing pressure and stress to follow rules and meet standards, individual academicians will surely feel motivated and encouraged when they look to the examples and models around them to do the best they can in teaching, research, and service.

Reform 4: Allow for Deviations

Status Quo. While they are not always clear about what they want, academic institutions can often become stubbornly intolerant of what does not seem to be usual or what appears to be unfamiliar. A research university may make someone feel unwelcome who proves to be a wonderful source of inspiration for students inside and outside the classroom yet fails to publish in designated academic journals. A small liberal arts college, on the other hand, may threaten to deny tenure and promotion to a faculty member who publishes controversial research in prime outlets yet does not perform well as a classroom instructor.

Reform. Academic institutions should remain flexible enough to accommodate reasonable deviations from standard practice. A research university ideally looks for people who excel in scholarship, perform well in teaching, and respond regularly to service. It is still to its advantage, however, to retain someone who turns out unique, innovative, or revolutionary research products even though he or she does not know how to handle people-to-people situations inside and outside the classroom. A teaching institution may stipulate in its employee guidebook that faculty members are encouraged or expected to make scholarly contributions to their respective discipline. It is nonetheless in its interest to keep some faculty who do not actively engage in research but always deliver inspiring lectures and interact well with students in classroom settings. In reaction to some considerable patterns of deviations in enforcement, academic institutions may revisit their policies and create new categories to facilitate unique individual career development and identity formation. For example, research institutions may adopt a tenure-rank system for research scientists parallel to that for conventional professorships. A teaching university may allow master classroom teachers to acquire tenure and proceed from junior lecturer to lecturer to senior lecturer, a ranking sequence comparable to the dominant assistant-to-associate-to-full professorship system in the United States.

Significance. Scholarly identity is developed and formed in the human dynamics of contrast and comparison. Providing a standard model while allowing for deviations, an academic institution will create a situation where the majority of its members follow the model, a few find their unique talents outside the model, and one serves as the other's reference and motivation in their respective realization of scholarly goals or actualization of academic identity. For example, an inspiring classroom performer who sees most of his or her colleagues publish in prime outlets may become ever more determined to excel in teaching whereas a stellar researcher who witnesses master classroom performance by the majority of his or her fellow faculty members may only want to be more productive or innovative in scholarship. The ultimate beneficiary will certainly be the academic institution that allows for this kind of self-motivated comparison and competition.

Reform 5: Promote Diversity and Vitality

Status Quo. Men have long dominated the knowledge enterprise. In mixed populations, it is often peoples of racial and ethnic minorities that are underrepresented in academic institutions. With more women as well as more members of minorities joining the quest for knowledge, there is a phenomenal lack of relevant role models for individual academicians of various origins, backgrounds, and orientations. Most critically, because no one inside the system or high up in the hierarchy can genuinely serve as their patrons, mentors, or models, women and minority scholars may suffer both implicitly and explicitly in publication, teaching, service, promotion, tenure, awards, and other areas of interest fundamental to a successful career.

Reform. There is obviously a widespread need to increase the presence as well as the influence of people of different demographic characteristics across the academic landscape. In the beginning, there should be preferential policies to recruit underrepresented groups so that people in those groups can find their way to academia, a place that may still appear foreign to their underrepresented origin or status. There also ought to be protective measures to retain and promote underrepresented members of the faculty in every academic institution because it often takes extraordinary courage and effort for those minority members to build a professional network, to find a sense of belonging, and to develop a scholarly identity in settings where no close model is available for reference.

However, to ensure vitality in academia, diversity must not be pursued in any way or to a degree that compromises quality. In recruitment, basic requirements must be maintained so that every academic entrant, regardless of gender, race, ethnicity, or other status, faces the same test of competency, commitment, and potential for success. Over the process of retention and promotion, some universal performance standards must be established so that every scholarly candidate has to pass the same barriers in his or her movement up the professional ladder as well as across the managerial hierarchy. In fact, hiring an incompetent applicant into the faculty of a university from an underrepresented group may only cause damage to the public image of that particular group within and outside the university. On the other hand, promoting a bright and outperforming minority member to a high level in rank or to a top position in academic management can inspire all, both the majority and the minority, and hence bring about vitality and vibrancy to a whole institution and beyond.

Significance. Diversity goes hand in hand with vitality. A diverse faculty provides the ultimate engine for vitality in an academic institution. And a vital institution calls constantly for diversity, an all-way inclusion of various groups and orientations in its general membership. Promoting diversity and vitality, academic institutions will attain quality, excellence, and influence on the basis of inclusion rather than exclusion, pluralism rather than elitism, and representation rather than domination. Individual practitioners, in the meantime, will find multiple sources of encouragement, inspiration, and stimulation in their search for model, reference, and identity throughout academic careers.

CONCLUSION

Making an academic career in the contemporary era is not just an individual endeavor. It involves three basic agents and agencies: academicians and their actions, institutions and their requirements, and the larger social structure and its dynamics.

Academicians choose to make a scholarly career. In their career pathway, they attend school, learn knowledge and skills, and obtain degrees. They search for academic jobs, affiliate with universities, research institutes, and other professional groups, and pursue scholarship in organizational settings. They seek professional contacts, network with funding sources, publication outlets, and service communities, and develop scholarly visibility in the academic circle. From a structural point of view, degrees, positions, publications, teaching portfolios, presentations, service records, grants, awards, membership in academic associations, and tenure obtained or produced throughout the career-making process combine to form individually unique identities academicians strive to build for their scholarly career as well as in their mundane life.

Institutions provide training grounds, supply jobs, and offer media for career-making academicians. They establish standards, set rules, and impose requirements upon scholarly processes. They conduct assessments, evaluations, and judgments that are essential to personal motivation, academic productivity, occupational mobility, and self-identity. They control resources, opportunities, and rewards that are indispensable to task performance, job success, professional accomplishment, and self-fulfillment. A few elite universities send their graduates to high-ranking institutions, placing them in a network that affords them prestigious points of contact for top-rated funding, sponsorship, research projects, and publication outlets. A multitude of ordinary programs, on the other hand, dispose of their students anywhere in the labor market or the knowledge enterprise without much regard for whether they can do something, work for a living, or just survive as an academic professional. Whereas institutions with high concentrations of talents may simply focus on productivity, quality, success, and merit, institutions of more ordinary performers may often falter in individual stagnation, interpersonal envy, group conflict, political friction, and overall mediocrity. Indeed, it is institutions that provide material conditions, spiritual sentiment, and a general environment in and by which career-making academicians work toward their career actualization in scholarship. A basically ordinary person may soar skyward if he or she happens to become part of a privileged network in a supportive institutional environment. An essentially brilliant person may disintegrate if he or she happens to fall into a destructive relationship in a swampy organizational milieu.

Following academicians in their career journey, institutions may eagerly recruit the bright, meticulously cultivate the promising, generously maintain the productive, and creatively promote the exceptional. They may also intentionally exclude the talented, maliciously abuse the innocent, unfairly treat the achiever, and ruthlessly persecute the innovator. Institutions and institutional practices vary tremendously in every aspect, from effectiveness, efficiency, productivity, rationality, fairness, and openness, to supportiveness. This volume has proposed a wide range of ideas and measures to established agents and agencies in academia to change and better their attitude, role playing, and performance or to reform and improve their system, operation, and service for career-making academic professionals. Agents to whom innovative ideas are addressed consist of department chairs, college deans, university presidents, manuscript reviewers, journal editors, book publishers, grant evaluators, program funding officers, foundation directors, association managers, association presidents, and other stakeholders in academia. Agencies to which reformative measures are presented include colleges, universities, research institutes, publishing houses, private foundations, public funding offices, professional associations, and other institutional establishments involved in the production and distribution of knowledge in contemporary society.

All innovative ideas and reformative measures are conceived and proposed from the perspective of academic careers and career-making scholars. While some proposals are simple, straightforward, and ready for immediate adoption and implementation, others are complex, complicated, and in need of careful research and planning. However, no matter whether any proposed ideas and measures are sensible, practical, and applicable, academic agents and agencies must have necessary openness, vision, and courage to recognize that there are always different, oftentimes better, ways of doing things. Once the benefit of a new idea or measure is recognized, academic agents and agencies then need to commit sufficient time, manpower, and resources to implement it amid various dynamic forces within an institution, across a discipline, or throughout the whole community of scholarship. For example, tenure has existed for generations. But the system does not have to continue into the future if it does not serve well either individuals or institutions in higher education. Use of personal recommendation prevails in academia as well as across the professional community. But the practice does not have to go any further if it places too much burden on individuals while offering too little benefit to institutions. Recruitment of academic administrators from the outside has been a standard from institution to institution. But the rule does not have to hold any longer if it only creates a group of privileged "entrepreneurs" in the academic market who move into powerful positions with high salaries from one institution to another and who during a term of five years or so may rob an academic institution of its own functionality, stability, and continuity. In fact, no system, no tradition, and no practice should ever be taken for granted. Reform, renovation, renewal, and rebirth should be an out-and-out theme for all academic institutions in their drive for scholarly excellence and organizational efficacy.

The large social structure supports the knowledge enterprise because it consumes knowledge. It supplies resources for scholarly institutions because it needs academic personnel. The social structure expands in scale and scope as more and more academic institutions come into existence. The social process perpetuates itself as more and more career-making academicians flock to the knowledge enterprise with creative input and effective output. Social authority, control, and dominance increase while individuals and individuality become less important, insignificant, and negligible. Although no single academic institution, much less any individual academician, is able to curb, abort, or even reverse the general social process, its development or trend, every scholarly agent and agency should stay alert and be aware of the negative cycle in contemporary academia. A positive cycle is never impossible: The more career-making academicians there are, the more they contribute, the stronger the knowledge enterprise is to become; and the stronger the knowledge enterprise becomes, the more support the academic establishment is able to provide for its individual participants, the more career-seekers are to be attracted, motivated, and encouraged to make greater and more varied contributions.

In all, this volume serves its purpose if some of its readers, whether they are ordinary career-making professionals, powerful stakeholders in academic establishments, or keen observers and advocates of science and scholarship, say it makes them think again about what they do, how they operate in organizational settings, and how they relate to knowledge, the knowledge enterprise, and larger social dynamics.

REFERENCES

Abel, E. K. (1984). *Terminal degrees: The job crisis in higher education.* New York: Praeger.

Acker, D. (2006). *Can state universities be managed?: A primer for presidents and management teams.* Westport, CT: Praeger/American Council on Education.

Alley, M. (2007). *The craft of scientific presentations: Critical steps to succeed and critical errors to avoid.* New York: Springer.

Alstete, J. W. (2000). *Posttenure faculty development: Building a system for faculty improvement and appreciation.* San Francisco: Jossey-Bass.

Altbach, P. G., Berdahl, R. O., & Gumport, P. (2005). *American higher education in the twenty-first century: Social, political, and economic challenges.* Baltimore, MD: Johns Hopkins University Press.

Arreola, P. A. (2006). *Developing a comprehensive faculty evaluation system: A guide to designing, building, and operating large-scale faculty evaluation systems.* Bolton, MA: Anker Publishing.

Baez, B. (2002). *Affirmative action, hate speech, and tenure: Narratives about race, law, and the academy.* New York: Routledge Falmer.

Bain, K. (2004). *What the best college teachers do.* Cambridge, MA: Harvard University Press.

Baldwin, R. G., & Chronister, J. L. (2001). *Teaching without tenure: Policies and practices for a new era.* Baltimore, MD: Johns Hopkins University Press.

Barnard, M. (1990). *Magazine and journal production.* New York: Van Nostrand Reinhold.

Barnes, S. L. (2007). *On the market: Strategies for a successful academic job search.* Boulder, CO: Lynne Rienner Publishers.

Baudrillard, J. (1988). *Selected writings* (M. Poster, Ed.). Palo Alto, CA: Stanford University Press.

Bauer, D. G. (1999). *The "how to" grants manual: Successful grant-seeking techniques for obtaining public and private grants.* Phoenix, AZ: Oryx Press.

Becher, T. (1989). *Academic tribes and territories: Intellectual enquiry and the cultures of disciplines.* Bristol, PA: Society for Research into Higher Education.

Becker, H. S. (1998). *Tricks of the trade: How to think about your research while you're doing it.* Chicago: University of Chicago Press.

Beckham, J. (1986). *Faculty/staff nonrenewal and dismissal for cause in institutions of higher education.* Asheville, NC: College Administration Publications.

Bennett, J. B. (2003). *Academic life: Hospitality, ethics, and spirituality.* Bolton, MA: Anker Publishing.

Bianco-Mathis, V., & Chalofsky, N. (1999). *The full-time faculty handbook.* Thousand Oaks, CA: Sage Publications.

Blaxter, L., Hughes, C., & Tight, M. (1998). *The academic career handbook.* Philadelphia, PA: Open University Press.

Bok, D. (2003). *Universities in the marketplace: Commercialization of higher education.* Princeton, NJ: Princeton University Press.

Bolek, C. S., Bielawski, L., Niemcryk, S., Needle, R., & Baker, S. (1992). Developing a competitive research proposal. *Drugs and Society, 6*(1/2), 1–22.

Bowen, W. G., & Rudenstine, N.L. (1992). *In pursuit of the Ph.D.* Princeton, NJ: Princeton University Press.

Bowen, W. G., & Sosa, J. A. (1989). *Prospects for faculty in the arts and sciences: A study of factors affecting demand and supply, 1987 to 2012.* Princeton, NJ: Princeton University Press.

Bresciani, M. J., & Wolff, R. A. (2006). *Outcomes-based academic and co-curricular program review: A compilation of institutional good practices.* Sterling, VA: Stylus Publishing.

Bright, D. F., & Richards, M. P. (2001). *The academic deanship: Individual careers and institutional roles.* San Francisco: Jossey-Bass.

Brodkey, L. (1987). *Academic writing as social practice.* Philadelphia, PA: Temple University Press.

Brown, D., & Brooks, L. (1996). *Career choice and development.* San Francisco: Jossey-Bass.

Brown, R. H., & Schubert, J. D. (2000). *Knowledge and power in higher education: A reader.* New York: Teachers College Press.

Buller, J. L. (2006). *The essential department chair: A practical guide to college administration.* Bolton, MA: Anker Publishing.

Busch, F. (1986). *When people publish: Essays on writers and writing.* Iowa City: University of Iowa Press.

Cantor, J. A. (1993). *A guide to academic writing.* Westport, CT: Greenwood Press.

Carrigan, D. P. (1991). Publish or perish: The troubled state of scholarly communication. *Scholarly Publishing, 22*(3), 131–142.

Cartter, A. M. (1976). *Ph.D.'s and the academic labor market.* New York: McGraw-Hill.

Caughey, J. L. (2006). *Negotiating cultures and identities: Life history issues, methods, and readings.* Lincoln: University of Nebraska Press.

Chait, R. P. (2005). *The question of tenure.* Cambridge, MA: Harvard University Press.

Clark, M. J., & Centra, J. A. (1985). Influences on the career accomplishments of Ph.D.'s. *Research in Higher Education, 23*(3), 256–269.

Clark, S. M., & Lewis, D. R. (1985). *Faculty vitality and institutional productivity: Critical perspectives for higher education.* New York: Teachers College Press.

Clark, W. (2006). *Academic charisma and the origins of the research university.* Chicago: University of Chicago Press.

Cohen, S. (1997). Conference life: The rough guide. *The American Sociologist, 28*(3), 69–84.

Coiner, C., & George, D. H. (1998). *The family track: Keeping your faculties while you mentor, nurture, teach, and serve.* Urbana and Chicago: University of Illinois Press.

Conley, V. M. (1997). *Characteristics and attitudes of instructional faculty and staff in the humanities.* Washington, DC: U.S. Department of Education.

Coser, L. A., Kadushin, C., & Powell, W.W. (1982). *The culture and commerce of publishing.* New York: Basic Books.

Cotten, S. R., Price, J., Keeton, S., Burton, R. P. D., & Wittekind, J. E. C. (2001). Reflections on the academic job search in sociology. *The American Sociologist, 32*(3), 26–42.

Cownie, F. (2004). *Legal academics: Culture and identities.* Portland, OR: Hart Publishing.

Cox, J. B. (2007). *Professional practices in association management: The essential resource for effective management of nonprofit organizations.* Washington, DC: ASAE & Center for Association Leadership.

Cox, J., & Cox, L. (2006). *Scholarly publishing practice.* Brighton, UK: Association of Learned and Professional Society Publishers.

Darling, D. (2005). *Networking for career success.* New York: McGraw-Hill.

Davis, G. B., & Parker, C. A. (1997). *Writing the doctoral dissertation: A systematic approach.* Hauppauge, NY: Barron's Educational Series.

Dewsbury, D. A. (1996). *Unification through division: Histories of the divisions of the American Psychological Association.* Washington, DC: American Psychological Association.

Di Leo, J. R. (2003). *Affiliations: Identity in academic culture.* Lincoln: University of Nebraska Press.

Diamond, R. M. (2002). *Serving on promotion, tenure, and faculty review committees: A faculty guide.* San Francisco: Jossey-Bass.

Dickeson, R. C. (1999). *Prioritizing academic programs and services: Reallocating resources to achieve strategic balance.* San Francisco: Jossey-Bass.

Digiusto, E. (1994). Equity in authorship: A strategy for assigning credit when publishing. *Social Science and Medicine, 38*(1), 55–58.

Dore, R. P. (1976). *The diploma disease: Education, qualification, and development.* Berkeley: University of California Press.

Editorial Board. (1993). *The awards almanac.* Chicago: St. James Press.

Eggins, H. (2003). *Globalization and reform in higher education.* Berkshire, UK: Open University Press/Society for Research into Higher Education.

Elliott, A. (1996). *Subject to ourselves.* Cambridge, MA: Blackwell Publishers.

English, J. F. (2005). *The economy of prestige: Prizes, awards, and the circulation of cultural value.* Cambridge, MA: Harvard University Press.

Engvall, R. P. (2003). *Academic identity: Place, race, and gender in academia.* Cresskill, NJ: Hampton Press.

Epstein, D., Kenway, J., & Boden, R. (2007). *Writing and publishing (academics support kit).* Thousand Oaks, CA: Sage.

Eurich, N. (1981). *Systems of higher education in twelve countries: A comparative view.* New York: Praeger.

Fairweather, J. S. (1996). *Faculty work and public trust: Restoring the value of teaching and public service in American academic life.* Boston: Allyn & Bacon.

Feldman, B. (2000). *The Nobel prize: A history of genius, controversy, and prestige.* New York: Arcade.

Fenton, N., Bryman, A., Deacon, D., & Birmingham, P. (1997). 'Sod off and find us a boffin': Journalists and the social science conference. *The Sociological Review, 45*(1), 1–23.

Finkelstein, M. J., Seal, R. K., & Schuster, J. H. (1998). *The new academic generation: A profession in transformation.* Baltimore, MD: Johns Hopkins University Press.

Finkin, M. W. (1996). *The case for tenure.* Ithaca, NY: ILR Press.

Flemons, D. G. (1998). *Writing between the lines: Composition in the social sciences.* New York: W. W. Norton.

Formo, D. M., & Reed, C. (1999). *Job search in academe: Strategic rhetorics for faculty job candidates.* Sterling, VA: Stylus Publishing.

Fox, M. F. (1985). *Scholarly writing and publishing: Issues, problems, and solutions.* Boulder, CO: Westview Press.

Garber, M. B. (2001). *Academic instincts.* Princeton, NJ: Princeton University Press.

Golde, C. M., & Walker, G. E. (2006). *Envisioning the future of doctoral education: Preparing the stewards of the discipline.* San Francisco: Jossey-Bass/Carnegie Foundation for the Advancement of Teaching.

Goldsmith, J. A., Komlos, J., & Gold, P. S. (2001). *The Chicago guide to your academic career: A portable mentor for scholars from graduate school through tenure.* Chicago: University of Chicago Press.

Gornitzka, A., Kogan, M., & Amaral, A. (2007). *Reform and change in higher education: Analyzing policy implementation.* New York: Springer/Consortium of Higher Education Researchers.

Gosling, P. A., & Noordam, B. D. (2006). *Mastering your PhD: Survival and success in the doctoral years and beyond.* New York: Springer.

Gossett, J. L., & Bellas, M. L. (2002). You can't put a rule around people's hearts . . . can you?: Consensual relationship policies in academia. *Sociological Focus, 35*(3), 267–284.

Gould, R. (1978). *Transformations: Growth and change in adult life.* New York: Simon and Schuster.

Grant, W., & Sherrington, P. (2006). *Managing your academic careers.* Hampshire, UK: Palgrave Macmillan.

Greenwood, D., & Levin, M. (2001). Re-organizing universities and 'knowing how': University restructuring and knowledge creation for the 21st century. *Organization, 8*(2), 433–440.

Hamilton, N. W. (2002). *Academic ethics: Problems and materials on professional conduct and shared governance.* Westport, CT: Praeger/American Council on Education.

Haskell, T. L. (2000). *The emergence of professional social science: The American Social Science Association and the nineteenth-century crisis of authority.* Baltimore, MD: The Johns Hopkins University Press.

Heap, B. (2004). *University scholarships and awards.* Surrey, UK: Trotman Publishing.

Heiberger, M. M., & Vick, J. M. (2001). *The academic job search handbook.* Philadelphia: University of Pennsylvania Press.

Heinz, W. R., & Marshall, V. W. (2003). *Social dynamics of the life course: Transitions, institutions, and interrelations.* Hawthorne, NY: Aldine de Gruyter.

Henson, K. T. (2004). *Writing for publication: Road to academic advancement.* Boston: Allyn & Bacon.

Hermanowicz, J. C. (2002). In the shadows of giants: Identity and institution building in the American academic profession. In R. A. Settersten & T. J. Owens (Eds.), *Advances in life course research: New frontiers in socialization* (pp. 133–162). Oxford, UK: JAI.

Hines, E. R., & Hartmark, L. S. (1980). *Politics of higher education.* Washington, DC: American Association for Higher Education.

Huer, J. (1991). *Tenure for Socrates: A study in the betrayal of the American professor.* New York: Bergin & Garvey.

Hyland, K. (2006). *English for academic purposes: An advanced resource book.* New York: Routledge.

Ibarra, H. (2004). *Working identity: Unconventional strategies for reinventing your career.* Cambridge, MA: Harvard Business School Press.

Joughin, L. (Ed.). (1967). *Academic freedom and tenure: A handbook of the American association of university professors.* Madison: University of Wisconsin Press.

Kalman, C. S. (2007). *Successful science and engineering teaching in colleges and universities.* Bolton, MA: Anker Publishing.

Kaplowitz, R. A. (1986). *Selecting college and university personnel: The quest and the questions.* Washington, DC: Association for the Study of Higher Education.

Kerr, C., Gade, M. L., & Kawaoka, M. (1994). *Higher education cannot escape history: Issues for the twenty-first century.* Albany: State University of New York Press.

Kitchin, R., & Fuller, D. (2005). *The academic's guide to publishing.* Thousand Oaks, CA: Sage.

Krahenbuhl, G. S. (2004). *Building the academic deanship: Strategies for success.* Westport, CT: Praeger/American Council on Education.

Lattuca, L. R. (2001). *Creating interdisciplinarity: Interdisciplinary research and teaching among college and university faculty.* Nashville, TN: Vanderbilt University Press.

Leaming, D. R. (2003). *Managing people: A guide for department chairs and deans.* San Francisco: Jossey-Bass.

Leap, T. L. (1995). *Tenure, discrimination, and the courts.* Ithaca, NY: ILR Press.

Levinson, D. J. (1978). *The seasons of a man's life.* New York: Ballantine Books.

Lewis, L. S. (1975). *Scaling the ivory tower: Merit and its limits in academic careers.* Baltimore, MD: Johns Hopkins University Press.

Lewis, M. (1997). *Poisoning the ivy: The seven deadly sins and other vices of higher education in America.* Armonk, NY: M. E. Sharpe.

Licata, C. M., & Morreale, J. C. (2007). *Post-tenure faculty review and renewal: Experienced voices.* Washington, DC: American Association of Higher Education.

Lindholm-Romantschuk, Y. (1998). *Scholarly book reviewing in the social sciences and humanities: The flow of ideas within and among disciplines.* Westport, CT: Greenwood Press.

Locke, L. F., Spirduso, W. W., & Silverman, S. J. (2007). *Proposals that work: A guide for planning dissertations and grant proposals.* Thousand Oaks, CA: Sage.

Long, J. S., McGinnis, R., & Allison, P. D. (1993). Rank advancement in academic careers: Sex differences and the effects of productivity. *American Sociological Review, 58*(5), 703–722.

Lucas, A. F. (2000). *Leading academic change: Essential roles for department chairs.* San Francisco: Jossey-Bass.

MacDonald, S. (1994). *Professional academic writing in the humanities and social sciences.* Carbondale and Edwardsville: Southern Illinois University Press.

Macfarlane, B. (2007). *The academic citizen: The virtue of service in university life.* New York: Routledge.

Maki, P. L., & Borkowski, N. A. (2006). *The assessment of doctoral education: Emerging criteria and new models for improving outcomes.* Sterling, VA: Stylus Publishing.

Marx, K. (1967). *Capital* (S. Moore & E. Aveling, Trans.) New York: International Publishers.

McGinty, S. (1999). *Gatekeepers of knowledge: Journal editors in the sciences and the social sciences.* Westport, CT: Bergin & Garvey.

Meiners, R. E. (2004). *Faculty towers: Tenure and the structure of higher education.* Oakland, CA: Independent Institute.

Mortimer, K. P., Bagshaw, M., & Masland, A. T. (1985). *Flexibility in academic staffing: Effective policies and practices.* Washington, DC: Association for the Study of Higher Education.

Newman, F., Couturier, L., & Scurry, J. (2004). *The future of higher education: Rhetoric, reality, and the risk of the market.* San Francisco: Jossey-Bass.

Nilson, L. B. (2007). *Teaching at its best: A research-based resource for college instructors.* San Francisco: Jossey-Bass.

Noble, K. A. (1994). *Changing doctoral degrees: An international perspective.* Bristol, PA: Open University Press.

Paechter, C. (2001). *Knowledge, power, and learning.* Thousand Oaks, CA: Sage.

Parsons, P. (1989). *Getting published: The acquisition process at university presses.* Knoxville: University of Tennessee Press.

Piper, D. W. (1992). Are professors professional? *Higher Education Quarterly, 46*(2), 145–156.

Popkewitz, T. S., & Fendler, L. (1999). *Critical theories in education: Changing terrains of knowledge and politics.* New York: Routledge.

Powell, W. W. (1985). *Getting into print: The decision-making process in scholarly publishing.* Chicago: University of Chicago Press.

Professional Convention Management Association. (2006). *Professional meeting management: Comprehensive strategies for meetings, conventions, and events.* Dubuque, IA: Kendall/Hunt Publishing.

Rajagopal, I., & Lin, Z. (1996). Hidden careerists in Canadian universities. *Higher Education, 32*(3), 247–266.

Readings, B. (1996). *The university in ruins.* Cambridge, MA: Harvard University Press.

Reinhart, S. M. (2002). *Giving academic presentations.* Ann Arbor: University of Michigan Press.

Rendle-Short, J. (2006). *The academic presentation: Situated talk in action.* Burlington, VT: Ashgate Publishing.

Rhode, D. (2006). *In pursuit of knowledge: Scholars, status, and academic culture.* Stanford, CA: Stanford University Press.

Rhodes, F. H. T. (2001). *The creation of the future: The role of the American university.* Ithaca, NY: Cornell University Press.

Ries, J. B., & Leukefeld, C.G. (1995). *Applying for research funding: Getting started and getting funded.* Thousand Oaks, CA: Sage.

Rosenwasser, D., & Stephen, J. (1997). *Writing analytically.* Fort Worth, TX: Harcourt Brace College Publishers.

Rossides, D. W. (1998). *Professions and disciplines: Functional and conflict perspectives.* Upper Saddle River, NJ: Prentice-Hall.

Sachs, M. (1990). *World guide to scientific associations and learned societies.* New York: K.G. Saur.

Savage, J. D. (2000). *Funding science in America: Congress, universities, and the politics of the academic pork barrel.* New York: Cambridge University Press.

Schuster, J. H., & Finkelstein, M. J. (2006). *The American faculty: The restructuring of academic work and careers.* Baltimore, MD: Johns Hopkins University Press.

Seldin, P. (2007). *The teaching portfolio: A practical guide to improved performance and promotion/tenure decisions.* San Francisco: Jossey-Bass.

Shattock, M. (2003). *Managing successful universities.* Berkshire, UK: Open University Press/Society for Research into Higher Education.

Shaw, V. N. (2002a). Peer review as a motivating device in the training of writing skills for college students. *Journal of College Reading and Learning, 33*(1), 68–76.

Shaw, V. N. (2002b). Counseling the university professor on the securing of research grants and the publishing of research products. *Education, 123*(2), 395–400.

Shaw, V. N. (2002c). Essential social sciences skills in college and university education. *Contemporary Education, 72*(1), 39–43.

Shaw, V. N. (2001a). Training in reading skills: An innovative method from classroom instruction. *Reading Improvement, 38*(4), 188–192.

Shaw, V. N. (2001b). Training in presentation skills: An innovative method from classroom instruction. *Education, 122*(1), 140–144.

Shaw, V. N. (2000). Toward professional civility: An analysis of rejection letters from sociology departments. *The American Sociologist, 31*(1), 32–43.

Shaw, V. N. (1999). Reading, presentation, and writing skills in content courses. *College Teaching, 47*(4), 153–157.

Shoenfeld, C., & Magnan, R. (2004). *Mentor in a manual: Climbing the academic ladder to tenure.* Madison, WI: Atwood Publications.

Silverman, F. H. (2001). *Publishing for tenure and beyond: Strategies for maximizing your student ratings.* Westport, CT: Bergin & Garvey.

Slaughter, S., & Rhoades, G. (2004). *Academic capitalism and the new economy: Markets, state, and higher education.* Baltimore, MD: The Johns Hopkins University Press.

St. John, E. P., & Parsons, M.D. (2004). *Public funding of higher education: Changing contexts and new rationales.* Baltimore, MD: Johns Hopkins University Press.

Stephens, M. D. (1989). *Universities, education, and the national economy.* London and New York: Routledge.

Stinchcombe, A. L. (1999/2000). Making a living in sociology in the 21st century (and the intellectual consequences of making a living). *Berkeley Journal of Sociology, 44,* 4–14.

Sweet, S. (1998). Practicing radical pedagogy: Balancing ideals with institutional constraints. *Teaching Sociology, 26*(2),100–111.

Talburt, S. (2000). *Subject to identity: Knowledge, sexuality, and academic practices in higher education.* Albany: State University of New York Press.

Taylor, S. (2005). *A handbook for doctoral supervisors.* New York: Routledge.

Tierney, W. G. (2006). *Governance and the public good.* Albany: State University of New York Press.

Tierney, W. G. (2004). *Competing conceptions of academic governance: Negotiating the perfect storm.* Baltimore, MD: Johns Hopkins University Press.

Tierney, W. G. (1991). *Culture and ideology in higher education: Advancing a critical agenda.* New York: Praeger.

Tierney, W. G., & Bensimon, E. M. (1996). *Promotion and tenure: Community and socialization in academe.* Albany: State University of New York Press.

Tinkler, P., & Jackson, C. (2004). *The doctoral examination process.* Berkshire, UK: Open University Press.

Toren, N., & Moore, D. (1998). The academic 'hurdle race': A case study. *Higher Education, 35*(3), 267–283.

Wasserman, P., & McLean, J. W. (Eds.). (1978). *Awards, honors, and prizes.* Detroit, MI: Gale Research Co.

Weber, M. (1930). *The protestant ethic and the rise of capitalism.* New York: Scribner.

Weddle, P. (2007). *2007/8 guide to association websites.* Stamford, CT: Weddle's.

Weingartner, R. H. (1999). *The moral dimensions of academic administration.* Lanham, MD: Rowman & Littlefield Publishers.

White, V. (1983). *Grant proposals that succeeded.* New York: Plenum Press.

Wildavsky, A. B. (1989). *Craftways: On the organization of scholarly work.* New Brunswick, NJ: Transaction Publishers.

Wolverton, M., & Gmelch, W. H. (2002). *College deans: Leading from within.* Westport, CT: Oryx Press/American Council on Education.

Young, M. L. (1985). *Scientific and technical organizations and agencies directory.* Detroit, MI: Gale Research Co.

Young, S., & Shaw, D. G. (1999). Profiles of effective college and university teachers. *Journal of Higher Education, 70*(6), 670–686.

Zemsky, R., Wegner, G. R., & Massy. W. F. (2005). *Remaking the American university: Market-smart and mission-centered.* Piscataway, NJ: Rutgers University Press.

ABOUT THE AUTHOR

Victor N. Shaw, Ph.D., is a professor of sociology at California State University-Northridge. Dr. Shaw is interested in the study of crime, deviance, social control, organizational behavior, higher education, and public policy, and has published widely in those areas. Dr. Shaw's recent book, *Substance Use and Abuse: Sociological Perspectives,* appeared in "Outstanding Academic Titles, 2003," *CHOICE: Current Reviews for Academic Libraries,* the Association of College and Research Libraries.

Printed in the United Kingdom
by Lightning Source UK Ltd.
130293UK00001B/43/P